God and Human Responsibility

Voices of the African Diaspora

This series presents the development of the intellectual tradition of the African diaspora. The series will bring together a variety of disciplines, including literary and social/cultural criticism, anthropology, sociology, religion/philosophy, education, political science, psychology, and history—by publishing original critical studies and reprints of classic texts. The reprints will include both nineteenth- and twentieth-century works. The goal is to make important texts accessible and readily available both to the general reader and to the academic.

Chester J. Fontenot, Jr.
Series Editor

God and Human Responsibility

David Walker and Ethical Prophecy

Rufus Burrow, Jr.

Mercer University Press
Macon, Georgia

MUP/H643   P260

First Edition.

∞The paper used in this publication meets the minimum requirements of
American National Standard for Information Sciences—Permanence of Paper
for Printed Library Materials, ANSI Z39.48-1992.

Library of Congress Cataloging-in-Publication Data

Burrow, Rufus, 1951-
 God and human responsibility : David Walker and ethical prophecy /
Rufus Burrow, Jr.— 1st ed.
    p. cm.
Includes bibliographical references and index.
 ISBN 0-86554-852-8 (hardcover : alk. paper) — ISBN 0-86554-892-7
(pbk. : alk. paper)
1. Walker, David, 1785-1830—Religion. 2. Antislavery movements—United
States—History. 3. Antislavery movements—Moral and ethical aspects—United
States. 4. Slaves—Emancipation—Moral and ethical aspects—United States.
I. Title.
E446.W178B87 2003
261.7'092—dc22

                                                              2003022640

Contents

Preface vii

Acknowledgments xi

Introduction 5

Chapter 1. Born "Free" in Slavery 17

Chapter 2. Ethical Prophecy: Setting the Stage 41

Chapter 3. Elements of Ethical Prophecy in the *Appeal* 75

Chapter 4. Walker's Call for Black Self-Determination 129

Chapter 5. Moral Pretentiousness of White Christianity 157

Chapter 6. The Relevance of Ethical Prophecy for Today 175

Select Bibliography 209

Index 217

Preface

I have in my lifetime known but two pastors whose life and ministries exemplify what I call *ethical prophecy*; that is, prophecy modeled after that of Amos, Isaiah, Micah, Ezekiel, and Hosea. They were pastors who believed in the necessity of speaking God's truth to the people and to the world, no matter the cost to themselves. And they did so in love. But make no mistake about it. They preached—and one continues to preach—the Word of God, come hell or high water. One, Reverend Robert A. Mulligan, a retired United Methodist pastor in Savoy, Illinois, who is eighty-eight years-old at the time this book is being published, has given me hope that God can and does get through to an Anglo pastor every now and then.

The other minister, Reverend William W. Hannah, was a pastor in the Christian Church (Disciples of Christ) for nearly forty years. Bill Hannah (as I called him) was my pastor at Faith United Christian Church in Indianapolis, Indiana. The truth is that I was attracted to that congregation only because of his presence. Having heard about him in the mid-1980s, I heard him preach one Sunday morning and simply fell in love with him; with his courage and ability to speak God's truth in a way that congregants had to work very hard *not* to understand the proclaimed "thus says the LORD." Sunday after Sunday Hannah preached God's Word with a clarity seldom heard in contemporary sermons. No one had to guess at what the preacher was trying to convey, especially when it was time to utter words of prophecy relative to what God expects of the urban-American church. I've heard many sermons preached by others who so sugarcoated the Word in an endeavor not to offend congregants that, when the sermon was over, I left the building wondering what the preacher was really trying to convey. When Hannah preached, one knew that he loved his God and he loved the people. Because he loved God, he was compelled to preach the Word "in season and out," no matter the cost. Because he loved the people, he was obligated to feed them with God's Word. There is absolutely no question in my mind that Bill Hannah was one of God's "bad boys." That is, he could tell the Jewish, Christian, and African American story. Always weaving together bits and pieces of his experiences growing up in West Virginia and his young adult life in Cleveland, Ohio, where he was called by God to establish a church in that city, Hannah told God's story wherever he went. He was not interested in being popular. He wanted to be obedient and faithful to God. He was not one for theatrics in the pulpit. He was all business, although he always allowed for spontaneity and gave free reign to the Spirit.

Even in retirement, Hannah was the quintessential prophet. By the time I met him in the mid-1980s, I was already teaching a course on ethical prophecy at Indianapolis' Christian Theological Seminary. I was immediately attracted to him because he generally preached prophetic sermons, which is why I invited him to lecture to my class on that subject on 30 April and 1 May 1986. On those days I sat, listened, and took notes as he made his presentations from a very rough outline. He began by telling us that prophetic ministry is very difficult. Such a ministry, he said, is always "on the cutting edge" and its proponents are "always in trouble with the authorities." He paused for a moment, and then said: "In fact, if you're not in trouble in ministry, you're not doing what you ought to be doing."

Hannah lectured on Ezekiel during those two days. He brought that prophet to life for the students and me in a way that we had not before experienced. He characterized Ezekiel as "a unique kind of prophet;" different from all of the other prophets in the Bible, inasmuch as "he didn't act like anybody else." Perhaps this was so because Ezekiel prophesied during a period of intense political crisis. In light of this, Hannah said that his study and reflection on Ezekiel revealed five characteristics of prophecy. In those days I was not yet using the term "ethical prophecy," but the traits that he identified are not different from those discussed in this book. According to Hannah, these include: *the call, the commission, the anger, the judgment*, and *hope or redemption*. He said that in the black church context the call is absolutely essential before one could even think about doing anything else in ministry. He believed that part of the difficulty in ministry today is that there are many who have been counseled to go into ministry, but have not been called.

Ezekiel was commissioned or instructed by God to "eat the Word of God" (Ezek 3:1-3), Hannah said. Out of obedience to God, the prophet ate the word and concluded that it was very good. Despite the national arrogance of his day, and amid intense political crises, Ezekiel preached doom but also saw reason for hope or redemption. God loved the people and preferred that they be saved rather than destroyed. Indeed, had God not said through the prophet, "Know that all lives are mine; the life of the parent as well as the life of the child is mine…"? (Ezek 18:4) But it is important to remember that ethical prophets *do* preach and "warn about impending danger." According to Hannah, this means that the church is to always be on watch. Tragically, the church instead tends to join those who oppress and demean people. Hannah was certain that in his reading of the prophets, pastors who are truly called "must be willing to sit where the people sit." That is, they must be willing to go out among the people and be with them, especially in very difficult times.

Prophets do preach doom, but in the end they always preach words of hope—hope that the people will return to covenant relationship with God and with each other. Indeed, one who is called to ministry frequently exhibits what is perceived by others to be "insanity." Hannah believed it to be the highest compliment when somebody called him "a fool for God." The prophet does not know any better than to do exactly what she believes God requires of her. She always works on the assumption that *God is*, and that "God knows what God is doing." But the prophet also always assumes that "God needs the prophet."

Finally, for Hannah, Jesus Christ brought the entire prophetic tradition together by telling the story, showing us the way, and doing what God requires. Hannah was not, however, a supersessionist. He believed God's Word is revealed in both testaments of the Christian Bible. In any case, he believed that in Jesus we see at once the prophetic stance (declared word) and the prophetic act (deed). We have in Jesus, then, the chief exemplification of ethical prophecy. "Jesus came to liberate a 'dry bones' society," said Hannah. This means that the ethical prophet is always busy, and thus is "never unemployed." Because the prophet is human, he is sometimes discouraged; but God always empowers him to do what he is called to do.

Hannah's final words in his lectures on Ezekiel were that one who is called by God ought always to exhibit "enthusiasm" about the Word and work of God. "Even if the Word itself is soft-spoken, it must nevertheless be done with excitement and energy." When one is called by God, she speaks God's truth and does God's work, "no matter the cost."

During the last two years of his life, I had the privilege and honor of working with Hannah on two books in which the basic ideas of ethical prophecy are explored in detail. The books will be published posthumously, inasmuch as my pastor recently heard "the roar of the chariots" stopping by his home early on a Sunday morning to return him to the One for whom he worked so enthusiastically, obediently, and vigilantly for so many years in this world.

Much of what the reader finds in this book is consistent with Hannah's understanding of the importance of ethical prophecy for ministry. The book itself is much influenced by his witness to God's truth for the world. I am both humbled and honored to dedicate this book on David Walker to my friend, surrogate father, and my pastor, the late William (Bill) W. Hannah (1927–1998).

Acknowledgments

There are simply no words in the English language to adequately express appreciation for my good friend, colleague, and perpetual social gadfly, Chester J. Fontenot, editor of the Mercer University series: Voices of the African Diaspora. He has reminded me time and time again over the years that for Afrikan Americans, *la lucha* (the struggle) is our life. No matter the racial and cultural insensitivity that Afrikan American scholars experience in our respective institutions, he has always reminded me that the struggle is not *just* about me. It is about all those Afrikan American ancestors, as well as a few well meaning Anglos, for whom *la lucha* was also their life. Therefore, my role is to remember that I stand on the shoulders of giants who made amazing sacrifices to open the way for me, and my generation. My responsibility is both to remember, and to open the way for those who follow in my path.

In the writing of this book, Professor Fontenot has cheered me every step of the way, believing from the beginning that this project would see the light of day through publication. For his willingness to be a brother (and only *brothers* can understand what I mean by this), I am both humbled and grateful. What he has done in the way of being supportive of this long distance colleague is truly the quintessential model for collegiality.

Marsha M. Luttrell did an excellent job of guiding me through the process at Mercer University Press. She was the one who kept me informed of next steps, deadlines, etc. She easily conveys a sense of cool professionalism and commitment to excellence regarding her work with the Press.

The copyeditor who worked through the early drafts of this book is simply superb at the editorial task. I can't say enough about Tom Harrington's sense of what I really want to convey in this book, and his uncanny ability to make some of my ideas clearer to me. For the chiding questions and prodding that prompted me to think just a little bit deeper in a number of places, I am forever grateful to this editorial sage.

Introduction

This book is a study in "prophetic ethics." I define the term in chapter 2. Most readers, however, will have some idea of its meaning. My hope is that this book will contribute toward helping to further clarify the meaning of prophetic ethics, and what I have chosen to call *ethical prophecy*. Most books and anthologies published on Christian and theological ethics do not address prophetic ethics.[1] Furthermore, with the exception of more recent anthologies on Christian ethics, we do not find the inclusion of selections by African Americans, whose work would most likely resemble prophetic ethics. This omission is indicative of the shameful lack of notice given to that particular community regarding the subject by much of Western scholarship.

Historically, African American Christians and religious scholars have had a strong affinity with the tradition of eighth-century BCE Hebrew prophecy. From the time of American slavery through the present, there has been a deep appreciation among many African Americans for the prophetic tradition of the Jewish and Christian faiths. The Hebrew prophets' emphases on God's expectation that justice be done, and that God's people were to maintain a righteous spirit in the world, met the first African Americans at a place of great agony during their enslavement. Because they were treated inhumanely, unjustly, and without dignity, the enslaved Africans easily resonated to the prophets'

---

[1] For example, see *Readings in Christian Ethics*, ed. J. Philip Wogaman and Douglas M. Strong (Louisville KY: Westminster/John Knox Press, 1996).

cry for immediate justice in God's world. Just as the ancient prophets were not concerned about justice beyond the grave but in *this* world, so too were the enslaved Africans who endured unspeakable hardship. From the very beginning of their enslavement, the Africans protested their lot. When they began to be converted to Christianity and were able to read the Bible for themselves, it was not long before they were prophesying about God's expectation that they be freed and that justice be done. Indeed, considerable activity of this type occurred before Walker's appearance.

David Walker, like the ancient Hebrew prophets, did not merely appear out of thin air prophesying God's call for justice and righteousness. He was the product of a culture and tradition from which issued a number of outstanding black predecessors in the eighteenth century. These had spoken forcefully against the injustice and inhumanity of slavery, especially in light of American democracy and Christianity. Walker stood within a long tradition of protest and criticism against religious and political hypocrisy. He was not the first person of African descent to speak of a wrathful, angry, impatient God whose fundamental nature is love. Indeed, Prince Hall, "Othello," and Nathaniel Paul had already done so long before Walker began to make his presence felt as forcefully as he did. Walker was not the first to preach resistance. There was before his time a long history of black agitation against slavery.[2] Walker was therefore not the initiator but the product of the black resistance tradition. As important as was his theologico-political treatise, the *Appeal*, its publication was not the root instigator of black resistance in the 1820s and 1830s. The *Appeal* was, however, a significant document around which many blacks—the enslaved and the nominally free—could and did rally.

Yet David Walker's *Appeal* should not be viewed only as a political document, but a as theological treatise as well. Indeed, in the work of African Americans historically and presently, it is not unusual for this to be the case. It has always been the African view that there is one world, and that it belongs to God. For example, blacks historically have not cared about Western distinctions between a sacred and secular or profane world. There is one world, and whatever happens in it may well have

---

[2] Peter P. Hinks, chap. 6 in *To Awaken My Afflicted Brethren: David Walker and the Problem of Antebellum Slave Resistance* (University Park PA: Pennsylvania State University Press, 1997).

political, sociological, economic, and other implications. Accordingly, all that happens in the world has in some way to do with God. Conversely, the viewpoint argues, all that happens in the world also affects God in some way. In my judgment that makes whatever happens in the world fundamentally theological in nature, for it has to do with God, with God's world, and with God's people, since all people and this world belong to God. Such is also the case with Walker's *Appeal*; it has very much to do with the reality of the African American in slavery and with God.

The *Appeal* did challenge the political and economic arrangement of whites over blacks in America during the second and third decades of the nineteenth century. At the same time, however, virtually every page of the document contains significant God-talk, including statements about God's displeasure with slavery. One also finds numerous passages that have clear-cut theologico-ethical implications. In this regard, J. Philip Wogaman and Douglas M. Strong were quite right to include a selection from Walker in their anthology on Christian ethics.[3] Although Walker was primarily self-taught, there is no question that he had read and understood the Bible as well as any of his white contemporaries who were formally educated. An open-minded reading of the *Appeal* easily leads one to conclude that, despite a lack of formal training, Walker would today be deemed a theologian or religious ethicist.

Prophecy of the type discussed in this book is never done in a social vacuum. It is always done in a particular socio-cultural context. It is inevitably informed by that which came before it, i.e., a particular history and tradition. It is always as if God, the author and source of all legitimate prophecy, is always working to prepare the way for prophecy, including the women and men chosen to declare "thus says the LORD." It was no different in the case of David Walker.

Walter Rauschenbusch (1861–1918), a leader in the social gospel movement during the first two decades of the twentieth century, characterized the eighth-century prophets as "the beating heart of the Old Testament."[4] Without the contributions of the Hebrew prophets, the Bible might well not be as significant as it has been and is to millions of persons since biblical times.

---

[3] See Wogaman and Strong, *Readings in Christian Ethics*, Part 4, Selection 41.

[4] Walter Rauschenbusch, *Christianity and the Social Crisis* (New York: Macmillan, 1907) 3.

Much of the core of the Bible's ethical teachings is found in the prophets, upon whom Jesus depended so much in his ministry and teachings. Indeed, in the Gospel of Luke it is reported that Jesus began his ministry with a statement of profound ethical significance that drew on the prophet Isaiah: "The Spirit of the Lord is upon me, because he has anointed me to bring good news to the poor. He has sent me to proclaim release to the captives and recovering of sight to the blind, to let the oppressed go free, to proclaim the year of the Lord's favor" (Luke 4:18–19; cf. Isaiah 61:1–2). Short of that influence, one wonders whether we would have been blessed with the famous Sermon on the Mount and the Beatitudes (Matt 5). Of the extant teachings of Jesus, that passage comes closest to providing an outline for ethical guidelines for behavior consistent with his understanding of God's expectations for human existence and relating in the world. Jesus clarified what the Jewish religious law required, but in every case he pushed beyond minimal legalistic requirements to explore God's maximized expectations of those who choose to live within the declared Realm of God and by its standards.

Rauschenbusch held that without the contributions of the prophets "there would be little left to appeal to the moral and religious judgment of the modern world."[5] In order for one to adequately understand the moral message of Jesus and that of the Christian faith it is necessary, Rauschenbusch maintained, to understand and appreciate the contributions of the Hebrew prophets. Although prophetic inspiration did not cease after the time of the Hebrew prophets, it may be argued that it was reinvigorated and energized in the life and teachings of Jesus and in the work of the early Church.

There are a number of approaches to the study of prophecy in a Jewish and Christian context. I want here to distinguish between two: *higher morality* and *divine pathos*. The former is the old line approach to prophecy and is represented in the work of Julius Wellhausen and his disciples during the early part of the twentieth century. According to this approach, the most distinctive contribution of the eighth-century prophets was their emphasis on social morality and the consequent penchant to apply a hermeneutic of moralization to religion and life.

---

[5] Ibid., 3.

The prophets, according to the higher morality view, were essentially social reformers. Proponents of this stance claim that, prior to the appearance of the eighth-century prophets, there was little or no emphasis on ethical and righteous teaching and living among the people of Israel. Therefore, goes the argument, it was the eighth-century prophets who first articulated this prophetic message. "Social gospel" thinkers such as Rauschenbusch were adherents of this view. For example, Rauschenbusch made the claim that the basic conviction of the prophets was that God demanded righteousness, and righteousness only.[6] Similarly, Harry Emerson Fosdick, the great inspirational social gospel preacher who was pastor of the famous Riverside Church in New York City, once proclaimed: "The greatest single contribution of the Hebrew prophets to human thought was their vision of the righteous nature of God and of his demands on men. Their supreme abhorrence was unmoral religion."[7] According to the higher morality theory, it was the eighth-century prophets who lifted religion and life to the moral plane.

Gerhard von Rad was among the leading critics of the higher morality theory. He argued that its proponents failed to acknowledge that the prophets did not simply enter history and begin prophesying. They, like everybody else, were recipients of history and tradition. For example, Amos, Hosea, and Jeremiah were influenced by the Exodus-Sinai tradition. Isaiah and Micah were influenced by the David-Zion tradition, while Ezekiel and Deutero-Isaiah were influenced by a combination of these traditions.[8] But the prophets were also persons living within social contexts. That is, they contributed to the making of their cultures, even as they were influenced and shaped by those cultures. Invoking the best of their received cultures and traditions, the prophets were able to reinterpret the society of their contemporaries on the basis of the best of the long held cultural values of the people. This is all to say that the prophets did not prophesy in a socio-cultural vacuum, an observation that was an important aspect of von Rad's critique of the higher morality theory.

---

[6] Ibid., 4.

[7] Harry Emerson Fosdick, *The Meaning of Service* (New York: Association Press, 1921) 8.

[8] Bruce C. Birch, *Let Justice Roll Down: The Old Testament, Ethics, and Christian Life* (Louisville KY: Westminster/John Knox, 1991) 256.

Von Rad may have overemphasized the role of received traditions and history with respect to the prophets. He may not have given enough attention to their self-determination and ability to interpret formative influences, all the while calling the people to accountability in the here and now. Nevertheless, von Rad's basic criticism was on target. He sought to show that it was not that the eighth-century prophets were needed to tell the people of Israel what "thus says the Lord God." *The people already knew what God required.* Instead, it was in part the prophets' task to say in new, more intelligible ways what God expected of the people. Therefore the eighth-century prophets, according to von Rad, were not the first to intervene on behalf of the voiceless and the weak. Nor were they the first to stress ethical religion and God's requirement that justice be done in ways that are consistent with a righteous spirit. These things had previously been heard in Israel. After King David committed adultery with Bathsheba, wife of Uriah, the LORD sent the prophet Nathan to tell him a parable about a rich man's abuse of the poor that outraged David's moral sense. David declared that the villain in the parable deserved to die. Of course, Nathan had to tell him: "You are the man" (2 Sam 12:7).

Nathan was unquestionably a forerunner of the ethical prophets of the eighth century. Yet it may be added that the Hebrew prophets differed from their predecessors and less ethically inclined contemporaries in that they lived in perpetual outrage against injustice, without regard to the perceived extent of the injustice being committed. Injustice was injustice—period. In a way and to a degree that others were not, these prophets were obsessed with justice and righteousness. Injustice was not something that one periodically and conveniently became morally outraged about, only to return easily and calmly to habitual ways of living as if nothing of consequence had really happened. The point is well made by Rabbi Abraham Joshua Heschel (1907–1972), a model and masterful interpreter of ethical prophecy:

> That justice is a good thing, a fine goal, even a supreme ideal, is commonly accepted. *What is lacking is a sense of the monstrosity of injustice.* Moralists of all ages have been eloquent in singing the praises of virtue. *The distinction of the prophets was in their remorseless unveiling of injustice and oppression, in their comprehension of social, political, and religious evils.*

They were not concerned with the definition, but with the predicament, of justice, with the fact that those called upon to apply it defied it[9] (emphasis mine).

The prophets conveyed the message that God is outraged about injustice and always considers it to be scandalous. Unlike human beings, God never gets used to injustice and the dehumanization of persons. As will be seen later, none was more outraged and more incensed about the injustices committed against his people by white proponents of Christianity, than was David Walker. Indeed, Walker was obsessed, filled with what he considered the divine mandate that the preciousness of all persons be acknowledged and that justice be done.

A second interpretive approach to prophecy sees *divine pathos* as the regulating ideal. Heschel is its most prominent advocate. It maintains that the most distinct feature of the prophets was their declaration of God's relentless care and concern for persons, and that God is in no instance indifferent to evil. The prophets declared *the evil of indifference*, as well as God's concern about even the most trivial things that adversely affect persons. Divine pathos also proposes to convey God's need of persons. This is a repudiation of the classical Greek and Roman stances that advocated a perfectly powerful, immutable, impassable, uncaring, impersonal, and distant deity who had no need whatever for persons. This classical deity was totally indifferent to persons and their circumstances in the world. Unfortunately, strands of this conception of the divine found their way into early Jewish and Christian thought. Remnants of this understanding of God exist even today in some prominent quarters of Jewish and Christian thought, especially among religious fundamentalists associated with those traditions.

Divine pathos, however, conveys the opposite view of God. God is not only personal and immanent in the world and among persons. God cares about persons and the world. In addition, and unlike the older truncated classical view, *God needs persons*. Because persons are not created as unthinking automatons, because they are free within limits to contribute (or not) to the remaking of the world, they can be co-workers with God. If nothing else, persons can, said Heschel, work to make the world worthy of being redeemed by God.

---

[9] Abraham J. Heschel, *The Prophets* (New York: Harper, 1962) 204.

Heschel was essentially in agreement with von Rad's critique of the higher morality theory. While it was never his intention to undermine the ethical emphasis in prophetic religion (and he never did!), Heschel stressed divine pathos and thus achieved a grounding of prophecy in theology. That is, Heschel's was a staunchly theocentric approach to prophecy, which for our purpose means that God is the ground or center of prophecy. God is prophecy's reason for being. God's relentless care, faithfulness, and compassion for persons, is absolutely matchless. No matter how stupidly we humans behave, no matter how persistently we turn away from God, God forever turns toward us. God pursues us in the hope that we will hear and obey the call to return to covenant relationship with God and with each other; that we will resume obedience and faithfulness to God. Even when it seems that there is absolutely no hope of saving the people, God's inexhaustible love bursts forth. Nowhere is this better illustrated than in the Book of Hosea: "How can I give you up, Ephraim? How can I hand you over, O Israel? ... My heart recoils within me; my compassion grows warm and tender. I will not execute my fierce anger; I will not again destroy Ephraim; for I am God and no mortal, the Holy One in your midst, and I will not come in wrath" (Hos 11:8–9).

According to the approach of divine pathos, it was not humans who initiated a relationship with God or who first turned toward God. It was God who initiated the relational turn toward persons and began an unending pursuit for their love. Heschel's term for this divine turning toward persons is *anthropotropism*. According to this point of view, the ancient Hebrew prophets sought to convey to the people the drama of the divine pathos, that God had persistently turned toward them in love. Conjointly, the representatives of the priestly office, through ritual acts, worship, prayer, and meditation, helped the people in their quest for communion with God. By this interpretive model, the prophet speaks for and represents God to the people; the priest speaks for and represents the people to God.[10]

This book is much influenced by the second of the two approaches to prophecy. Although David Walker did not use the language of Heschel's concept of *divine pathos*, there is no question that the theme of

---

[10] Abraham J. Heschel, "Prophetic Inspiration: An Analysis of Prophetic Consciousness" in *To Grow in Wisdom: An Anthology of Abraham Joshua Heschel*, ed. Jacob Neusner and Noam M. M. Neusner (New York: Madison Books, 1990) 66.

God's relentless love, care, and concern for enslaved Africans of his day is pervasive in his *Appeal*. In this sense, Walker anticipated Heschel's doctrine of divine pathos. In addition, there is implicit in Walker's insistence on black self-determination the idea that God needed the enslaved Africans, both because of God's love for them and because of what they themselves ultimately could contribute to their socio-political salvation. What I endeavor to do in this book is to situate and establish Walker in the tradition of eighth century or ethical prophecy. I also list and discuss criteria that any person would have to satisfy in order to be considered a prophet within this tradition. It is my position that true prophets—past and present—are ethical prophets, reflecting the characteristics found within the traditions of Hebrew prophecy. In other words, I discuss the criteria that establishes and legitimizes a true prophet.

I am not a Bible scholar, but a theological social ethicist who defines his discipline along interdisciplinary lines. I am therefore bound to be conversant with the methods and substantive contributions of other fields of thought, e.g., biblical studies, theology, theological ethics, the social and behavioral sciences, philosophy, church history, social philosophy, and history. I seek what Walter G. Muelder—a pioneer in Christian social ethics in this country—sought, namely "a new level of interdisciplinary integration" with a view to "emergent coherence."[11] As a theological social ethicist, I consider the contributions of Bible scholars, theologians, ethicists, and even literary artists in my effort to devise a means for thinking about and determining when ethical prophecy is being done, or when one is in the presence of a true prophet. I endeavor to take from each relevant field of thought appropriate ideas and mold them into the most reasonable, coherent statement on the meaning and relevance of ethical prophecy.

When in the mid-1980s the Christian Theological Seminary invited me to teach a course titled "Prophetic and Ethical Witness of the Churches," I was both ecstatic and *very* anxious. I believed that such a course could make a real difference in the way pastors-in-training and others pursuing ministerial vocations think about and do ministry.

In part, I was anxious because I realized that this kind of course could shatter students' worldviews and confront old ways of thinking in

---

[11] Walter G. Muelder, *Foundations of the Responsible Society: A Comprehensive Survey of Christian Social Ethics* (New York: Abingdon Press, 1959) 9.

their journey toward ministry that seldom gave place to the prophets. It seemed to me that such a course would be especially useful for those who understood that ministry is much more than a profession; that it is fundamentally a vocation or call, and that God does the calling. The student who understood her calling as such would already have a sense that what she was being called to was in every sense counter-cultural and therefore necessarily posed a direct challenge—indeed, by some perspectives, a threat—to a *status quo* ethic in church and society.

I was anxious for another reason as well. The truth is that I simply did not know how to teach such a course. The course as previously taught did not seem to focus enough on the prophetic ethics that I believed so essential to the subject matter. Part of the struggle, one in which I was also to share, was that no book had been written on the subject of the prophetic and ethical witness of the church. It was, for all intents and purposes, unexplored territory.

I wanted the course to have a strong, coherent theologico-social ethics component, and provide an opportunity for the students to see ethical prophecy in action. One way to get at this was through assigning specific readings and the exploration of materials available in different types of communications media. Substituting the term "theological" for "Christian" ethics gave me the space to consider a broader range of readings for the course, not all of which had to be by Christian authors. For example, I could have the students read literature by Jewish, Muslim, East Indian, American Indians, and non-Christian African writers. At all times, however, the learning aim would be to determine what it meant to be prophetic or to do prophetic ministry in ways consistent with the ethical teachings of the Hebrew prophets and Jesus Christ.

I had taught the course for several years before I stumbled upon Abraham Joshua Heschel's work while reading about Martin Luther King, Jr. Hurried library research revealed that Heschel published *The Prophets* in 1962. I was intrigued by his approach and emphasis on divine pathos. I was also aware that Heschel and King were key presenters at the 1963 Conference on Religion and Race in Chicago (where they first met), and that Heschel had marched with King in Selma in 1965. I have since learned from biographical statements by Susannah Heschel that her father was at that time an older man and "not able to protect himself physically," a matter that worried her and her mother a great deal during the few days he was in Selma.[12] In 1964, King became the first gentile to receive an honorary degree from Jewish Theological Seminary in New York City, where Heschel taught, an honor to which the latter gave primary personal sponsorship.[13] The two men would be together for the last time on the evening of 25 March 1968, ten days before King was assassinated.[14]

What Heschel and King most shared in common was "a commitment to the language and experience of the Hebrew prophets."[15] Heschel's daughter has reflected on what she believed led to the close relationship between her father and King.

> The preference King gives to the Exodus motif over the figure of Jesus certainly played a major role in linking the two men intellectually and religiously; for Heschel, the primacy of the Exodus in the civil rights movement was a major step in the history of Christian-Jewish relations. King's understanding of the nature of God's involvement with humanity, derived from the black church, bears striking similarities to Heschel's concept of divine pathos and provided the basis of the spiritual affinity they felt for each other...nurtured by the surprising spiritual connections informing their understandings of the Bible.[16]

The prophets had come to tell the people that God cares about them; that God is involved in all that happens to them; and that God requires and expects that justice to be done. No one in the tumultuous period of struggle for civil rights in the United States was more committed to this way of thinking or more willing to demonstrate it in their ministries than were Heschel and King.

---

[12] Abraham J. Heschel, *God in Search of Man: A Philosophy of Judaism*, (1955; reprint, with a foreword by Susannah Heschel, Northvale NJ: Jason Aronson, 1987) xxxii.

[13] Taylor Branch, *Pillar of Fire: America in the King Years, 1963–65* (New York: Simon and Schuster, 1998) 327.

[14] See the partial transcription of "Conversation with Martin Luther King" in *The Eyes on the Prize Civil Rights Reader*, ed. Clayborne Carson et al. (New York: Penguin Books, 1991) 393–409.

[15] Branch, *Pillar of Fire*, 22.

[16] Quoted in Marc Schneier, *Shared Dreams: Martin Luther King, Jr. and the Jewish Community* (Woodstock VT: Jewish Lights Publishing, 1999) 137.

What I found in the very first pages of Heschel's *The Prophets* convinced me that his was an approach to the prophets that, though novel to me, had the strong ethics component I was seeking. Unlike the older and familiar higher morality theory related to the Personalism[17] developed at Boston University from the latter part of the nineteenth century through the 1960s, the doctrine of divine pathos insists that God cares about persons and all that happens to them in the world. I provide an in-depth discussion of these two approaches to prophecy in chapter 2.

A course that deals with such a subject will be successful only if it challenges students to engage the topic beyond the mere exercise of intellect. True, ethical prophecy according to the model of the Hebrew prophets is what one embraces in the delivery of legitimate ministry. The charge from God was not that prophets think, theorize, or write about justice, but that they *do* justice in a spirit of lovingkindness (cf. Mic 6:8). They were to be concerned about the eradication of concrete forms of injustice and the establishment of justice among the people. This lofty goal was also David Walker's aim. All that he did was for the purpose of the complete liberation of his people from the smoldering cauldron of slavery and all its related manifestations of injustice.

The tendency is to apply the term "prophet" to anyone who brings systematic criticism of social entities or religious bodies from within the ranks of those institutions. The type of prophecy discussed in this book does not take criticism as such to be its chief criterion. There is much more to it than this, not least of which is the *reason* for and the *authority* on which criticism purported to be prophetic is offered. In addition, it will be seen that the type of prophecy discussed in these pages does not seek ways of prophesying that neither offend or upset those to whom it is declared—whether these are among those who most need a word of hope or those who have the means and the willingness to oppress others.

The eighth-century prophets declared God's expectation that the people would return to covenant relationship with God and each other, and that justice and righteousness prevail among them. My aim is to

---

[17] See Albert C. Knudson, *The Beacon Lights of Prophecy* (New York: Eaton & Mains, 1914) and *The Prophetic Movement in Israel* (New York: The Methodist Book Concern, 1921). Also, Francis J. McConnell, *The Prophetic Ministry* (New York: Abingdon Press, 1930). Each of these texts by noted Personalists stress a form of the higher morality theory. For a more recent discussion on the philosophy of Personalism, see my *Personalism: A Critical Introduction* (St. Louis: Chalice Press, 1999).

consider the meaning of this divine expectation or point of view in specific contexts of contemporary times. The question to address is this: In light of this or that social issue, e.g., racism, sexism, heterosexism, spousal and child abuse, what does biblical or ethical prophecy require of persons and the institutions of which they are a part? Virtually every representative group engaging in behavior contradictory to the divine edict that justice be done is called to task in light of the Hebrew prophetic tradition of the Bible and the best conscience of the Christian church.

One who examines the work of any one or more of the Hebrew prophets can fairly easily identify the criteria that establishes whether an individual stands within the tradition of a true prophet. These include but are not limited to: declaration of God's steadfast care and concern for persons; evidence of a sense of call; call to the people to return to covenant relationship with each other and with God; focus on the dignity and sacredness of persons; emphasis on God as personal; call to justice; an emphasis on divine wrath; the expression of ultimate hope.

A staunch Christian in the Methodist tradition, having been influenced by the Methodist Episcopal Church in Wilmington, North Carolina, and the African Methodist Episcopal Church in Charleston, South Carolina, David Walker was a militant abolitionist who sought to apply his faith to the liberation project of his people. Although nominally free, Walker was never at peace—indeed, he was outraged—with the idea of his people being enslaved by those who claimed to be Christians. Answering what he believed to be a call from God, and believing that he would either kill or be killed if he remained in the South, Walker relocated to Boston where he became the owner of a secondhand clothing store. He devoted most of his spare time to devising means for the emancipation of his people. His most noted written work, commonly known by its short form title, the *Appeal*, was a major contribution to this endeavor.

One finds in the *Appeal* not only a radical political treatise for its day, but an impassioned pro-abolition argument based on firm theological and ethical convictions. It is grounded in the idea of the God of love and justice who is not pleased with the practice of the enslavement of blacks. Because David Walker believed slavery to be an abomination and sin against God and humanity, he did not hesitate to prophesy divine wrath on those who refused to liberate the enslaved

Africans. Nor was he apprehensive about suggesting that if whites would not willingly set free their captives—and he had neither reason nor evidence to believe that most ever would—blacks were morally obligated to take their destiny into their own hands. Even though Walker invoked divine wrath on whites, in the spirit of the Hebrew prophets he did not see this as the last word. He hoped that whites would hear his prophecy, repent, and liberate the enslaved. Walker, like the Hebrew prophets, began with words of doom, but kept open the door of hope for the salvation of those whites who might repent and set free those they dehumanized through slavery.

Over the years I have read a number of works that only half-heartedly referred to David Walker as a prophet. I have discovered no publication that makes the claim that Walker was a prophet and goes on to develop an argument that substantiates the claim. That, in part, is the purpose of this book. Examining the *Appeal* and a number of other sources, I try to support the claim that Walker was indeed an ethical prophet in the tradition of Amos, Micah, Jeremiah, Isaiah, and Hosea. My hope is that the criteria set forth in this book will be useful in helping us to determine, especially today, who is a true prophet, and who is not.

I take it as a given that there are false prophets and there are true *prophets*. That is, there are many, e.g., politicians or even cultic leaders like Jim Jones and David Koresh, who by virtue of their speech and behavior have been characterized as prophets. This book is about one specific type of prophet, namely the Hebrew prophet. Prophets in this tradition are ethical prophets, inasmuch as they prophesy in ways that are consistent with God's love and concern for persons and the divine requirement that love and justice be done in the world. There are specific criteria that one must meet in order to be considered a prophet in the tradition of Amos. Politicians generally, and cult leaders such as Jim Jones and David Koresh specifically, do not meet the criteria of ethical prophecy as set forth by the eighth-century BCE Hebrew prophets. They may meet the criteria of some other type of prophet, but that is a topic for another study. This book examines ethical prophecy, considers it in light of one nineteenth-century African American representative, David Walker, and applies it as a standard for those who would become true prophets.

I intend in this discussion to address a half-dozen of the criteria that, at a bare minimum, must be to some degree present if one is to be identified as a true prophet in the vein of the Hebrew forebears. While not given any particular order of priority, I consider each criterion to be important in determining one's legitimate claim as a true prophet.

Chapter 1 provides some biographical background on David Walker and endeavors to further clarify what we know about him. This will sometimes mean challenging more traditional beliefs, e.g., that he married a slave sweetheart after moving to Boston, and that he was poisoned to death a year after the publication of the *Appeal*.[18] In chapter 2 I lay the foundation for this study by defining and setting the parameters for the meaning of ethical prophecy in this book.

Chapter 3 is the pivotal chapter of this work because it lists and discusses some of the key criteria for determining whether one is an ethical prophet. The purpose of this chapter is to help us answer the question: Who may be considered a true prophet? Although Walker wrote a number of articles for the first black paper, *Freedom's Journal*, he only wrote one book, *Appeal to the Colored Citizens of the World*, which underwent two revisions in less than a year. The discussion in chapter three is based primarily on this book and shows the presence of elements of prophecy in the *Appeal*.

Chapter 4 presents a discussion on Walker's call for black self-determination. This is a theme that has been present in all subsequent forms of Black Nationalism in the United States. Walker may be considered the spiritual father of Black Nationalist thought in this country.

Chapter 5 addresses the issues of the moral pretentiousness of white Christianity and the sense in which Walker declared blacks to be morally superior to whites. Walker charged white enslavers with hypocrisy and espousing an inauthentic version of Christianity, one that essentially required that the Africans serve them their entire lives. The discussion also explores Walker's declaration that his people were morally superior to whites. Was he making a fundamental theological claim, or was it one based only on experience and history?

Finally, in chapter 6, I consider the relevance of David Walker's ethical prophecy for today. What is its meaning for the African American community in particular at a time when racial discrimination still

---

[18] In this discussion I have found the recent work by Peter P. Hinks to be helpful: *To Awaken My Afflicted Brethren: David Walker and the Problem of Antebellum Slave Resistance* (University Park, Pennsylvania: Pennsylvania State University Press, 1997).

harasses and hounds its members in every moment of their lives? What are we to say when the leading cause of death in the African American community is not a physical malady, such as heart disease, strokes, or diabetes, but—especially among black males between the ages of 15–24—intra-community homicide? What might we learn from David Walker's prophetic voice that may help African Americans to reverse the more deadly trends that adversely affect the black community from within and from without?

Chapter 1

Born "Free" in Slavery

David Walker's Birth

Until recently most scholars of black history accepted Henry Highland Garnet's claim, made in 1848, that David Walker was born in 1785. Garnet made this statement in *A Brief Sketch of the Life and Character of David Walker*.[1] A contemporary historian, however, argues against the traditional dating, arguing it is more likely that Walker was born in 1796 or 1797. Peter P. Hinks bases this theory on his close examination of census and poll tax records in North Carolina (the state of Walker's birth) in the late eighteenth and early nineteenth centuries. Hinks became troubled when these and other records did not account for Walker's absence from them, given the assumption of his birth in that region in 1785. If an adjustment were made to his date of birth, Hinks argues, that "might make his absence from crucial records in North Carolina more understandable."[2] If Walker left home in the late 1810s

---

[1] The full text of Garnet's assertion is included in Herbert Aptheker, *One Continual Cry* (New York: Humanities Press, 1965) 40–44.

[2] Peter P. Hinks, *To Awaken My Afflicted Brethren: David Walker and the Problem of*

and was born in 1796 or 1797, "that would make his absence more plausible, because he would be too young to appear on all but a few tax lists and could not have been listed on the 1810 census as head of a household."[3] A poll tax was required of all "free" blacks in the state during that period. That Walker's name is conspicuously absent from those and other census records seems to support the revised year of birth proposed by Hinks.

Apart from rudimentary teaching by his mother, David Walker was self-taught. He was tall, slender, and dark complexioned. It is generally presumed he was born to a "free" black woman in Wilmington, North Carolina. There remains considerable obscurity concerning his father. It has long been held that his father was a slave, who died just prior to David's birth. Walker's father might have been Anthony Walker, an Ibo of Nigeria, bought and owned by John Walker, who later sold him, along with the plantation, to a Revolutionary War hero, Major General Robert Howe. This, however, is speculation.[4]

It was the law in North Carolina, as in much of the South, that the black child takes the status of the mother rather than the father. Walker, the child of a "free" black, was therefore himself born "free." He was, however, reared in a place where large numbers of his people were enslaved. Walker, then, witnessed how his people were treated, both in the South and in other places he traveled.

Walker's travels convinced him that "the colored people" of the United States were "the most degraded, wretched, and abject set of beings that ever lived since the world began...."[5] Walker found what he considered to be more than adequate support for this belief through his study of history. He studied Greek and Roman forms of slavery and became convinced that no other enslaved people in the history of civilization had been as meanly and brutally treated as the enslaved Africans in the United States. Walker was both appalled and angered by this discovery, especially since many of his white countrymen who

Antebellum Slave Resistance (University Park PA: Pennsylvania State University Press, 1997) 11.

[3] Ibid., 11.

[4] Ibid., 12.

[5] David Walker, *Appeal to the Colored Citizens of the World, But in Particular, and very Expressly to those of the United States,* in *Great Documents in Black American History,* ed. George Ducas and Charles Van Doren (New York: Praeger Publishers, 1970) 59. The entire text of Walker's *Appeal* is reproduced in this anthology.

enslaved Africans claimed to be Christians. His own understanding of Christianity convinced him that one could not at the same time be a Christian and one who enslaved others. Only a "pretended" Christian enslaved another person. Walker wanted white Christians to live up to the true meaning of the Christian faith with respect to slavery. According to his understanding of that faith, slavery was both a crime against humanity and a sin against God.

Nowhere to Run to Freedom

David Walker was born "free" in slavery. He was free only in the sense that his mother was free, and the law said the black child assumed the status of the mother. As he would find out upon moving to Boston, however, there was no place in the United States of the 1820s that even nominally free blacks were treated as beings of dignity who warranted respect because they were imbued with the image and fragrance of God. Walker instead discovered that no matter where he traveled, blacks were harried and harassed, regardless of their social status. There is no question that Walker absolutely loathed slavery and the way in which his people generally were treated by whites. He reserved special disapproval for enslavers and other advocates of the "peculiar institution" who espoused the Christian faith. He frequently referred to these as the "pretenders" of Christianity. They were at best "false Christians" and, he opined, God would not take seriously their petitions as long as they owned or otherwise benefited from trafficking in human cargo.

Walker's eyewitness accounts of the behavior of white Christians toward his people made it impossible for him to remain in the South. He undoubtedly came to believe that if he remained, he would either kill one or more whites, or be killed. If he were going to play any part at all in the liberation of his people, he would have to leave. He moved to Boston, naively thinking that because slavery was outlawed there, blacks would not be subjected to racial injustice and prejudice. It was not long before he encountered much racism and racist violence in that city. Boston, much like the rest of the country, was no safe haven for blacks seeking refuge from violence and injustice at the hands of whites.[6]

Not long after arriving in Boston in late 1824, Walker opened a secondhand clothing shop—a popular business among blacks in that

---

[6] Hinks, *To Awaken My Afflicted Brethren*, 89.

city[7]—from which he earned a respectable living. Because of his financial resources and his deep commitment to the liberation of his people, Walker did not hesitate to assist runaway slaves. He was among those who supported a fund to buy the freedom of George Horton, a North Carolina slave reputed to be the greatest black poet since Phyllis Wheatley.[8] Walker's abolitionist activities led him to become the Boston agent of the country's first black newspaper, *Freedom's Journal*, launched in New York by Samuel Cornish and John Russwurm in 1827. Walker contributed several articles to the journal. Despite failing after only a brief period, the newspaper played an important role in paving the way for the publication of Walker's signature work in 1829, *Appeal to the Colored Citizens of the World, But in Particular, and Very Expressly to those of the United States*. It is commonly referred to by the short-form title, *Appeal*.

Marriage and Family

On 23 February 1826 David Walker married Eliza Butler in Boston.[9] Scholars of African American history believed for a long time that Walker fell in love with a slave woman before moving to Boston, and that it was she that he married.[10] Taking a clue from Martha Gruening's

---

[7] Ibid., 66–67.

[8] Benjamin Quarles, "Abolition's New Breed," in *Afro-American History Past to Present*, ed. Henry N. Drewry and Cecelia H. Drewry (Princeton NJ: Princeton University Press, 1971) 58.

[9] Hinks, *To Awaken My Afflicted Brethren*, 269.

[10] Henry Highland Garnet, "A Brief Sketch of the Life and Character of David Walker," in *Walker's Appeal/Garnet's Address*, preface by William Lorenz Katz (New York: Arno Press and the *New York Times*, 1969) 7–9. In 1848 Garnet wrote that Walker married a "Miss Eliza" in 1828. He made no reference to her maiden name. This omission is what prompted some scholars to surmise that it was intentionally omitted because Eliza was an escapee from slavery, and her life would be endangered had her maiden name been given. Herbert Aptheker observed that Martha Gruenig, "in her sketch of Walker in the *Dictionary of American Biography*, finds strange the omission of the maiden name of Walker's wife. No doubt she was herself a fugitive slave; hence the use of only a first name may have been considered a necessary security measure—even in 1848" (Aptheker, *One Continual Cry* [New York: Humanities Press, 1965] 42n.) This has been the traditional view held by scholars, put forth as recently as 1993 by James Turner, who contends that "speculation" has it that Eliza was a fugitive from slavery (See James Turner, *David Walker's Appeal*, introduction [Baltimore MD: Black Classic Press, 1993] 11–12). But it seems to me that the research by Peter Hinks into census data and other

biographical sketch of Walker in the *Dictionary of American Biography*, Herbert Aptheker argues that the fact Walker only referred to his wife by her first name suggests "she was herself a fugitive slave; hence the use of only a first name may have been considered a necessary security measure."[11] Peter Hinks, to the contrary, argues that Eliza Butler was a member of a well-established black family of Boston; that she was born, raised, and died in that city.[12] As with establishing the year of Walker's birth, Hinks bases this position on a thorough examination of associated census records, and marriage and death certificates. If Walker married into a well-established black Boston family, it also meant that he had gained entreé into that city's black community. His marriage into such a family also would have aided his efforts to establish himself in the secondhand clothing business.

The federal census of the 1820s reveals that two boys and a girl, all under the age of ten, were living in the Walker household.[13] Before the publication of Hinks' book on Walker, scholars generally did not mention his daughter, and only one of the sons. James Turner follows this line in his 1993 "Introduction" in *David Walker's Appeal*.[14] This precedence was set by Garnet.[15] Hinks' meticulous research strongly suggests it is more likely that the Walkers had three children.

The Walkers' infant daughter, Lydia Ann, died of lung fever the week before David Walker himself succumbed to what was for his day a common pulmonary disease, viz., consumption.[16] It is believed that one of the couple's sons, Edwin, became one of Boston's most outstanding African American citizens in the post-Civil War era. He excelled in the

---

legal documents pertaining to the Walkers in Boston provides the more "definitive" account, viz., that Eliza was born, reared, and died in Boston.

[11] Aptheker, *One Continual Cry*, 42n.

[12] Hinks, *To Awaken My Afflicted Brethren*, 69. Some scholars had thought that Eliza was an enslaved woman that Walker fell in love with in Wilmington, South Carolina. This, they argued, might explain why he only mentions her first name in the *Appeal*, and did not say where she was from. If she was in fact enslaved and transported to a "free" state by a "free" black, she could have been legally and forcibly returned to Wilmington and severely punished.

[13] Hinks, *To Awaken My Afflicted Brethren*, 69–70.

[14] Turner, *David Walker's Appeal*, 19n.3.

[15] Garnet in fact said that, "the son of the subject of this Memoir, was a posthumous child" (Garnet, "A Brief Sketch," in Aptheker, *One Continual Cry*, 41].

[16] Hinks, *To Awaken My Afflicted Brethren*, 269.

leather trade and had more than a dozen employees. He studied law and successfully passed the bar in 1861. Only the third black attorney of that period in Boston's Suffolk County, Edwin Walker was also eventually elected to the state legislature.[17]

Mysterious Death

Following Hinks, I indicated above that the cause of Walker's death was consumption. But, this is not the traditional viewpoint long espoused by many students of the period. Some of the lore surrounding David Walker maintains that factions in the white South put out a reward for his murder or live kidnapping. According to this account, with its primary source in Henry Highland Garnet, Walker was allegedly poisoned or otherwise murdered. In his sketch of Walker's life, Garnet wrote: "A company of Georgia men then bound themselves by an oath, that they would eat as little as possible until they had killed the youthful author. They also offered a reward of a thousand dollars for his head, and ten times as much for the live Walker."[18]

With good reason, some scholars maintain that much mystery surrounds the death of Walker. Not long after he completed the third and final edition of the *Appeal* in 1830, he was found dead near the entrance to his used clothing shop.[19] According to Herbert Aptheker, a black citizen of Boston "reported in the *Liberator* Jan. 22, 1831, that it was believed Walker had been murdered. A rumor was current that some person(s) in the South had offered $3,000 reward to the individual who would kill him."[20]

Aptheker[21] and Sterling Stuckey[22] are proponents of the view that Walker's was a mysterious death. These scholars take their position based on information culled from Garnet's biography of Walker. Here Garnet reported the common view among blacks in Boston: "It was the opinion of many that he was hurried out of life by the means of poison,

[17] Ibid., 270–71.

[18] Garnet, "A Brief Sketch," in Aptheker, *One Continual Cry*, 43.

[19] Turner, *David Walker's Appeal*, 17.

[20] Herbert Aptheker, *The Negro in the Abolitionist Movement* (New York: International Publishers, 1941) 34n.

[21] Aptheker, *One Continual Cry*, 52–53.

[22] Sterling Stuckey, "David Walker," in *Dictionary of American Negro Biography*, ed. Rayford W. Logan and Michael Winston (New York: W.W. Norton, 1982) 623.

but whether this was the case or not, the writer is not prepared to affirm."[23] Garnet made it clear; he could not substantiate the claim that Walker was poisoned. Although the accusation was hearsay, the prevalent opinion nevertheless became, and persisted to more recent times, that David Walker was poisoned at the instigation of Southern whites.

There is not sufficient evidence to say conclusively how David Walker died. Hinks argues convincingly that although *the door of suspicion surrounding Walker's death cannot be closed*, the available evidence suggests that he died of natural causes, quite possibly, consumption. This was a disease that was commonplace in those days and took the lives of many.[24] According to Hinks, what little evidence there is gives reasonable support to the natural cause of death theory rather than to mysterious cause allegations.

Hinks is careful to leave open the door regarding the mysterious death theory. Walker's *Appeal* was branded by many as "seditious" and "incendiary." These believed it posed a serious threat to the system of slavery and the economic livelihood of enslavers and their northern business connections. It is not beyond belief that determined advocates of slavery might well have taken drastic measures to eliminate the author of such a "dangerous" treatise. Furthermore, these would have done so with no pangs of conscience nor moral reprobation from an enculturated Christian religion that first and foremost served the enslavers' economic and social interests.

It would not be fair or accurate to say that Aptheker was any more a proponent of the mysterious death theory than is Hinks. Even Garnet did not say unequivocally that Walker was murdered. Aptheker himself points to "the mystery of Walker's death," noting that opinions range from natural to mysterious causes, i.e., murder. Clearly in the mysterious cause camp, Aptheker—himself a careful and meticulous historian—does not close the door completely on the natural cause theory. The uncertainty of a conclusive finding regarding Walker's death is somewhat obscured in Hinks' discussion. Aptheker's conclusion is: *"The verdict of 'cause for suspicion, but no definite conclusion is possible'...seems to be the soundest one given available evidence."*[25]

---

[23] Garnet, "A Brief Sketch," 9 (emphasis added).

[24] Hinks, *To Awaken My Afflicted Brethren*, 269–70.

[25] Aptheker, *One Continual Cry*, 52 (emphasis added).

Reasonably certain that conclusive evidence to the contrary is not forthcoming, Aptheker writes, "Deep mystery surrounds the manner of David Walker's death in his 44th year."[26]

While Hinks may have correctly reported the cause of Walker's death as noted on his death certificate, there is still the strong possibility that the stated "official" cause of death was a cover-up engineered by the period's white "powers that be." I say this because I am haunted by the fact that blacks of that period were murdered for much less than what Walker did by publishing and disseminating the *Appeal*. Considering that whites controlled the record keeping, whether in the coroner's office or elsewhere, it was fairly easy to make "official" anything that whites put into those records. Even if Walker had in fact been murdered by poisoning or some other mysterious means, the white coroner could have written in "natural causes" as the "official" cause of death. He could have done this and not ever have been challenged. So it seems that the only reasonable conclusion is that a good deal of mystery surrounds Walker's death even to this day, and that circumstantially, at least, one can make a case for either the natural or the mysterious cause theory of his death.

Walker and the Slave Ethos

Since Walker was born "free," one might be tempted to conclude that he did not know the ethos of slave culture to the extent that the enslaved did. To be sure, Walker and other free blacks were only nominally free. Their freedom was subject to numerous limitations in the social, economic, and legal environs of that day. Since "free" blacks frequently did not have firsthand experience with slavery, how would they be able to know much about the beliefs and practices of the enslaved? Stuckey argues that knowledge of African religious and cultural practices was nearly non-existent among nineteenth-century free blacks.[27]

Hinks provides an instructive commentary on this point: "Any sense of connectedness with Africa and its triumphs was almost totally obscured. Save for scattered articles in newspapers and fledgling efforts by *Freedom's Journal* and *The Rights of All* (which succeeded the short-

---

[26] Ibid., 53.

[27] Sterling Stuckey, *Slave Culture: Nationalist Theory and the Foundations of Black America* (New York: Oxford University Press, 1987) 109.

lived *Freedom's Journal*), there were hardly any texts that represented African American history or culture in any favorable light, or even threw a sop to them for having persevered against adversity."[28]

Little was known of or published about the Africans' existence prior to their forced enslavement. Nearly all that was known about their experiences and culture in this country until the 1820s was primarily shaped by their experience in slavery. In this regard, it was as if the Africans had no existence at all prior to slavery. This idea was intentionally impressed upon them by many whites. The real trouble, as Walker perceived it, was that large numbers of the Africans accepted this view of themselves. It was this theft of historical and cultural identity against which Walker contended so vehemently. That is, he was relentless in his efforts to eradicate the tendency of blacks to think of themselves as slaves and as inferior beings. White enslavers had done a very thorough job of brainwashing many blacks to think of themselves as inherently inferior. Why else, Walker wondered, would they even abuse each other only because a white man required it under threat of punishment for disobedience?

Notwithstanding, it is fair to say that Walker was more exposed to the cultural dimension of slave life than was previously known.[29] While growing up in Wilmington, North Carolina, he not only had frequent contact with his enslaved people, but he often witnessed whites' cruel and inhumane treatment of them. Indeed, this daily experience of observing his people being brutalized is what led Walker to the decision to leave the South and his commitment to liberate them. Said Walker, "If I remain in this bloody land, I will not live long. As true as God reigns, I will be avenged for the sorrow which my people have suffered. This is not the place for me—no, no. I must leave this part of the country. It will be a great trial for me to live on the same soil where so many men are in slavery. Certainly I cannot remain where I must hear their chains continually, and where I must encounter the insults of their hypocritical enslavers. God I must."[30]

---

[28] Hinks, *To Awaken My Afflicted Brethren*, 216.

[29] Stuckey, *Slave Culture*, 111.

[30] Walker quoted in Garnet, "A Brief Sketch," 7.

Charleston, South Carolina

Before traveling to Boston, however, Walker left Wilmington between 1815–1820 for Charleston, South Carolina. Charleston was thought to have a large community of free blacks and better employment opportunities. The white establishment in that city allowed the free blacks to organize in order to support each other through various cooperative ventures. In addition, the free black community of Charleston interacted closely with that city's many enslaved Africans. The Charleston free blacks, despite the "largess" of the whites, were committed to liberating their enslaved sisters and brothers and eradicating slavery.[31]

Many of Charleston's free blacks possessed deep religious convictions, and saw no contradiction between their faith and their actions to liberate the enslaved. Blacks controlled their own churches in that city and did not care to leave the fate of their enslaved people in the hands of any institution controlled by whites. As a result, the black churches actively took part in the liberation process. This, in part, is why it has been argued that a black church was involved in the planning of the Denmark Vesey uprising of 1822. For example, Hinks contends, "One can legitimately call the Charleston AME Church the center of the Vesey conspiracy."[32]

It was this type of religion that most influenced Walker when he finally relocated to Boston. There was nothing politically conservative about Walker's evangelicalism. As tends to be the case with most evangelicals, Walker's chief authority was the Bible. But unlike many white evangelicals, he saw clear political implications in the Scriptures that served to bolster his case against slavery. Walker not only sought employment opportunities in Charleston, but also desired to clarify the meaning of his own blackness and of freedom in a society that enslaved and dehumanized the vast majority of his people.[33]

Who Was Enlightened?

There is evidence in Walker's writing that he believed whites to be enlightened, and his own people to be ignorant. He implied that because

---

[31] Hinks, *To Awaken My Afflicted Brethren*, 62.

[32] Ibid., 38.

[33] Ibid., 20–21.

whites were enlightened, they were by moral responsibility obligated to enlighten the Africans. But instead of doing so, white enslavers and their supporters took advantage of the Africans, further contributing to the misery of their condition of enslavement.

> The Christians and enlightened of Europe, and some of Asia, seeing the ignorance and consequent degradation of our fathers, instead of trying to enlighten them, by teaching them that religion and light with which God had blessed them, they have plunged them into wretchedness ten thousand times more intolerable, than if they had left them entirely to the Lord, and to add to their miseries, deep down into which they have plunged them, tell them, that they are an *inferior* and *distinct race* of beings, which they will be glad enough to recall and swallow by and by.[34]

To the extent that the Africans were not socialized into the Anglo-Saxon mores of thinking, living, and relating, it can be said that they were ignorant of such ways. It can also be said that whites were just as ignorant of the ways of the free and enslaved Africans. It would seem that Walker was actually responding to the reality that Africans had been forced into slavery, and that many who were nominally free had not done enough to learn the ways of the whites as a means for the survival and ultimate liberation of the masses of blacks.

Walker was primarily addressing his comments to blacks rather than to whites. What he said, however, implied his own ignorance of the ways and accomplishments of Africa. As noted earlier, such knowledge was not generally available to blacks in this country in the early nineteenth century. Had Walker been more knowledgeable in this regard, he might well have proceeded to argue a case for spiritual, intellectual, cultural, and moral parity between the races. Even though his knowledge of his people's African heritage was limited, Walker was aware of some of their larger historic and social accomplishments. He refers, for example, to the construction of the Egyptian pyramids "and other magnificent buildings"[35] on the African continent.

---

[34] Walker, *Appeal*, 70.
[35] Ibid.

The Damning Impact of Slavery on the African Psyche

Despite such notable accomplishments, Walker knew how difficult it would be for his people to change the skewed self-perception imposed upon them by white enslavers. That is, the perception that blacks were inferior, subhuman, and thus fit only to exist as slaves and servants to whites. "Part of the horrible brutality of American slavery was the manner in which it could transform blacks—despite their showing clear signs of individual and group strengths and resourcefulness—into the believers and even the agents of their own degradation."[36] Walker, like Malcolm X over a century later, knew better than most that blacks were vulnerable to internalizing these damning perceptions of themselves to the extent that it would be a task of gargantuan proportions to eradicate such notions and reawaken in blacks a sense of humanity and dignity. Slavery destroyed black personhood, "leaving it little to stand on by way of its own making and thus more receptive to development by white masters."[37]

Despite the cruelty and dehumanization to which blacks were subjected in slavery, David Walker never believed that they were merely passive receptacles to be filled and molded by whites or instructed by them on what it really means to be persons. The fact that there was so much evidence of their ability as workers, as productive agents of change, and as people who were special to God,[38] convinced Walker that weariness and apparent submission were not the ultimate responses of blacks to their enslaved condition. It never was the case that all blacks submitted to and uniformly internalized whites' perceptions of them. Walker himself was a perfect example of a black person who was relentless in his efforts to define his own humanity, while rejecting whites' perceptions of him or their systemic attempts to mold him into their image.

Love for His People

Although David Walker was born "free," he identified with and loved his people, regardless of their status or his own geographic location once removed from the South. He did not hesitate to express his love for the

---

[36] Hinks, *To Awaken My Afflicted Brethren*, 217.

[37] Ibid., 218n. 34.

[38] Ibid.

people and pride that he was of African descent. Like Malcolm X, whom he preceded, he was less concerned about expressing hatred for whites than admonishing his people to love and regard one another with respect. Any hatred that Walker might have had for whites was in response to white hatred for and enslavement of his people.[39] That is, what hate was present in him was a reaction of revulsion to whites' inhumane treatment of blacks. Walker was less motivated by hatred for whites or a desire to teach his people to hate them, than by his deep love for and desire to be in total solidarity with his people. Historian Vincent Harding concurs: "He was impelled not by hatred of white America, but by a profound love and compassion for his people. It was this commitment to black people, and his unshakable belief in a God of justice, which led inevitably to an urgent statement of black radicalism, a call for uprooting and overturning of the system of life and death that was America."[40] Walker was animated and driven by the core values of his religious faith, love for his people, and the conviction that they possessed a fundamental humanity and dignity that ought to be acknowledged and respected—by themselves, as well as by whites.

As noted, this was an attitude and stance that anticipated by more than 125 years the outlook Malcolm X favored. Walker did not hesitate to criticize his people when they passively yielded before their white enslavers, or left unchallenged white society's insistence that blacks were somehow a lesser form of humanity. For Walker, those who refused to do all in their power to remove the chains of oppression deserved everything that the white system of dehumanizing slavery did to them. Walker reasoned that it was a violation of God's will and expectation for blacks to passively accept whites' perception of them, as well as the vicious form of enslavement to which they were subjected. This stance led him to declare: "The man who would not fight under our Lord and Master Jesus Christ, in the glorious and heavenly cause of freedom and of God—to be delivered from the most wretched, abject and servile slavery, that ever a people was afflicted with since the foundation of the world, to the present day—ought to be kept with all of his children or family, in slavery, or in chains, to be butchered by his *cruel enemies*."[41]

---

[39] Walker, *Appeal*, 100.

[40] Vincent Harding, *There is a River: The Black Struggle for Freedom in America* (New York: Vintage, 1981) 87.

[41] Walker, *Appeal*, 66.

Since blacks too were creatures of inestimable worth according to God's creative intent, Walker argued passionately for the practice of self-defense among his people. Better to be killed defending one's humanity and dignity, or for trying to liberate oneself from slavery than to passively accept the daily violence slavery imposed on one's personhood. Walker concluded that "the man who will stand still and let another murder him, is worse than an infidel, and if he has common sense, ought not to be pitied."[42]

Once again, Walker's emphasis was not on hatred of whites as such, or a desire to use violence for its own sake in the overthrow of slavery. His focus was on the necessity that his people reclaim and honor their God-given sense of humanity and dignity.

It is the case, however, that Walker was not opposed to violent overthrow of the slavocracy if other means failed. He preferred nonviolence to avoid the loss of human life, regardless of race. Walker's point was that whites themselves controlled the means to the imminent overthrow of slavery in the sense that they were the oppressors and possessed all of the resources of socio-political and economic power to ameliorate the injustice. It was as well within their power and means to emancipate the slaves nonviolently.

Walker wanted only that his people be freed from slavery and enabled to live with dignity. Those who maintain that he was largely a bitter, militant abolitionist who called for violence against whites overstate the matter. Indeed, no less an eminent scholar than John Hope Franklin is guilty of characterizing Walker as such.[43] Earl Ofari does similarly when he writes, without qualifying his statement, that Walker called for the violent overthrow of slavery.[44] By failing to give the appropriate context to Walker's rhetoric, these scholars mislead us to conclude that the black abolitionist was just another irresponsible militant, vengefully bent on killing whites. To the contrary, Walker's first preference was the voluntary manumission of the enslaved. He was, however, enough of a realist to know that his greater hope was but wishful thinking.

---

[42] Ibid., 74.

[43] John Hope Franklin and Alfred A. Moss, Jr., *From Slavery to Freedom*, (New York: Alfred A. Knopf, 1988) 167.

[44] Earl Ofari, *"Let Your Motto Be Resistance": The Life and Thoughts of Henry Highland Garnet* (Boston: Beacon Press, 1972) 41.

Black Nationalist Revolutionary

David Walker was among the earliest African American nationalist revolutionaries, though much black nationalist revolutionary activity preceded him—indeed, paved the way ahead of him. One need only recall, for example, the direct measures against enslavers taken by Gabriel Prosser in 1800 and Denmark Vesey in 1822. In fact, there is strong evidence that Walker—who left Charleston not long after the trial of Vesey and his comrades—had firsthand knowledge of the planning of the conspiracy.[45] Furthermore, the Vesey conspiracy was not Walker's only knowledge of or exposure to such revolutionary activity by his people. Indeed, he "grew up in a region of the South that had a long tradition of slave resistance, conspiracies, and marronage."[46]

David Walker was the first black American of African descent to produce and publish a sustained revolutionary political treatise: *Appeal to the Colored Citizens of the World, But in Particular, and Very Expressly to Those of the United States of America* (hereafter, *Appeal*). Less than 100 pages in length, the *Appeal*, the "volume on which Walker's reputation as the harbinger of militant abolitionism rests...,"[47] sent shock waves of fear throughout the white South, prompting some Southern politicians to write to the governor of Massachusetts (where the *Appeal* was written) pleading that he outlaw the text and ban it from publication. Although steps were taken by the whites in the South to minimize the reach of the *Appeal* in that region, enough copies had circulated so that the damage was already done.

Considered by one scholar to be a major black religious leader of his time,[48] and by another to be "the John the Baptist of the antislavery crusade,"[49] i.e., its chief forerunner, Walker, in his militant approach, his insistence on speaking primarily to his own people, and his belief in their inherent dignity, anticipated much of the approach taken by black nationalists of the 1960s. Historian John Hope Franklin has characterized Walker's *Appeal* as one of the most vigorous denunciations of slavery

---

[45] Hinks, *To Awaken My Afflicted Brethren*, 39, 62; entirety of ch. 2.

[46] Ibid., 40.

[47] Stuckey, *Slave Culture*, 120.

[48] Henry J. Young, chap. 3 in *Major Black Religious Leaders: 1755–1940* (Nashville: Abingdon Press, 1977).

[49] Lerone Bennett, Jr., *Before the Mayflower: A History of Black America* (Chicago: Johnson Publishing, 1970) 132.

ever published in the United States,[50] and noted its appearance at a time when it was literally life-threatening to engage in such an undertaking.

Walker's *Appeal* continues to be one of the most passionate and persuasive defenses of the humanity and dignity of Africans in *diaspora*. This theologico-political treatise provides considerable information about Walker's views on God and black personhood, which contributes to understanding his role as ethical prophet. His view of God shared much in common with the eighth-century prophets. God, for Walker, was steadfast, exhaustless in compassion, love, and justice. One could not play this God for a fool, or persistently disobey God's dictates without suffering severe consequences. Walker understood that divine wrath or judgment was something that God allows to happen only when people persist in disobedience and unfaithfulness to God's expectation that justice be done in the world. On the other hand, Walker believed God's essential nature to be characterized by love, justice, and compassion. Therefore, he did not include wrath as a fundamental attribute of God's nature.

In addition, Walker emphasized the idea of the sacredness of all persons. A number of passages in the *Appeal* makes it clear that he grounds the idea of the sacredness of all persons in the fundamental theological principle that God willingly and thoughtfully creates and imbues every individual with the divine image. Not only is this divine image *in* every person, but every person *is* the image of God. An important theological implication of this is that every person is a being of infinite and inviolable worth.

Excursus
David Walker's Influence on Maria W. Stewart

Walker's political analysis in the *Appeal*, as well as his witness of and crusade for the acknowledgement of the humanity and worth of his people and their desire for total liberation, had a profound influence on this country's "first black woman political writer," Maria W. Stewart (1803–1879). Walker was a close friend of Stewart and her husband, James. The two men worked together in the Massachusetts General Coloured Association in Boston. It might well have been Stewart, a

---

[50] Franklin, *From Slavery to Freedom*, 159.

"professional ship outfitter," who helped Walker smuggle copies of the *Appeal* onto ships leaving Boston harbor bound for the South.[51]

Maria Stewart was "the first black American to lecture in defense of women's rights...,"[52] and most particularly the rights of black women. She was also the first woman in this country to lecture to a mixed-gender audience of blacks and whites.[53] She did so at a time when patriarchal practices did not grant women such public voice. As enlightened as some early white abolitionists and their newspapers were, even these foes of slavery could not bring themselves to support public political outspokenness among women. Four months before Stewart addressed an audience in 1832, "the most progressive of the abolitionist newspapers, the *Liberator*, counseled: 'The voice of woman should not be heard in public debates, but there are other ways in which her influence would be beneficial.'"[54]

Like Walker, Stewart primarily addressed nominally free black audiences as a means of educating them about their humanity and worth as God's creations; the need to take their own destiny into their hands; and their need to be supportive of each other. She urged those with resources to do more in support of uplifting all black people.

Having experienced what was for her a sure sense of the prophetic divine call,[55] Stewart could be as "caustic" and candid in her socio-political analysis of the causes of the black condition of oppression as was Walker. Since her views—and sometimes her means of expressing them—went against the grain of the times, she alienated many people, including her own. It was not Stewart's intention to alienate others, but the nature of her message and her prophetic voice necessarily caused

---

[51] Turner, *David Walker's Appeal*, 18n. 1.

[52] Marilyn Richardson, ed., *Maria W. Stewart, America's First Black Woman Political Writer: Essays and Speeches* (Bloomington IN: Indiana University Press, 1987) xiii.

[53] *The Public Years of Sarah and Angelina Grimké: Selected Writings 1835–1839*, ed. Larry Ceplair (New York: Columbia University Press, 1989) xiii; Darlene Clark Hine and Kathleen Thompson, *A Shining Thread of Hope: The History of Black Women in America* (New York: Broadway Books, 1998) 105.

[54] See Paula Giddings, *When and Where I Enter: The Impact of Black Women on Race and Sex in America* (New York: Bantam Books, 1984) 49–50.

[55] Maria Stewart, "An Address Delivered before the Afric American Female Intelligence Society, of Boston," in *Spiritual Narratives*, ed. Sue E. Houchins (New York: Oxford University Press, 1988) 59.

many to part company with her. Stewart believed she answered only to God in answering her call, maintaining that she was "a strong advocate for the cause of God, and for the cause of freedom."[56]

Stewart, like Walker, was convinced that the condition of her people was nothing short of a state of emergency. She was therefore not prone to softening her language,[57] and was even less concerned about what people thought of her. Indeed, she was just as straightforward about identifying her people's suffering as she was about proposing solutions to their plight.

Stewart insisted, like Walker, on the necessity of *naming* both the culprits and the fundamental causes of blacks' oppression as prerequisite to proposing solutions.[58] Especially during the nineteenth century, this was a dangerous practice for blacks. It will be recalled that the mysterious circumstances of Walker's death not long after the publication of the *Appeal* are attributed to his daring outspokenness.

One sees the influence of Walker's ideas and approach in a number of Stewart's writings and speeches. In addition, there are two explicit references to Walker in her 1831 essay, "Religion and the Pure Principles of Morality, The Sure Foundation on which We Must Build." Stewart's essay appeared one year after Walker's death on 6 August 1830. In one passage, she tells readers that although Walker was dead, "his name shall be had in everlasting remembrance."[59] In another passage she makes clear her intention to fight for the liberation of her people, even to the point of being martyred: "Many will suffer for pleading the cause of oppressed Africa, and I shall glory in being one of her martyrs; for I am firmly persuaded, that the God in whom I trust is able to protect me from the rage and malice of mine enemies, and from them that will rise up against me; and *if there is no other way for me to escape, he is able to take me to himself, as he did the most noble, fearless, and undaunted David Walker.*"[60] Stewart was every bit as religious as David Walker, and like him she put her faith wholly in God, whom she believed would protect and deliver her from her enemies. Both her religious faith

---

[56] Stewart, "Female Intelligence Society," 59.

[57] See Hine and Thompson, *A Shining Thread of Hope*, 106.

[58] Richardson, *Maria W. Stewart*, 12–13.

[59] Ibid., *Maria W. Stewart*, 40.

[60] Ibid., *Maria W. Stewart*, 30. (emphasis added)

convictions and her commitment to her people gave her the courage to speak out, demanding justice and liberation on their behalf.

Although Stewart was significantly influenced by Walker, it is important to emphasize that she was her own person, did her own thinking, and spoke her own convictions. She transcended Walker's influence to the extent that she, like Anna Julia Cooper, Sojourner Truth, and a number of other nineteenth-century black foremothers, was explicit in proclaiming the right of black women to join the ranks of leadership with black men in the struggle for socio-political and human rights. In spirit, attitude, and behavior, Stewart and these other women anticipated the present day Womanist Movement, i.e., a way of thinking and behaving free of male domination that is being promulgated by African American women in and outside of the academy.

Stewart addressed abolition, black autonomy and self-determination, economic independence, race pride, and the rights of women. Like Walker, she excoriated blacks who depended solely on whites rather than look to themselves and God for their socio-political salvation. Stewart was critical of black men for failure to prepare themselves to be leaders, and for wasting their money and time in gambling establishments and dance halls.[61] She strongly urged blacks to use their money to support educational institutions for their children. In addition, Stewart insisted on the need for the involvement of black women in politics, business, and education. Moreover, she maintained blacks should adhere to the highest moral standards, as means to proving wrong the many whites who believed them to be inferior intellectually and morally.[62]

In every era of black African presence in this country, there have been black women who have been as devoted and committed to the cause of black humanity, dignity, and liberation as black men. Maria Stewart was such a woman. Until relatively recent times, the tendency of black historians and other writers of African descent was to name and discuss the contributions of black men only, thereby failing to acknowledge the contributions of black women. The practice generally was to consider, but only briefly, the contributions of one or two of the better known black women, e.g., Sojourner Truth and Harriet Tubman. Even black

---

[61] Stewart, "An Address Delivered at the African Masonic Hall," in *Spiritual Narratives*, 67.

[62] Stewart, "Religion and the Pure Principles of Morality," in *Spiritual Narratives*, 21.

history, when written by black hands, was largely written by men who essentially told the story of the contributions of black men. In this regard, the practice and behavior of black men historically has differed little from that of white men.

Basic American Political Documents

Before proceeding to the discussion of ethical prophecy in the work of David Walker, it may be helpful to comment on a common practice of black reformers in the nineteenth century, including Frederick Douglass. Because for many black reformers slavery was fundamentally a moral and theological problem, their basic argument against it was couched in the language of the Jewish and Christian faith traditions. They naturally looked to the Bible and to moral-ethical principles derived therein to express their convictions. The reformers also appealed to the ideas in major American political documents to further substantiate their claim that the Africans were fully human and equal before God. That additional source of constructing logical appeals for black African liberation and elevation presented its own unique challenges, as we will see.

At the conclusion of the *Appeal*, Walker included an addendum—a commentary on the Declaration of Independence. He believed he could rely on that historic document's language—"We hold these truths to be self-evident that all men are created equal"—as a means of further supporting his theologico-ethical argument against slavery, and for the absolute dignity of blacks—indeed, for that of *all* persons. This seems on the surface a reasonable approach to enhancing the argument against slavery and the social deprivation free blacks endured. Walker, Frederick Douglass,[63] and others who appealed to the nation's founding documents cannot be blamed for using everything at their disposal to argue against and contribute to the defeat of the slavocracy. One has to wonder,

---

[63] See Frederick Douglass's oration, "The Constitution of the United States: Is it Pro-Slavery or Anti-Slavery?" delivered in Glasgow, Scotland, 26 March 1860 in *The Life and Writings of Frederick Douglass*, ed. Philip S. Foner (1950; reprint, New York: International Publishers, 1975) 2:467–80. In fairness, however, it should also be noted that in an 1886 address Douglass was critical of the US Constitution, stating that it "has been slain in the house of its friends. So far as the colored people of the country are concerned, the Constitution is but a stupendous sham, a rope of sand, a Dead Sea apple, fair without and foul within, keeping the promise to the eyes and breaking it to the heart." (See Foner, *The Life and Writings of Frederick Douglass*, 4:431.)

however, about the wisdom of that approach given that the Declaration of Independence was not intended to include the Africans at all.

As noted previously, during the early 1800s, Africans were considered by many whites to be subhuman at best. In light of that, blacks were not even citizens at the writing of the Declaration of Independence, for *they were not thought to be persons.* That being the case, blacks could not legally claim for themselves the rights advocated in the Declaration and the Constitution. If they were recognized as whole and fully persons, however, the claim was on solid ground from a moral perspective, even if denied legal standing by the white powerbrokers of the day.

We should remember that Chief Justice Roger B. Taney refused to acknowledge the humanity of the Africans during slavery. This was made crystal clear in 1857 when Taney read the majority opinion of the Supreme Court in *Dred Scott vs. Sanford.* Scott charged that because he traveled with his owner in 1834 from the slave state of Missouri to Illinois, a free state, and then to the Wisconsin Territory where slavery was forbidden by the Compromise of 1820, this in fact made him a free man. There was legal precedence for Scott's claim, since prior to the 1850s Missouri courts ruled that owners who took their slaves to a free state effectively liberated them. By the 1850s, however, the courts were reversing this trend and ruling predominantly in favor of enslavers. Nevertheless, when Scott was returned to Missouri in 1846, he filed suit.

When the Supreme Court issued its ruling, Taney argued that persons of African descent were not citizens of the Colonies when the Declaration of Independence and the Constitution were written. Therefore, Dred Scott and other blacks could not bring suit against whites in the courts. Furthermore, the Court said that even if Scott had the right to sue, the fact that he lived in Illinois and the Wisconsin Territory did not make him free. Essentially this meant that an enslaved African was the property of her owner, and the Constitution protected a person's property, while it did not acknowledge and protect the humanity and rights of the Africans. Therefore, a property owner could take his property anywhere in the United States, but this would not affect the legal status of the property itself. It remained property.

According to Chief Justice Taney, Africans were by far the inferiors of the white race and therefore granted no rights either in the Declaration or the Constitution.

It is true, every person, and every class and description of persons, who were at the time of the adoption of the Constitution recognized as citizens in the several States, became also citizens of this new political body; but none other; it was formed by them, and for them and their posterity, but for no one else. And the personal rights and privileges guaranteed to citizens of this new sovereignty were intended to embrace those only who were then members of the several state communities, or who should afterwards, by birthright or otherwise, become members, according to the provisions of the Constitution and the principles on which it was founded....

In the opinion of the court, the legislation and histories of the times, and the language used in the Declaration of Independence, show, that neither the class of persons who had been imported as slaves, nor their descendants, whether they had become free or not, were then acknowledged as a part of the people, nor intended to be included in the general words used in that memorable instrument....

They had for more than a century before been regarded as beings of an inferior order; and altogether unfit to associate with the white race, either in social or political relations; and *so far inferior that they had no rights which the white man was bound to respect*; and that the negro might justly and lawfully be reduced to slavery for his benefit... This opinion was at that time fixed and universal in the *civilized* portion of the white race. It was regarded as an axiom in morals as well as in politics, which no one thought of disputing, or supposed to be open to dispute; and men in every grade and position in society daily and habitually acted upon it in their private pursuits, as well as in matters of public concern, without doubting for a moment the correctness of this opinion.[64]

Since they were not recognized as full persons, the Africans were thought to have extrinsic or instrumental value only. That is, their value was based on their economic worth to whites.

---

[64] From Chief Justice Roger B. Taney's reading of the Supreme Court's ruling in *Dred Scott* v. *Sanford*, in *Documents of American History*, ed. Henry Steele Commager (New York: Appleton-Century-Crofts, 1963) 341–42 (emphasis added).

While in fairness to Walker it should be said that his interpretation of the human rights clause in the Declaration came nearly thirty years before the Court's ruling in the Dred Scott case, it should also be remembered that Walker was familiar with Thomas Jefferson's opinions about blacks in *Notes on the State of Virginia*. One of the founding fathers, Jefferson also believed the Africans to be so far inferior to whites that their condition of servitude was warranted.

Consequently, it appears that Walker's appeal to the Declaration of Independence was unreasonable, since those who drafted its language did not consider the Africans to be persons. Because of this stance, the drafters of the Declaration concluded that they could treat the Africans as they wanted without fear of legal, moral, or other repercussions. There were no laws against enslaving those who were declared essentially non-persons or chattel property.

If, as it indeed seems, the nation's founders did not recognize the full humanity of the black African—whether free or slave—in America, then Walker's admonition that whites compare the language of the Declaration with their cruel, inhumane treatment of blacks really meant nothing in terms of providing further support for his argument that it was illegal and immoral for blacks to be enslaved. The most Walker logically might have argued is that the intent of the Declaration's language *should have* included the Africans, and that any reference in the document to persons or human beings should have been to all or to none. While modern American society may find it is repugnant to disallow any person their humanity, such was not the case in David Walker's day.

What we need to remember is that the most significant source of Walker's belief in the absolute dignity of his people—indeed, of all people—came not from whatever value he found in the basic American political documents, but from his religious and theological convictions. Walker believed in the God of the eighth-century prophets, the God of Jesus Christ (Jn 20:17). This was the God of all persons, or of no persons. Every person possessed a trace of the divine, and none was the superior or inferior of any other before God. Walker's argument for the categorical application of the equality principle and for the humanity and dignity of his people stood on firmer theological and biblical grounds than on appeals to the Declaration of Independence and the Constitution.

What follows is a more explicit examination of the framework and definition of ethical prophecy, as well as criteria or principles that must be met if one is to be considered an ethical prophet in the tradition of Hebrew prophecy. The criteria to be examined are not exhaustive. Chapter 2 will thereby set the stage for an examination of ethical prophecy in light of the life and work of David Walker.

Chapter 2

Ethical Prophecy

Setting the Stage

Ethical prophecy or prophetic ethics is a subject that might be examined from the perspective of any number of academic disciplines in a university or seminary curriculum. Ethical prophecy, however, has its most natural place in theological social ethics, a discipline that is intentionally interdisciplinary.[1] Social ethics, when studied in a predominantly Christian context, seeks to be open to and conversant with the methodologies and contributions of biblical studies, theology, Christian education, church history, and the social and behavioral sciences. Because theological social ethics is intentionally interdisciplinary, the subject of ethical prophecy might be taught by one individual or jointly by persons representing different academic disciplines. Prophetic ethics is more naturally a type of theological

---

[1] See Walter G. Muelder, *Foundations of the Responsible Society: A Comprehensive Survey of Christian Social Ethics* (Nashville: Abingdon Press, 1959) 9. See also "An Autobiographical Introduction: Forty Years of Communitarian Personalism," in his *Ethical Edge of Christian Theology* (New York: Mellen Press, 1983) 25–26.

ethics, because implicit in it is the imperative to be and to act in the world in light of God's Word and expectations as voiced through the teachings of the eighth-century prophets and others in that lineage.

Personal-Communal Nature of Ethics

It is important to understand that ethical prophecy lifts up the principle, first and last, that all ethics are personal-communal. At the end of the day, it comes down to one individual making a moral decision in the context of one or more communities. That is, first and last, each individual decides to do or not do this or that, and she chooses in the context of some community. Perhaps it will be helpful to illustrate what this might mean when applied to a specific moral issue.

Racism is endemic to American society and all of its major institutions. While it is true that ultimately there must be revolutionary change in these institutions and the white community that they by and large represent, at bottom it comes down to what a critical mass of individual whites will do about their racism. This challenges their level of commitment to radically altering the institutions and structures from which they continue to reap hefty, unearned benefits in the areas of education, employment, housing, etc. Structural and systemic change of the most radical nature are necessary if there is to be change in race relations which will put us on the path to meaningful human relations. This notwithstanding, it will be just as important for a significant number of individual whites to decide against racism in all of its forms, and then be courageous and willing enough to act individually *and* collectively against racial prejudice and discrimination.

To say that all ethics are, first and last, personal-communal means, for example that Quincy Viktor the white person has to *confess* his role in racism and how he benefits from it. But this is not all. In addition, he must be willing to talk about, and work at, his racism. Without this sort of individual or personal confession, one must wonder about the point of whites participating in strategy sessions ostensibly intended to bring about racial justice and reconciliation. If those doing the strategizing have not acknowledged, confessed, and sought forgiveness for their own complicity in racism and the privileges it makes available to them, it is inconceivable that any amount of strategizing, however well intentioned, will make any meaningful, lasting difference in race relations. One has to say, finally, "I am not myself *intentionally* racist in my attitudes and practices. However, I am aware that by virtue of my white skin and the fact that I benefit from racism whether I like it or not, I confess my complicity in it." Finally, one must be courageous enough to proclaim: "I am for racism," or, "I am against racism." Furthermore, he must say: "It is I who must take radical actions against all forms of racism. I must be vigilant at the point of self-criticism."

Naomi Wolf, a white feminist, suggests an excellent way for whites to begin grappling with their racism. She proposes that like herself, all "well meaning white people" (her phrase) must, rather than theorizing about racism or merely speaking and writing about it as if it were an abstraction that does not really have anything to do with them, begin instead to talk openly and straightforwardly "about what their own racism looks like, sounds like, feels like."[2] They must be courageous enough to openly own the part they play in racist ideology and practices. Only then, Wolf maintains, will it be possible to really begin liberating oneself from racism. This idea is consistent with the concept that all ethics, finally, are personal-communal. That is, all ethical decisions are inevitably made by individuals in the integral context of one of their communities.

Prophetic ethics maintains that the individual is the fundamental moral unit, which is similar to what we find in personalistic ethics[3] (which is not synonymous with individualistic ethics, but is more closely aligned with communitarian ethics). This means that even in the context of group decision-making, it is still the individuals in the group who, in the end, do the choosing and deciding. This is the case despite the texture and the pressure of the group. The emphasis is on the person as the moral unit-in-community, not on a kind of selfish individualism.

The importance of this principle is not difficult to determine. It means that no person, no group, gets off the moral hook easily (if at all).

---

[2] Naomi Wolf, "The Racism of Well-Meaning White People," in *Skin Deep: Black Women & White Women Write About Race*, ed. Marita Goldman and Susan Richards Shreve (New York: Anchor Books, 1995) 44.

[3] See related discussions in: Borden P. Bowne, "Ethics of the Individual," chap. 8 in *The Principles of Ethics* (New York: American Book, 1892); Edgar S. Brightman, "The Law of Individualism," chap. 13 in *Moral Laws* (New York: Abingdon Press, 1933); Peter A. Bertocci and Richard Millard, "Duties to Oneself: Individuality," chap. 26 in *Personality and the Good* (New York: David McKay, 1963); Walter G. Muelder, "Moral Laws: The Personalistic Aspect," chap. 6 in *Moral Law in Christian Social Ethics* (Richmond VA: John Knox Press, 1966).

That is one of the most important lessons of ethical prophecy. For example, it might be that only a small number of persons contribute to and benefit materially from the causes reeking devastating destruction on the environment. Even so, in prophetic ethics the entire human race is responsible for the way it responds to this or any similarly culpable tragedy. This is the case especially if it is our intention to continue living in this world; a world which is part of a moral universe; a world and all of its inhabitants—human and non-human—that belongs to the God of the Hebrew prophets. Because the world belongs to and is loved by God, and because God has put persons in the world as stewards or caregivers, we are finally responsible for what happens in and to the world. Therefore, as far as persons are able to bring it about, this must be a world with a reasonably safe environment in which to live if we are to live at all. No matter what happens in God's world because of the human hand, we are all, each of us, implicated in one way or another, if only in the way we respond to what happens with or without our direct involvement.

Prophetic ethics maintains that not only is God the moral governor of the universe, but that God has established the universe on a moral foundation. The social gospeler Washington Gladden (1836–1918) put it this way while reflecting on the moral consequences of mistreating a race of people: "We shall get it hammered into our heads one of these days that this is a moral universe; not that it is going to be, by and by, but that it is moral now, moral through and through, in tissue and fiber, in gristle and love, in muscle and brain, in sensation and thought; and that no injustice fails to get its due recompense, now and here."[4] Gladden was making not an empirical, but a fundamentally metaphysical claim about the nature or structure of the universe. As the author and judge of the universe, God has established it on a moral basis, which means that very much of what persons do in the world has moral implications. It means that nothing we do to self, to each other, to the plants and animals of our world, or to the larger environment escapes God's notice. This means that there are objective moral laws that govern the universe, and such laws are "an expression of a Holy Will which can be neither defied nor mocked."[5] In the end, then, the moral law wins out; justice and love win out, for God is "on the side of righteousness." Justice may be

---

[4] Washington Gladden, *Recollections* (Boston: Houghton Mifflin, 1909) 371.

[5] Bowne, *Principles of Ethics*, 201.

periodically delayed, but in the broader scheme of things it will have the last say.

To say as Martin Luther King, Jr. said, viz., that, "reality hinges on moral foundations,"[6] means that the entire universe is value-fused. What persons do in the world has moral implications, no matter how much we pretend otherwise. There are consequences for our moral misbehaving, as well as for the way we respond to the moral misbehaving of others. Because prophetic ethics maintains that the universe is grounded on a moral foundation, and that persons are created in freedom to be free, we cannot pretend that what happens in the world has nothing to do with us. Nor can we claim that we are not in some way morally culpable if we are not intentionally engaged in activity to eradicate this or that immoral behavior.

Ethical prophecy as such is thoroughly grounded in the conviction that God is characterized and motivated by love.[7] How else can we characterize the God who, according to the Hebrew prophets, relentlessly turns toward and searches for us and extends a welcoming hand to wayward humanity? How else do we explain the fact that God never gives up on us, is always hoping even against hope, that we will be reconciled to each other and to God? God is love. Emil Brunner made a helpful statement in this regard when he wrote, "God's love is not just an *attitude*; it is not just an act of God, it is the very essence of God. *God is love*. God is will, and the direction of his will is outgoing, sharing, self-communicating."[8]

In this view, precisely because God is love, we must take this to mean that God loves all persons thoroughly and equally, and expects that each person will be respected, accorded dignity, and treated justly. This

---

[6] Martin Luther King, Jr., "Rediscovering Lost Values," in *A Knock at Midnight*, ed. Clayborne Carson and Peter Holloran (New York: Warner Books, 1998) 10–14.

[7] In this instance the claim that God is love is a metaphysical one. While it is true that the Hebrew prophets stress God's *hesed* and never-ceasing compassion, we must be able to see that God does not merely *become* love in the second Testament. The God of the Hebrew prophets is the Lord of Jesus Christ, and thus is love. This is not a God who simply loves. Rather, God loves as God does because God *is* love and is the ground of love. While the claim that God is love is found only in the Second Testament (1 Jn 4:8), this is also the only explicit reference to that regard. My understanding of the Jewish and Christian traditions and my own faith convince me that God's essence always has been and always will be love.

[8] Emil Brunner, *Faith, Hope, and Love* (Philadelphia: Westminster Press, 1956) 66.

means that persons have the responsibility for "doing" love and justice to each other through all their religious and societal institutions. It means that individuals and the institutions that form the bases of their societies—whether church, school, or marketplace—bear moral responsibilities and obligations to each other in the name of the God of the Hebrew prophets.

God's Expectation of Persons in the World

Ethical prophecy—that is, true prophecy—is that way of being and living in the world that requires one to proclaim God's expectation that persons return to covenant relationship with each other and with God. It also requires that one proclaim God's steadfast love and concern for persons, and that justice be done in the world in ways that are consistent with the spirit of righteousness. That is, God expects not merely that justice be done, but that it be done in ways that exhibit respect for the humanity and dignity of all persons.

Nowhere is this principle stated with more clarity than the Book of Micah. A peasant farmer who lived in the countryside and who was the voice of the inhumanely and unjustly treated poor and oppressed, Micah proclaimed divine judgment on rulers who rendered justice for a bribe; on priests who taught for a fee; and on those so-called prophets who prophesied for money (Mic 3:11). Though making it clear that God threatened judgment against unrighteousness, the Book of Micah also insists that God does not *want* to execute judgment upon the people. Micah sums up what God considers acceptable behavior by the people: "To do justice, and to love kindness, and to walk humbly with your God" (Mic 6:8).

A prophet is one who speaks God's words, i.e., God's point of view, to the people about the need to return to covenant relationship with God and with each other. The prophet warns the people to stop their acts of injustice in the world and admonishes them to establish justice, and to do so in tender and loving ways. The prophet generally experiences a *call* from God and has a clear sense that the words she speaks are not hers, but God's. God speaks through her as if hers is God's voice to the people. She endeavors to convey to the people not their own or even her own understanding of human existence. Instead, the prophet's charge from God is that she clarify for the people *God's understanding of human existence and what God expects* in human relations and behavior.

The prophet's task, then, is to understand and communicate God's understanding and expectations of persons, and their being and living in the world.

Abraham Joshua Heschel captured the meaning of this when he wrote that prophecy "may be described as *exegesis of existence from a divine perspective.* Understanding prophecy is an understanding of an understanding rather than an understanding of knowledge; it is exegesis of exegesis. It involves sharing the perspective from which the original understanding is done."[9] The prophet's task, then, is to understand and communicate God's perspective on all things that are relevant to human existence.

The prophet reminds the people of God's steadfast love and compassion for them; that God is always pursuing them in the hope that they will hear, obey, and return to covenant relationship. He assures the people that God never gives up on them despite their hardheartedness and persistent disobedience. God proclaimed through the prophet Hosea that God cannot, indeed will not, give up on the people (Hos 11:8). Ethical prophecy takes the view that God is always turning toward the people. The prophet is careful to remind the people that God needs them to do all they can to make the world worthy of redemption. One who consistently exhibits such a stance is an ethical, or true prophet, for his is primarily a moral and theological concern that is grounded in the love and justice of the God of the eighth-century prophets.

I believe that prophetic inspiration did not end with the last of the biblical prophets, but continues even to this day. Therefore, I think it is possible to identify personalities throughout history who are in the lineage of the eighth-century prophets. There are a number of criteria that one must meet, however, in order to be a true and powerful ethical prophet. I discuss six of these criteria in chapter 3: the call and commission, divine justice, divine wrath, emphasis on the sacredness of persons, God's relentless love and compassion, and hope.

Ministry is primarily a social affair, i.e., a communal event. It is not something that one typically accomplishes alone or in a social vacuum. Every person who claims to be Christian, who has a sense of Jesus' legacy as prophet and priest, must understand that each individual is to this social extent invited to share in Christ's ministry. Each is an active

---

[9] Abraham J. Heschel, *The Prophets* (New York: Harper, 1962) xviii.

witness to the good news proclaimed in the gospel; a witness that extends beyond the walls of the local church. David Walker was such a witness.

Broad Responsibilities of Ministry

Pastors, as well as individual members of churches, have broad responsibilities in ministry. The black church tradition contends that the work of the pastor does not begin and end on Sunday morning. Martin Luther King, Sr. reflected on this in his autobiography as he thought about what he had learned from his father-in-law, the Reverend A. D. Williams, about the larger responsibilities of the preacher: "It was through him that I came to understand the larger implications involved in any churchman's responsibility to the community he served. Church wasn't simply Sunday morning and a few evenings during the week. It was more than a full-time job. *In the act of faith, every minister became an advocate for justice.* In the South this meant an active involvement in changing the social order all around us."[10]

Ministry, then, is not just a job that one does a few hours during the week. It is a way of being and relating that supports what God expects of persons. In the broadest sense, to minister means simply to serve, and to do so in the conviction that it is required by God. Any minister, any Christian worthy of the name, is bound by the prophetic tradition of the church and the gospel to stand up for justice for those counted among the least of the sisters and brothers. In any event, I want to hazard the statement that every person who claims to be Christian—or better, a disciple of Jesus Christ—is a minister in the sense that each is expected to engage in service in the name of Jesus Christ wherever she finds herself. Although ministry is essentially a communal affair, every individual Christian is expected to participate in some way in the service of ministry; not ministry for ministry's sake, however, but for the sake of the One whose unending love, compassion, and faithfulness is always in search of lost humanity.

The Value of Prophecy

In a world where oppression and social injustice of one kind or another is ubiquitous, every Christian should have and express a focused sense of

---

[10] Martin Luther King, Sr., *Daddy King: An Autobiography*, with Clayton Riley (New York: William Morrow, 1980) 82 (emphasis added).

moral outrage. No Christian should, for the sake of their own convenience, make peace with injustice of any type. Believers must take proactive steps to make themselves aware of what is happening around them with respect to how their society treats people from a variety of cultural, ethnic/racial, religious, economic, and social backgrounds.[11]

That being said, taking steps to enhance one's level of awareness of what is going on around him is only the beginning. It is also necessary to develop the sense that it is one's religious and moral responsibility to be outraged about the inequities and injustices one has become aware of, and to begin seeking ways to join in the struggle to liberate and empower those who are beaten and crushed to the earth.

Prophetic Ethics Are Not Synonymous with Works Righteousness

Contrary to what some may surmise, prophetic ethics is not about "works righteousness." That is, the concern here is not with earning God's favor or somehow working to ensure that when this life is over heaven or some such place will be one's reward. Indeed, what is important is that individuals know they have ready access to divine grace, for God has already promised its availability to any who would ask it. One is justified not through works, but by grace through faith alone. Martin Luther stressed this doctrinal assertion in his famous 1531 lectures on the Book of Galatians. Luther did not reject the doing of good works and charitable deeds in and of themselves, but he saw justification as central. Persons are saved or justified "by faith only in Christ."[12] Accordingly, there is nothing that individuals can do to actually earn divine grace. This does not mean, however, that God's grace is cheap, without real and costly value. Having received God's grace, individuals ought not suppose they may go on living and behaving in the world as if the gift had not been given.

---

[11] One's awareness is enhanced through the reading of local, national, and international newspapers, supplemented by the reading of weekly newspapers, e.g., those published by African Americans and Latinos/as. In addition, magazines like the *Christian Century*, *Sojourners*, *Mother Jones*, and the *Other Side* frequently provide thoughtful Christian perspectives on socio-political and economic issues.

[12] Martin Luther, "A Commentary on St. Paul's Epistle to the Galatians," in *Martin Luther: Selections from His Writings*, ed. John Dillenberger (New York: Anchor Books/Doubleday, 1961) 116.

Few have characterized cheap and costly grace better than Dietrich Bonhoeffer (1906–1945), himself a twentieth-century paradigm of ethical prophecy. The church, according to Bonhoeffer, has no more deadly enemy than cheap grace. He argued that the church, as an institution, and individual believers must always fight for the recovery and health of costly grace. His words about both "types" of grace serve us well. Regarding cheap grace, he wrote:

> Grace without price; grace without cost! The essence of grace, we suppose, is that the account has been paid in advance; and, because it has been paid, everything can be had for nothing. Since the cost was infinite, the possibilities of using and spending it are infinite....
>
> Cheap grace means grace as a doctrine, a principle, a system. It means forgiveness of sins proclaimed as a general truth, the love of God taught as the Christian "conception" of God. An intellectual assent to that idea is held to be of itself sufficient to secure remission of sins....
>
> Cheap grace means the justification of sin without the justification of the sinner. *Grace alone does everything, they say, and so everything can remain as it was before....*
>
> Cheap grace is the preaching of forgiveness without requiring repentance, baptism without church discipline, communion without confession, absolution without personal confession. *Cheap grace is grace without discipleship, grace without the cross*, grace without Jesus Christ, living and incarnate.[13]

Costly grace is something altogether different. Christians may be easily swayed by the siren call of cheap grace, and consequently are susceptible to falling into works righteousness. Authentic disciples of Christ, however, are committed to costly grace, recognizing that there is a substantial price to be paid for following and living according to the teachings of Jesus Christ and all those who stand in the lineage of the eighth-century Hebrew prophets. Bonhoeffer had this to say about costly grace:

---

[13] Dietrich Bonhoeffer, *The Cost of Discipleship* (1937; reprint, New York: Macmillan, 1959) 35–36 (emphasis added).

Such grace is *costly* because it calls us to follow *Jesus Christ*. It is costly because it costs a man his life, and it is grace because it gives a man the only true life. It is costly because it condemns sin, and grace because it justifies the sinner. Above all, it is *costly* because it cost God the life of his Son: "Ye were bought at a price," and what has cost God much cannot be cheap for us.... Costly grace is the incarnation of God.

Grace is costly because it compels a man to submit to the yoke of Christ and follow him; it is grace because Jesus says: 'My yoke is easy and my burden is light.'[14]

In this vein, when God calls a person she is called to die to her old ways of living, to live evermore oriented to the new ways of life in Christ, and possibly even die a physical death.

That God's grace is not cheap means that once one turns toward God in Christ to receive the gift of grace and love, one's life ought to progressively reflect receipt of so precious a gift as this. Stated differently, once one chooses to receive God's grace, he can no longer engage in previously questionable behavior, e.g., racism, heterosexism, sexism, and other forms of abuse that minimizes and degrades the humanity of others.

It was precisely the failure of white proponents of the Christian faith to renounce racism during the early part of the nineteenth century that aroused David Walker's prophetic passion. None protested more vehemently than he American whites proclaiming adherence to the Christian faith while subjecting black Africans to dehumanizing slavery. The claim of Christianity by whites meant that they acknowledged receipt of God's grace. Walker concluded that the way they lived and behaved after receiving God's grace should have been radically altered, even if only gradually. With most whites of that period, however, religious conversion led to no significant changes in their behavior toward the Africans. Indeed, the enslaved Harriet Jacobs reported in her narrative that it was often the case that once slave owners claimed a Christian conversion, they not only continued to hold the Africans in slavery but subjected them to even greater brutalities.[15]

---

[14] Bonhoeffer, *The Cost of Discipleship*, 37 (emphasis added).

[15] Harriet A. Jacobs, *Incidents in the Life of a Slave Girl*, ed. Jean Fagan Yellin

This discussion is not an apology for "works righteousness." It is, however, unashamedly and profoundly concerned with *righteous works*, or the lack thereof, in persons who claim to be Christians. It seems that at bare minimum righteous works are required of those who claim to be recipients of God's love and grace. Once one willingly accepts God's love and grace, expressed in the Christian faith by belief in and discipleship under the authority of Christ, she is at once placed under heavy obligation to *live* as if she is a recipient of God's infinite grace and love. Although works righteousness is not the focus in this book, one must, once she accepts God's grace, be committed to engaging in righteous works, e.g., addressing issues of injustice and declaring, in the name of the God of the eighth-century prophets and of Jesus Christ, that justice be done. This is the burden that persons assume when they claim to be recipients of the gift of God's grace.

Need for Social Prophets

Persons generally do not come into the Christian community fully comprehending that theirs is to be both prophetic *and* priestly behavior and living. While almost every new convert understands that he is to be more intentional about altering his own personal sense of morality in light of the Christian ethic, the unique ground of this ethic and of all human action is located in divine actions and expectations. What persons do in the world, accordingly, is based on what God does and requires.[16] It is nearly impossible to live without violating some aspect of the perfecting standards of the Christian ethic. The ultimate objectives of the Christian love ethic are so demanding that they seem impossible to achieve. We can only hope to approximate the requirements of the love ideal, especially in group or collective relations.[17] The new Christian convert generally understands the importance of being intentional about

---

(Cambridge MA: Harvard University Press, 1987) 74.

[16] See Emil Brunner's helpful discussion on the meaning of Christian ethics in chap. 9 of *The Divine Imperative: A Study in Christian Ethics*, trans. Olive Wyon (London: Lutterworth Press, 1937).

[17] A point that the social ethicist, Reinhold Niebuhr, came to during his pastorate in Detroit, long before the publication of his provocative *Moral Man and Immoral Society* (1932), or his magnum opus, *The Nature and Destiny of Man* (1941, 1943). See, Reinhold Niebuhr, *Leaves from the Notebook of a Tamed Cynic* (New York: Willett, Clark & Colby, 1929) 85–86.

developing and exhibiting a sweeter spirit when relating to others. But most do not know about that aspect of the Jewish and Christian traditions that requires a genuine commitment to the establishment of just institutions and practices in all manifestations of societal and religious life. This lack of ethical comprehension demands that contemporary Christians be intentional about *recovering the tradition of Hebrew prophecy*. Once reawakened to the importance of prophecy for ministry and the Christian life, it will be necessary to take steps to help develop ethical or social prophets who understand themselves to be serving the Christ-like God; who will commit themselves to working deliberately and diligently to reflect this in all that they do. Every individual Christian has the responsibility to develop such an understanding of ministry and Christian living.

It is not that all believers are *called* to be prophets of the same sort, for persons possess different gifts, talents, and abilities. Further, it is the case that both ministry and the needs of persons and communities are broad and frequently complex. This means it will be necessary for there to be different understandings and approaches to ministry and the problems it seeks to address in church and society. Yet it does seem that every individual Christian, clergy and laity alike, should understand what prophecy is, and what it requires of them in ministry.

Having said that, there is need to make a much stronger statement. Although we are not all called to be prophets of the same sort, *the fact that one claims to serve Jesus Christ means that one is called to be prophetic*, especially in the face of injustice and any other behavior that undermines the humanity and worth of persons. Every individual Christian is called to respond favorably to God's expectation that a positive witness be made for God and the least of the sisters and brothers; to be courageous and exhibit holy rage when injustice exists, whatever form it takes. It is true that we cannot all be the proverbial celebrity prophet who receives national and international recognition. Nevertheless, if nothing else, every Christian can be a social critic who takes seriously the spirit of ethical prophecy and the life and teachings of Jesus Christ. We will see that none did this more faithfully and courageously than David Walker.

Prophet and Priest

It is not my intention to set up a dichotomy between the prophetic and priestly offices of the Christian church. Historically, however, actual practice reveals the existence of a pronounced dichotomy between these offices. Indeed, history has seldom produced persons in which there exists a healthy tension between prophetic and priestly offices. Conflict is the common denominator in such a relationship. Jesus Christ, foreshadowed in the Old Testament by unique personalities such as Samuel and Isaiah, is the epitome of the perfect type, i.e., the prophetic priest. The evidence of such like-minded personalities in history is more rare than common. Ministers today are usually one or the other, prophet or priest—more often priest. Many pastors view their primary role as providing comfort to and protection for their parishioners. Therefore, they tend to shy away from sermons and actions that might upset the social equilibrium in the churches they serve.[18] They avoid preaching sermons or taking action to confront major social problems, especially those from which their parishioners may draw some form of self-interested benefit.[19] In the same vein, many lay Christians expect their ministers to provide for them comfort rather than a challenge in the light of the radical Christian ethical imperative to "do" love and justice to the poor and the weak. Vocational ministry and laity thus facilitate one another in avoiding the demands of ethical prophetic Christian faith. Religious institutions, a corporate reflection of the individuals who populate their ranks, tend to concede to the conservative ethic of society.[20] Such a tendency is not, however, in keeping with the spirit of prophetic ethics, which is essentially a *counter-status quo ethic*.

It is important to keep before us the need for the offices of prophet and priest to remain wedded. The marriage need not (nor will it!) be a happy one at every moment, but it must be an enduring one. For just as sure as there is an urgent need for prophecy today in response to so much

---

[18] Charles Y. Glock and Rodney Stark, et al., "Ministers as Moral Guides: The Sounds of Silence" in *Religion in Sociological Perspective*, ed. Charles Y. Glock (Belmont CA: Wadsworth, 1973) 163–86.

[19] Charles Y. Glock and Rodney Stark, "Church Policy and the Attitudes of Ministers and Parishioners," in *Religion and Society in Tension* (Chicago: Rand McNally, 1965) chap.12.

[20] Charles Y. Glock and Rodney Stark, "Prejudice and the Churches" in *Religion American Style*, ed. Patrick McNamara (New York: Harper & Row, 1974) 305–14.

societal disfunction, there is as urgent a need for the priestly care, comfort, and nurture of souls. In addition, the priest can provide comfort for the weak and the poor, as well as for those who work relentlessly to liberate them. The weak and poor need loving and responsible comfort in their difficult circumstances. Those Christians who take seriously the work of prophecy frequently are weighed down, frustrated, and discouraged due to what must often seem an unending, fruitless struggle. They, too, should benefit from authentic Christian comfort.

Avery Dulles was not wrong when he said that if nothing else, we can *understand the necessity of being prophets*, or the need for prophets, even if we are not ourselves prophets.[21] We can be intentional in our efforts to understand that there is always a need for prophets. We may not be prophets ourselves, but there is a need to acknowledge the Christian mandate and responsibility to be prophetic when one comes face to face with injustice and human abuse. If nothing else, we can surely understand the importance of prophecy and can be supportive of those who have been called to that task in ways that surpass our own sense of calling. In other words, we can stand courageously with the woman who feels called, and thus compelled, to prophesy in and to the church and world.

Despite the ideal of unity between the priestly and prophetic offices, there remains an inescapable tension between them. Neither functions well without the energy, creativity, and the challenge of the other. The ultimate goals of prophetic and priestly ministries are similar. It is the responsibility of each manifestation of Christian ministry to help us find our way back to covenant relation with God and with each other. Both are concerned that persons heed the message of faithfulness and obedience to God's will. Honesty compels the acknowledgement that Christians frequently suppress prophecy in church and society.[22] Put colloquially, it is often the religious, not the irreligious, who seek to behead the prophet. This happens because prophecy is a "disturbing element" that invariably upsets the normal, accepted routines of a community's day-to-day living, even if those routines are routinely unjust or otherwise lacking ethical character.

---

[21] Avery Dulles, *The Survival of Dogma* (Garden City NY: Image Books, 1973), 136–37.

[22] Ibid., 136.

In the very best case scenario, the prophet is both social critic *and* priestly comforter or social physician. On the one hand he afflicts and challenges the comfortable and those who are in complicity with oppressive systems and practices. On the other hand he comforts marginalized persons and groups in church and world. It is therefore the case that the roles of priestly social physician and prophetic social critic are forever and necessarily intertwined.

It is important to remember that the prophet is a person—a flesh and blood being with sensibility as well as potential for rationality, morality, and self-determination. There is much more to the prophet than humanness—for the notes of his voice tend to be an "octave too high for our ears."[23] He tends to be iconoclastic, full of compassion for the people, and relishes in making what Heschel refers to as "sweeping allegations" or generalizations.[24] *That* he is human is of utmost significance. There can be no prophecy without the vessel, which is the human person; the vessel through which God conveys God's point of view to the world.

As a human being, then, the prophet will always experience the same emotions, including fear, as other persons. We need to remember, therefore, that *prophets are always, and only, persons.* Not super-persons. Persons. Insofar as prophets are called of God and respond to the divine mission appointed to them, they are able through resources not their own—that is, the power of divine grace and the working of the Holy Spirit—to find enough peace within themselves to stay the course directed by God, no matter what dangers they face. It is the responsibility of prophets—who always focuses on events in the here and now, in this the only world they know—to demand that the socio-political and economic orders conform as nearly as possible to the requirements of God's understanding of the new redemptive order for the world. This is an order [revealed through God's self-disclosure in the Scriptures and in the life of the obedient church,] that is based on the principles of dignity, equality, shared power and privilege, love, and justice done in the spirit of lovingkindness. Martin Luther King, Jr.'s nomenclature (following Josiah Royce) for this new order is the *Beloved Community*. It is not an overstatement to say that the prophet should be adamant in proclaiming

---

[23] Abraham J. Heschel, *The Prophets* (New York: Harper, 1962), 9.

[24] Ibid., 9–14.

God's expectation that the social order be rendered impartially, and that the image of God in every person be acknowledged and respected.

The ethically attuned social prophet is concerned with the establishment of social justice in religious as well as societal institutions. She is to be concerned with demanding individual and social transformation in light of the Hebrew prophets and Christ-like principles. In every case, she is to strive to insure that her actions are consistent with and based on those of God.

The priest, something of a social physician in contrast to being society's critic, primarily tends to be concerned with matters of forgiveness and reconciliation between the oppressor and the oppressed. The social prophet, however, does not allow us to lose sight of the fact that forgiveness and reconciliation, like Bonhoeffer's idea of "costly grace," cannot be had cheaply. That is, reconciliation will not likely materialize short of cross-like experiences (whatever one may think of the atonement tradition[25]). Applied to the human condition, we may say that oppressor and oppressed alike must go through the torture of the cross in the sense that historically and presently there will be suffering, sacrifice, and hard struggle before liberation and reconciliation becomes a reality. We should not delude ourselves about this: it must be a *shared suffering*. That is, mere apologies, regrets, and requests for forgiveness by members of an economically and politically privileged group after benefiting from centuries of the practice of excluding other groups, cannot be deemed adequate and ethically acceptable. Such persons are in position to discuss forgiveness and reconciliation *only* when they have done, in substantive ways, everything that can be done to develop genuine structures of love and justice. They must be the living examples and models of real participation and sharing in church and world.

What is here proposed is not impossible to achieve. There is no question, however, that it will not be easily achieved. The role or witness of the prophet that is modeled after the eighth-century prophets and the

---

[25] Here it is important to acknowledge the revisionist views of this tradition that are offered by white feminist, as well as womanist, theologians. See Joanne Carlson Brown and Rebecca Parker, "For God So Loved the World?" chap. 1 in *Christianity, Patriarchy, and Abuse: A Feminist Critique*, ed. Joanne Carlson Brown and Carole R. Bohn (Cleveland OH: The Pilgrim Press, 1989); and Delores S. Williams, *Sisters in the Wilderness: The Challenge of Womanist God-Talk* (Maryknoll NY: Orbis Books, 1993) 161–67, 199–201.

life and teaching of Jesus Christ does not generally lead to popularity, societal rewards, or even to longevity of life. On this point the philosopher Socrates reminded those committed to truth and the establishment of justice what they may expect from their world. Charged by an Athenian court in 399 BCE with corrupting youth and not believing in the gods of the state, he said: "No man on earth who conscientiously opposes either you or any other organized democracy, and flatly prevents a great many wrongs and illegalities from taking place in the state to which he belongs, can possibly escape with his life. The true champion of justice, if he intends to survive even for a short time, must necessarily confine himself to private life and leave politics alone."[26] The ethical prophet's way is not easy, either in the church or the world. Both venues resist the unfettered word of prophecy.

As one scholar reminds us, the prophet encounters resistance "on a massive scale." She is rejected as much as God is, for God not only gives her the message, but "God must be said to go with the word, so that in some sense God is absorbed into the very life of the prophet."[27] To begin to appreciate the mystery of the divine-human symbiosis in the person of the prophet, consider the relationship between God and Jeremiah, one in whom the person as an individual and office of the prophet coincided.[28] Although such union of person and office is clearly not the case with all prophets, an important point that applies to ethical prophets is that God does not simply impart the message to them and then hide away, absent from them and the world. Instead, God "leaves the word behind in the prophet. God calls the prophet to take the word received and embody that word from the moment of the call onward."[29] If God goes with the word and is indeed absorbed into the life of the prophet, this means that the resistance, suffering, and frustration experienced by the prophet is also experienced by God. When the prophet is mocked, God is mocked.

---

[26] Socrates, "Socrates' Defense (Apology)," in *The Collected Dialogues of Plato: Including the Letters*, ed. Edith Hamilton and Hunting Cairns (Princeton, NJ: Princeton University Press, 1971) 17.

[27] Terence E. Fretheim, *The Suffering God: An Old Testament Perspective*, (Philadelphia: Fortress Press) 153.

[28] "He is set apart to be a prophet before his birth, indeed before his conception (Jer 1:5). Prophethood thus defines his person from the very beginning; it is the essence of his very being. He is decisively shaped by God not just to be a certain kind of speaker, but a certain kind of person." Ibid., 152.

[29] Ibid., 151.

Furthermore, even when the prophet is no more, God's Word remains. "This is the great comfort of one who preaches," said Archbishop of El Salvador, Oscar Romero (1917–1980). "My voice will disappear, but my word, which is Christ, will remain in the hearts of those who have willed to receive it."[30]

Prophecy's roots are located deep in the best of biblical history, and should be taken seriously by all who join the ranks of the Christian community as disciples of Jesus Christ. God has never been without a prophet, i.e., a witness, and there is no indication that God will forego prophetic presence in the future. One never knows whether he will be chosen by God to bear the prophet's witness. Should the call come to individuals, it is crucial that they have an accurate appreciation of ethical prophecy's true costs.

The Prophet's Task and Its Cost

The prophet will not make accommodations for nor compromise with injustice or any system of oppression. This absolute refusal to accept anything short of the justice that God demands is frequently what keeps the prophet in the bad graces of rulers and the socially privileged. The prophet understands that every person belongs to and is loved and sustained by God. Therefore, with audacious courage she will be God's voice, lodging her protests against injustice wherever it is detected. Although she is fully human, the prophet will not be deterred because of threats to her life and well-being. As a human being it is natural that she may sometimes experience fear, but she will be comforted and energized when she remembers her faith commitment to God and that God sends the Holy Spirit to comfort her.

When they began their crusade against slavery and challenged the commonly held belief of their day that blacks were less human than whites, Sarah Grimké (1792–1873) and her sister, Angelina (1805–1879), were forbidden from ever again returning to their home in Charleston, South Carolina. The daughters of wealthy slaveholding Christian parents, these women had and expressed what they experienced as a deep sense of the immorality and sin of slavery even when they were

---

[30] Oscar Romero quoted in James R. Brockman, *Romero: A Life* (Maryknoll NY: Orbis, 1989) ii.

young girls. This was especially the case with Angelina, who was thirteen years younger than Sarah.

We marvel that such youthful individuals, who clearly benefited materially and in other ways from the stolen labor of the Africans, could be so resentful of slavery and have the audacity to express this sentiment to their parents. The sisters did most of their public abolitionist work between 1835–1839. Following those years, they continued to protest against slavery passionately, vociferously, and relentlessly throughout their adult lives.[31]

During the most active period of their involvement in the anti-slavery campaign and the struggle for women's rights, Angelina and Sarah were threatened with bodily harm a number of times.[32] Nevertheless, these former Episcopalians-turned-Quakers[33] were fearless and dauntless.

The sisters initially believed that the Quakers were free of race prejudice against the Africans, inasmuch as very many of them were against slavery. When the sisters discovered the existence of prejudice in their local meeting in Philadelphia and a refusal to actually fellowship with the two black women members, Sarah and Grace Douglass,[34] their commitment to the Quakers was shaken. Neither sister ever recovered from the disappointment.[35] They were eventually turned away from the Society of Friends when Angelina violated Quaker practice by marrying the non-Quaker, Theodore Weld, with Sarah in attendance.[36] More than most whites, the sisters were passionately vocal in their criticism of Northern churches' and pastors' silence on the issue of slavery in the

---

[31] See Gerda Lerner, *The Grimke Sisters from South Carolina: Rebels Against Slavery* (Boston: Houghton Mifflin, 1967).

[32] Angelina refers to one such instance during her 16 May 1838 speech at Pennsylvania Hall. See *The Public Years of Sarah and Angelina Grimké: Selected Writings 1835–1839*, ed. Larry Ceplair (New York: Columbia University Press, 1989) 319–20.

[33] Angelina's religious journey was actually from membership in the Episcopal Church to affiliation in the Presbyterian Church. Ultimately, she followed Sarah and became a Quaker.

[34] Lerner, *The Grimké Sisters*, 132–33.

[35] Lerner, *The Grimké Sisters,* chap. 6–8; also 132–33, 172, 256.

[36] Ibid., 255–57.

South, as well as in their critiques of prejudice and discrimination against blacks in the North.[37]

The Grimké sisters were determined to be God's voice speaking to their generations against slavery. They were also active in protesting the denial of human rights to *all* women, regardless of race and class. The sisters refused to compromise with the injustice and inhumanity of slavery. The enslavement of the Africans was for them a sin against God and humanity.[38] It was not just a socio-political problem, but a problem of faith—of morals and religion. As Angelina insisted, slavery was a contradiction of the Christian faith.[39] The sisters contended that slavery effectively dehumanizes persons and disregards their preciousness to God. Sarah wrote of the effect of slavery on the African in "An Epistle to the Clergy of the Southern States" in 1836. "Slavery has disrobed him of royalty, put on him the collar and chain, and trampled the image of God in the dust."[40]

The sisters were courageous and unrelenting in registering public protest against slavery, despite the cost to themselves. Angelina was prepared to give up friends, and even life itself, for the cause of the immediate—not gradual—emancipation of the enslaved Africans.[41] Indeed, her first letter (30 August 1835) to the noted abolitionist, William Lloyd Garrison, said: "If persecution is the means which God has ordained for the accomplishment of this great Emancipation; then, in dependence *upon him* for strength to bear it, I feel as if I could say, Let it come; for it is my deep, solemn, deliberate conviction, that this is a cause worth dying for."[42]

The Grimké sisters' work toward and commitment to the abolition of slavery, the overcoming of prejudice and discrimination against blacks, and the early women's suffrage movement in America is an outstanding example of choosing to take ethical and prophetic stances against the mainstream of society. No matter what one's race, gender, and socio-economic status, one has a choice in how to behave and live.

---

[37] See Sarah M. Grimké, "An Epistle to the Clergy of the Southern States" in *The Public Years*, 90–115; and Angelina Grimké, "An Appeal to the Christian Women of the South," ibid., 36–79.

[38] Ibid., 56, 71, 101.

[39] Ibid., 66.

[40] Ibid., 92.

[41] Ibid., 35.

[42] Ibid., 26.

In the case of the Grimkés, it was a series of choices that required a level of faithfulness that was rare, and whose scarcity may well continue in our day. The Grimkés knew that, first and last, ethics is personal-communal. They themselves had to choose. Indeed, they could not avoid choosing. Not to choose is in fact to make a choice! In the words of Jean-Paul Sartre, persons are "condemned forever to be free."[43] Recognizing that not choosing was not an option enabled the Grimké sisters to avoid the monstrous sin of indifference to injustice and other forms of social evil during their day.

There can be no question that one who is *called* to deliver God's message is obligated to do what Martin Luther King, Jr. did when he took a fateful detour to Memphis and his own death in 1968. On one level it may be argued that because King had freedom and autonomy of will, he did not have to go to Memphis. He could have chosen to remain focused on planning the Poor Peoples' Campaign to take place on the lawn of the nation's Capitol. It was, however, precisely because of the depth of King's religious faith, his sense of call, his commitment to what he considered to be God's will, in addition to his own unqualified belief in and support of the absolute dignity of all persons, that *he did in fact have to go to Memphis*. In this regard, the option not to go to Memphis was not within King's field of moral choice. He had long since chosen to be faithful to God, despite the cost. He chose to accept God's call, and in this respect he had to go to Memphis.

By now, the reader should sense that the type of prophecy discussed in this book necessarily leads the faithful to their own experience of what Jesus underwent at Calvary. This is part of the cost of prophecy. Here one need only recall the prophet Jeremiah's anguish and torment when the people refused to heed God's Word and were being punished for their disobedience and hard heartedness. Jeremiah asks at one point: "Is there no balm in Gilead? Is there no physician there?" (Jer 8:22)

Martin Luther King knew that there were threats against his life, and that those threats had become both more numerous and believable by the mid-1960s, especially following the Selma campaign in 1965.[44] Despite

---

[43] Jean-Paul Sartre, *The Age of Reason*, trans. Eric Sutton (New York: Bantam Books, 1967) 276.

[44] Jim Bishop, *The Days of Martin Luther King, Jr.* (New York: G.P. Putnam's Sons, 1971) 370–80; David J. Garrow, *Protest at Selma: Martin Luther King, Jr., and the Voter Rights Act of 1965* (New Haven CT: Yale University Press, 1978) 73; Martin Luther

the risk to his beloved family's well-being should something negative befall him, King also knew that there were sanitation workers—those counted among the "least of these"—who had no one to be their voice or witness before the abusive ruling powers in the city of Memphis.

Once in Memphis, King addressed a community rally at Mason Temple on the night of 3 April 1968. He recalled before his audience the parable of the Good Samaritan (Luke 10:30-37). He remembered how the priest and the Levite passed up the opportunity to help the man who was in need because they feared a trap. The man on the side of the road might well have been faking injury to lure the innocent and take advantage of their willingness to help. It was the Samaritan, one who himself had been disregarded and rejected by his society, who came by and gave an affirmative answer to the moral question. He thought not of his own well being and safety, but only of the man who had been beaten and robbed.

King traveled purposefully to a Southern city known for its active opposition to everything for which he stood for what some no doubt perceived as lowly, no-count garbage collectors. Some of King's advisors told him that he should not intervene in the sanitation workers' strike but should instead stay focused on the more important issues of immediate national consequence, such as planning for the Poor People's Campaign. After all, in Memphis it was only a matter involving unremarkable people who pick up the garbage.

A tired and weary Martin Luther King knew from the influence of his parents and grandparents, the teachings of the Ebenezer Baptist Church, and his seminary and graduate school training, that injustice anywhere is a threat to justice everywhere. He based this conviction on the fundamental Jewish and Christian belief that all reality is communal, and therefore all persons are inextricably and integrally interrelated,[45] God being at the center of the human community. The interrelated structure of reality means that justice is indivisible. Therefore what

---

King, Jr., *The Autobiography of Martin Luther King, Jr.*, ed. Clayborne Carson (New York: Warner Books, 1998) 278; Frederick L. Downing, *To See the Promised Land: The Pilgrimage of Martin Luther King, Jr.* (Macon GA: Mercer University Press, 1986) 255.

[45] Martin Luther King, Jr., "The Ethical Demands For Integration," in *A Testament of Hope: The Essential Writings of Martin Luther King, Jr.*, ed. James M. Washington (New York: Harper & Row, 1986) 122. See also King, "A Christian Sermon on Peace," ibid., 254–55.

affects one directly or indirectly affects all others, including God. This conclusion was consistent with King's conviction that the universe hinges on a moral foundation, that there is an objective moral order that has been established and is sustained by the God of Jesus Christ.[46]

Such strong convictions, therefore, did not give Martin Luther King the option of being indifferent to what was happening to the garbage collectors in Memphis. Indeed, is this point of view not a basic component of God's message to be delivered by the prophet? *God cares about it all; everything that happens to persons in the world*, and most particularly the poor and the oppressed. Abraham Joshua Heschel, who marched with King in Selma and became a close friend of the civil rights leader,[47] put it this way:

> The prophet's great contribution to humanity was the discovery of *the evil of indifference*. One may be decent and sinister, pious and sinful.
>
> The prophet is a person who suffers the harms done to others. Whenever a crime is committed, it is as if the prophet were the victim and the prey. ... All prophecy is one great exclamation: God is not indifferent to evil! He is always concerned, He is personally affected by what man does to man. He is a God of pathos.[48]

Indeed, according to Heschel, the great scandal of those days was the tendency of people becoming accustomed to a certain amount of injustice and other scandalous behavior.[49] Many social ills existed in King's day and continue to exist in our own precisely because so many

---

[46] See Rufus Burrow, Jr., "Personalism, the Objective Moral Order, and Moral Law in the Work of Martin Luther King, Jr.," chap. 5 in *The Legacy of Martin Luther King, Jr.: The Boundaries of Law, Politics, and Religion*, ed. Lewis V. Baldwin (Notre Dame IN: University of Notre Dame Press, 2002).

[47] Marc Schneier, *Shared Dreams: Martin Luther King, Jr. and the Jewish Community* (Woodstock VT: Jewish Lights Publishing, 1999). Rabbi Schneier's excellent book examines the mutual influence between King and the Jewish community. Chapter 14, especially, highlights the strong friendship that developed between King and Heschel.

[48] Abraham Joshua Heschel, *The Insecurity of Freedom: Essays on Human Existence* (Philadelphia: The Jewish Publication Society of America, 1966) 92.

[49] Abraham J. Heschel, *Moral Grandeur and Spiritual Audacity*, ed. Susannah Heschel (New York: Farrar, Straus, Giroux, 1996) 253.

proponents of religious faith are indifferent, willing to be patient with or make compromises that skirt the existence of these forms of injustice and race and class hatred. Without such indifference; without such patience and inclination to compromise with social evils, they would ultimately cease to exist for lack of toleration. King himself knew well the principle that Heschel expressed, namely, that the God of the Bible, the God of the prophets, "is *concerned with everydayness, with the trivialities of life.*" The true prophet, the ethical prophet, boldly confronts those whose actions minimize the dignity of others.[50] To demean any person's dignity is to demean the image of God that is a part of every person. "Wherever you see a trace of man," said Heschel, "*there is the presence of God.*"[51]

The decision to be faithful to what he believed to be God's will, to be the "voice of the voiceless" garbage collectors, cost Martin Luther King, Jr. his life in this world. The stance against slavery and advocacy for women's human and political rights cost Angelina and Sarah Grimké their lives, too; but in a different way. There is a price to be paid for taking prophecy seriously; for being prophetic. The cost is not always physical death. It may be psychological death. It may be the loss of one's inheritance, family, and friends, as in the case of the Grimké sisters. It may be the loss of one's church, as happened to some Southern white pastors during the civil rights movement when they decided to be faithful to God by speaking against racism and segregation, by declaring the contradiction between racist ideology and practice and the Christian radical imperative of *agapé* (utterly self-giving love).

Those who have been called, who understand the importance and the necessity of prophecy, must speak the truth in whatever way(s) they can speak it best. We are all different and have different experiences, cultural backgrounds, gifts, and talents. Although the prophetic message is the same, no two persons will speak it the same way. But we must speak it! The distinguishing mark of true prophecy was well described by Allan Boesak as "the constraint to speak YAHWEH's truth whatever the risks, even against one's own interests; daring to do what is right, trusting only in the God whose voice you have heard."[52]

David Buttrick hits the target dead center in his book, *Preaching Jesus Christ*. What he wrote about the church might also be applied to

---

[50] Heschel, *Insecurity of Freedom*, 102.

[51] Ibid., 94.

[52] Allan Boesak, *Walking on Thorns* (Grand Rapids: Eerdmanns Publishing, 1984) 5.

the individual, namely that in order to speak the truth it will be necessary to stop trying to get in on the power.[53] That is, neither the church nor the individual can retain its ethical-prophetic edge as long as they seek the approval and rewards of the powers that be. Martin Luther King, Jr. sought no such approval and rewards; nor did the Grimké sisters. The voice of authority in these women came from the Word of God. To seek approval or permission of the powerful and privileged in order to carry out the ethical and prophetic work of Christian ministry can lead only to the loss of one's sense of autonomy. In turn, this severely erodes and blunts one's prophetic edge.

In the face of injustice and oppression the prophet does not hesitate to make her prophetic witness; to proclaim God's understanding and God's expectations for persons and the world. When confronted with specific social evils, the prophet does not speak in generalities. When she protests, she protests against specific evils. Furthermore, when the time comes that she feels she can do nothing else because all her efforts at protest have failed to bring about a positive resolution, she leaves the church or organization while making the reasons for her departure clear. For example, the challenge issued by secular social scientist, Robert MacIver, was that no act of discrimination or prejudice go publicly unchallenged:

> Let us not passively accept actions of discrimination or prejudice practiced by those with whom we are associated, and particularly by the organizations to which we belong. Let us not think that it means nothing to us if a body to which we belong displays this spirit. It may be a club, or it may be a business group, or it may even be a church. Let us oppose it all we can. Let us make our protest heard in the clearest possible way. *And if we cannot make our protest felt in any other way, let us resign.*[54]

Let us not resign *before* we have made it crystal clear why we are doing so. The prophet has the courage to register his protests against injustice. He knows that if he must resign from some position or from membership in some organization—including the church—because all

---

[53] David Buttrick, *Preaching Jesus Christ* (Philadelphia: Fortress Press, 1988) 53.

[54] *Unity and Difference in American Life*, ed. Robert MacIver (New York: Harper, 1947) 157 (emphasis added).

other protest has been ignored, he must be courageous enough to state why he is leaving that organization. Resigning without stating one's reason(s), or giving a false reason because of a desire to avoid hurting another's feelings, or because of loyalty to a group "code of honor," wastes the impact and potential educational and moral value of the event for the powers that be and for those who are being trampled upon. The prophet gives explicit reasons for his resignation. Publicizing the reasons either in the presence of the powers that be, or in some other public forum, e.g., a retirement dinner, may be thought of by many to be uncouth, unprofessional, inappropriate, and politically incorrect. But only a response of the type just noted enhances the possibility of one's continued connection with the prophetic tradition and insures one's good standing before God. Generally, one cannot be a prophet and be popular at the same time. What is more, God requires not that one be "politically correct," but morally correct.

For the sake of the God who cares, as well as for those who are treated unjustly, the prophet does not wait for someone else to protest against injustice. A good rule of thumb is to assume at all times that if you do not do it, if you will not be the voice of those who have no voice in church and world, no one else will! This proactive perspective was eloquently articulated by Socrates:

> If you put me to death, you will not easily find anyone to take my place. It is literally true, even if it sounds rather comical, that God has specially appointed me to this city, as though it were a large thoroughbred horse which because of its great size is inclined to be lazy and needs the stimulation of some stinging fly. It seems to me that God has attached me to this city to perform the office of such a fly, and all day long I never cease to settle here, there, and everywhere, rousing, persuading, reproving every one of you.[55]

Socrates did not assume that others would take it upon themselves to try to open people's eyes to truth and knowledge. He saw the problem and went about trying to solve it. Just as there was a need for "stinging" social gadflies in Socrates' day, there is a need for such prophetic voices

---

[55] Hamilton, *Collected Dialogues*, 16–17.

today. I am confident that if we examine our own lives on the basis of what prophecy requires, and authentically apply ourselves to what is discovered therein, we will potentially enliven and generate significantly positive advancement in church and world.

Prophecy Requires that We Know what We See

We have become almost irreversibly accustomed to what we know. This makes it very difficult for us to know and to be transformed by what we see, i.e., by that which stares us in the face each and every moment. For example, we are taught in the most subtle ways, socialized at home, in school, in church, on the job—everywhere in society—that women are just a little bit lower on the scale of humanity than men. This is reflected in social and political policies, in law enforcement (and un-enforcement!), in judicial rulings, in our reading and interpretation of the Bible, and so on, *ad infinitum.* We have uncritically accepted and internalized what we "know" about women in this regard, and it affects everything that we see, hear, and do, as well as that which we fail to see, hear, and do. We cannot see the full humanity of women because we have always only known that they are not as fully human as men. Therefore, it does not seem to us that the exploitation of their labor is unjust or unfair. That is, there is nothing wrong with paying women less than men for equal work performed, even if women by-and-large perform better work. In this vein, it hardly matters if a woman's qualifications for that work are superior to those of a man. Federal employment and salary statistics bear out this sad reality.[56]

What we most readily see is what we have always known. This myopic vision blurs or blocks our ability to know what is staring us in the face, namely that inasmuch as women are created by the one God of the universe and imbued with as much of the divine image as men, they too are fully human and of infinite value to God. Heschel put it this way. "What impairs our sight are habits of seeing as well as the mental concomitants of seeing. Our sight is suffused with knowing, instead of feeling painfully the lack of knowing what we see. The principle to be

---

[56] See Daniel W. Rossides, *Social Stratification: The Interplay of Class, Race, and Gender*, 2nd ed. (Upper Saddle River, NJ: Prentice Hall, 1997); and Denny Brown, *The Rich Get Richer* 2nd ed. (Chicago: Nelson-Hall Publishers, 1997).

kept in mind is *to know what we see rather than to see what we know*."[57] In other words, we have been conditioned to see only the things we have always known as a result of a very thorough socialization process. The suffering of others is before our very eyes everyday, but we cannot see and feel their pain because of our conditioning. So we do not know what we see each day, i.e., the suffering that stares us in the face. We see only what we have been socialized to recognize.

The prophet's aim is to remove the perceptive blinders from our eyes. She introduces into the path of our vision "God's understanding of existence" and how persons should think of themselves and others in light of God's infinite love for them. Prophecy seeks to bring a new, redemptive order to interpersonal and social relations. Because of the difficulty we have in knowing what we see, this is not an easy task. Indeed, it is fair to say that to learn to know what we see is an important precondition to actually establishing a new order that is in tune with the realm of God. We must remember that it is not institutions or their representatives but God who calls and gives the charge to be prophetic. It is also the case that in every local congregation, the prophet must earn "the right" to be prophetic in that setting. One of the best ways to do this is to learn to love the people by moving among them in the daily routines of their lives,[58] keeping in mind that this relational process takes time.

Prophecy Seeks a New Order

David Walker prophesied against slavery, a religious and social order that contradicted God's understanding of what human relations should be. Walker preached the destruction of the slavocracy, and the establishment of an order of living and relating based on the recognition that all people are made in the image of God. For Walker, this implied the need to establish a social order based on the principles of justice, fairness, equality, and democracy for all. In his estimation, all people are precious to God because each is so highly valued and regarded by God.

The goal of prophecy and Christian social responsibility is not necessarily to make things easier for a particular group of persons, if by easier one means providing handouts without any intention in the first

---

[57] Heschel, *The Prophets*, xv.

[58] Dennis J. Geaney, *The Prophetic Parish* (Minneapolis MN: Winston Press, 1983) 47.

place of discovering the underlying causes for the need to give handouts. Rather, the goal is to make things better, which itself will make things easier for the poor and the weak. There is no doubt from the point of view of Christian theology why the goal should be to make things better for all people and construct a social order which will make it possible. People are interconnected by the will and love of God. We are of different genders, sizes, sexual orientations, colors, shapes, etc., but we are bound together by the common thread of divine love.

The goal of making things easier has often been translated into band-aid or stopgap approaches to problems like racial-ethnic and gender discrimination, poverty, and crime. It has often amounted to little more than tokenism, impersonal welfare programs, and little opportunity for the poor and underemployed to be gainfully and meaningfully employed. Making things better requires vision and imagination, short and long-term planning, followed by ongoing action through implementation of well constructed social policies and plans. It also requires shared suffering and shared power. Making things better in society goes beyond a mere ethic of survival in an economic system like Western capitalism that frequently subordinates the worth and importance of persons, the environment, and the animal kingdom.

This means that the prophet must be an advocate for the need to adopt an ethic of radical transformation. Such an ethic opens the door to the possibility of a new order of living and relating in the world based on divine expectations. The establishment of such an order will not be an easy task. It will require tremendous risks and sacrifices. There is great risk in seeking to eradicate the life-threatening elements of the present politico-economic order that is fuelled by a cut-throat ethic of rugged individualism. But, there is also risk in proposing and committing oneself to the establishment of a new way of living in the world based on justice and righteousness. One is likely to encounter enemies in both arenas.

Niccolo Machiavelli (1469–1527), considered to have been the "father of power politics," and himself no adherent of Christian ethical principles, wrote about just how difficult it is to inaugurate a new order of living arrangements in the world. If one who held that ethics had only a crudely utilitarian place in the arena of politics believed it to be difficult to establish a new order, those who do take ethics seriously need to understand this as well.

It must be considered that there is nothing more difficult to carry out, nor more doubtful of success, nor dangerous to handle, than to initiate a new order of things. For the reformer has enemies in all those who profit by the old order, and only lukewarm defenders in all those who would profit by the new order, this lukewarmness arising partly from fear of their adversaries, who have the laws in their favor; and partly from incredulity of mankind, who do not truly believe in anything new until they have had actual experience of it.[59]

The difficulty of establishing a new order is even more challenging for the disciple of Christ, for the ethic to which she adheres—and on which she would base such an order—is *agapé* love. This is a demanding ethic of perfectionism which society and many elements in churches resist like they would the plague.

A new order of things in God's world. Think about that! This is language that many do not typically like to speak or hear. According to the Book of Revelation, aging John, on the Isle of Patmos, spoke such language through the idiom of *a new heaven and a new earth* (Rev 21:1). What do you think Jesus' message, "The Kingdom of God is at hand; repent and believe," is all about? This was the announcement of the immediacy of God's new order for the world—of God's vision for the world, not next month or next presidential, senate, or congressional election, but right now! The Kingdom of God is at hand, right now! Jesus went to the cross, not just because he preached the Kingdom, but because he preached that it is *now* at hand. He preached it with a sense of urgency! Such an announcement, David Buttrick proclaims, "is bound to be intolerable to those who have over-invested themselves in 'this present age.'"[60] The announcement of the Realm of God was *bad news* for the privileged and powerful. It was (is!) *good news* for the poor and others counted among the least of the sisters and brothers.

It may be that two words upset Jesus' contemporaries more than any others regarding his preaching on the realm of God—*new* and *now*.[61] Proponents of the Christian faith somehow must catch the vision of this

---

[59] Niccolo Machiavelli, *The Prince and the Discourses* (New York: Modern Library, 1950) 21.

[60] Buttrick, *Preaching Jesus Christ*, 41.

[61] Ibid.

proclamation of the realm of God. This is why we need to resurrect the prophetic tradition of the church, and why we need the voice of prophecy today. It is the prophetic voice that proclaims forcefully and unequivocally that the dominion of God is at hand, right now.

It will indeed be difficult to establish a new order, particularly one based on the prophetic ethical principles of reverence for persons, equality, sharing, justice, and righteousness. It follows that the fate of the prophet who courageously and persistently insists on the need for such a radical new order is also uncertain in this world. Perhaps when we consider the fate of well known prophets of ancient and modern times, we will understand why so many in religious communities work so diligently and carefully to avoid prophetic ministry; why so many pastors and lay people seldom if ever preach and teach from the prophets; indeed, why so many work unceasingly to route out all vestiges of prophecy from the churches they attend.[62] This notwithstanding, there is a tremendous need for prophecy if there is to be hope for a new order of living and relating in both church and world. Martin Luther King, Jr. had this in mind in 1958 when he reflected on the Montgomery bus boycott.

---

[62] One need merely recall the plight of Jeremiah and other Hebrew prophets, as well as that of Jesus Christ. Martin Luther King, Jr., Oscar Romero, and others were martyred because of their prophetic voices. Avery Dulles reminds us that churches themselves generally squelch their own prophetic voices (see his *The Survival of Dogma*). Hans Kung writes of both the difficulty of prophecy for the church and the overwhelming need for prophets (see his *The Church*, trans. Ray and Rosaleen Ockenden [New York: Sheed and Ward, 1967] 433-34). Moreover, the prophetic ministry addresses forthrightly issues such as racism and sexism. Yet, sociologists of religion confirm that far too many churches fail in this regard (see Keith A. Roberts, *Religion in Sociological Perspective*, 3rd ed. (Belmont CA: Wadsworth, 1995] 298–333; C. Eric Lincoln and Lawrence Mamiya, *The Black Church in the African American Experience*, [Durham NC: Duke University Press, 1990] 274–308; Charles Y. Glock, Benjamin Ringer, and Earl Babbie, *To Comfort and to Challenge: A Dilemma of the Contemporary Church* (Berkeley/Los Angeles: University of California Press, 1967). Too numerous to list are the sociological studies confirming that churches generally shy away from prophetic ministry, especially regarding issues such as racism and sexism (including the recently heated debates surrounding sexual preference). To these, I can also add my own experience as a member of the Christian faith for several decades. The church that intentionally seeks to be prophetic is indeed rare. The pastor who preaches from the prophets on a routine basis is also rare.

Any discussion of the role of the Christian minister today must ultimately emphasize the need for prophecy. Not every minister can be a prophet, but some must be prepared for the ordeals of this high calling and be willing to suffer courageously for righteousness. May the problem of race in America soon make hearts burn so that prophets will rise up, saying, "Thus saith the LORD," and cry out as Amos did, "...let justice roll down like waters, and righteousness like an ever-flowing stream."[63]

In his day, David Walker responded to the need for prophetic ministry among the timid and the unrepentant, crying out for justice and demanding righteousness from the very ones who, claiming that theirs was the way of Christ, shamelessly stole the divine gifts of humanity, dignity, and freedom from others. The need for the courageous voice of the ethical prophet is no less needed in our day. One simply cannot talk about or represent the Christian faith sensibly and intelligibly if she fails to express the need for ethical prophecy at such a time as this, in such a world as this.

---

[63] Martin Luther King, Jr., *Stride Toward Freedom* (New York: Harper and Row, 1958) 210 (emphasis added).

Chapter 3

Elements of Ethical Prophecy in the *Appeal*[1]

Like many African Americans, past and present, David Walker was religiously and theologically conservative in matters pertaining to personal morality, e.g., the consuming of alcoholic beverages, gambling, and attending parties. During Walker's day, enslaved Africans were generally encouraged by white enslavers to consume alcohol, especially during extended holidays such as Christmas.[2] It was an inexpensive way of anesthetizing and controlling the enslaved during holiday seasons when there was a slowdown in plantation work. Walker, however, was totally opposed to drinking, especially among the enslaved. This stance was taken for religious and non-religious reasons. Walker knew, for example, that excessive drinking made the enslaved more docile and

---

[1] In this and subsequent chapters the numbers which appear in parentheses in the text refer to citations from the unabridged text of David Walker's *Appeal* which is reproduced in *Great Documents in Black American History*, ed. George Ducas and Charles Van Doren (New York: Praeger Publishers, 1970).

[2] None was more critical of this practice than Frederick Douglass, who wrote: "Judging from my own obsevation and experience, I believe those holidays were among the most effective means in the hands of slaveholders of keeping down the spirit of insurrection among the slaves" (Douglass, *Life and Times of Frederick Douglass* [1892; New York: Bonanza Books, 1962] 146–47).

easily controlled by their captors. It also led to disruption in their quarters, including unprovoked violent behavior toward other enslaved Africans. Walker was, understandably, opposed to any behaviors among his people that increased their vulnerability and made them even more susceptible to egregious manipulation. Such abuses only strengthened the cruel hands of the white enslavers, ultimately helping to keep the Africans in slavery.

Walker's stance, however, was anything but conservative when it came to socio-political matters, and most especially the enslaved condition of his people. Walker maintained that there was in his day a type of biblical Christianity that was "proper" or authentic; and another that was "improper" and thus inauthentic, propagated by white so-called Christians who enslaved Africans.[3] Proper Christianity had a strong message of liberation, stressed the image of God in all persons, and required that justice be done. The latter type—a malformed Christianity—justified the enslavement of the Africans by teaching that the image of God was in whites only, thus concluding that whites were superior to blacks in all ways. According to the white enslavers, the Bible taught that blacks should be obedient to whites, who were presumably their natural masters.

Politically, David Walker was not just liberal and-or progressive, but emphatically militant both in his views and in his willingness to take aggressive steps to bring about the liberation of his people. There was no dichotomy between Walker's religious beliefs and convictions and his commitment to issues of justice. Indeed, consistent with much of African American religious history, his commitment to social justice was grounded in his understanding of Christianity. Peter Hinks comments:

> Walker followed an African American tradition, evolving since the late eighteenth century, of employing evangelical religion not only for individual regeneration but also for radical social transformation. Influenced in part by the egalitarianism and support for rebellion espoused by many white evangelicals during the era of the American Revolution, Gabriel, the rebels of 1802, Vesey, Walker, and Turner crafted a doctrine of religion and rebellion that by 1831 was well established and gaining

---

[3] See Albert J. Raboteau, *Slave Religion* (New York: Oxford University Press, 1978) 295.

momentum as revivals and abolitionism converged in the social enthusiasms of the early 1830s.[4]

Of course, it was in 1831 that the famous Nat Turner rebellion occurred.

In any event, the linking of the evangelical Christian faith to the socio-political views and practices of Walker and others of his era was not—as some scholars maintain—just "incidental" to the functions of their religious faith. While evangelical religion had an "individual and communitarian" function for many blacks during this period, it also empowered the likes of David Walker to preach the destruction of evil social institutions such as slavery, and to substitute in their place structures based on a construct of Jewish and Christian justice and equality.[5]

Walker's stance was similar to that of notable biblical prophets, e.g., Amos, Isaiah, Jerermiah, Hosea, and Micah. Like the prophets, his insistence on the just and humane treatment of his people essentially was grounded not in political machinations, but in his theological and moral outlook. It cannot be argued that Walker believed the human rights and liberty of blacks were guaranteed by the Declaration of Independence and the Constitution of the United States. His moral-theological convictions, however, convinced him that in the end every person has such a guarantee because they are created, sustained, needed, and loved by God.

It is evident that the moral-theological stance of those in the tradition of the eighth-century prophets always has socio-political implications, and implies adherence to a higher ethic. At their best, politicians aim to do justice. But the prophetic individual reminds us that love is the higher, more radical imperative, and that justice is necessary but not sufficient by itself. Such a claim clearly has political implications. For it means that important as it is to achieve ever-higher degrees of justice, even politicians should not be satisfied with mere

---

[4] Peter P. Hinks, *To Awaken My Afflicted Brethren: David Walker and the Problem of Antebellum Resistance* (University Park PA.: Pennsylvania State University Press, 1997) 232.

[5] Ibid., 233. As Hinks puts it: "While aid to psychic and community stability was undeniably a critical service religion rendered African Americans, in the early decades of the United States those functions conjoined with a fierce religious impulse to destroy the social structures upholding degradation and submission and replace them with institutions based on Christian love and justice."

justice alone, at least according to the prophetic stance. Politicians, for example, may not be concerned about *how* justice is carried out. The ethical prophetic stance, on the other hand, requires that it be done righteously or with lovingkindness.

There are a number of important elements that characterize Hebrew prophecy, many of which are found in the *Appeal*. Six of these are examined in this chapter: 1) Divine Call and the Cost of Prophecy; 2) Divine Justice; 3) Divine Wrath; 4) Hope for Repentance of Evildoers; 5) Love and Compassion of God; and 6) Sacredness of Persons. Attention is especially given to 5 and 6, since these are crucial to the theologico-ethical grounding of prophecy.

Divine Call and the Cost of Prophecy

It quickly becomes clear that divine call actually implies cost in prophecy. It might even be argued that divine call necessarily implies the cost or the price to be paid by any person who enters the ministry and embraces its prophetic responsibilities. The call itself has implicit in it the idea that the one called should be prepared and willing to engage in a certain amount of prophetic daring. It is difficult to believe that any who spend time and energy trying to avoid such daring actually have experienced a divine call. It is understandable that human nature may cause one to question the place of prophetic daring in ministry. If, however, one truly understands what it means to be called by God, she will also know at the center of her being that prophetic daring is integral to the call to ministry.

One's sense of call is a fairly subjective experience. This means that it may not be possible for one person to determine with certainty whether a divine call has occurred or not in another. What we can be very sure of, however, is that without the legitimate presence of this sense of being called by God, one cannot be placed in the tradition of the eighth-century Hebrew prophets. Each of these prophets experienced a sense of being called by God—even when no clear account of a call narrative is included in the book that bears each figure's name. There are clear and explicit call narratives in the Books of Jeremiah (1:4-19) and Isaiah (6:1-13), for example, but not in the Book of Micah. Yet, any who read the latter and understand Micah can only conclude he was called and commissioned by God.

There is no question that David Walker was a man of deep and abiding religious faith. He was an active, faithful churchman. He had strong ties in the 4,000-member African Methodist Episcopal Church of Charleston, South Carolina. A number of the members, including Walker, were involved in the planning of the Denmark Vesey conspiracy of 1822.[6] Walker later attached himself to the Methodist Church in Boston. The pastor of that church was the Southern-born African American, Samuel Snowden.

There was no religious leader for whom Walker had more respect and admiration than Bishop Richard Allen (94), founder of the African Methodist Episcopal Church, officially organized in 1816. Walker devoted considerable space in the *Appeal* to discussing his admiration for Allen, a fact that implies the two men very likely had close contact during Walker's brief visit to Philadelphia as he made his way to Boston to establish his new home. There is also the strong likelihood that Walker was, at least in part, drawn to Charleston, South Carolina because of the well-established A.M.E. church in that city. Forty or more of the members of the congregation participated in one way or another in the Denmark Vesey conspiracy. We know from the *Appeal* that Walker was in Charleston not long before 1820 to attend a religious camp meeting. He relocated there sometime between 1815 and 1820 because of greater employment opportunities and a desire to determine for himself the meaning of being nominally free while so many of his people remained in slavery. But, he might well have been in Charleston for other reasons. For example, Hinks suggests: "A glaring symbol of black resistance to white hegemony, the church also stood as a constant reminder to all blacks of how they might seek out freedom together. The presence of large numbers of free blacks, numerous employment prospects, and the development of a church with black leadership all probably served to draw David Walker to Charleston in the late 1810s."[7]

---

[6] C. Eric Lincoln and Lawrence Mamiya have written about this church, its membership size, and the involvement of many of the members in the planning of the Vesey conspiracy. See their book, *The Black Church in the African American Experience* (Durham NC: Duke University Press, 1990) 52. They do not name David Walker as a member of that church, but we learn from the Hinks study, *To Awaken My Afflicted Brethren*, that there is strong likelihood that Walker was in regular attendance and likely participated in the planning.

[7] Hinks, *To Awaken My Afflicted Brethren*, 28–29.

It is not clear whether Walker actually joined Charleston's prominent A.M.E. church. We do, however, know at least two things. First, he received his first initiation to religious teachings in a black-led Methodist church in North Carolina.[8] Second, his disgust over the way his people were being treated by whites surely made him susceptible to being influenced by the commitment that the Charleston church had to the liberation of enslaved blacks.

One cannot read the *Appeal* and fail to appreciate that David Walker's energy for his mission came from the fact that he had experienced God and the Christian faith for himself. Because he could read and study the Bible and history, he had a good sense of what it meant to be a follower of Jesus Christ. This helps to explain Walker's frequent use of Christian mores to attack slavery and the mistreatment of Africans in America and the Western hemisphere in general. He also repeatedly used religious appeals to establish and defend the rights of his people. Indeed, not only did Walker use the Christian religious tradition as a weapon against slavery and in defense of black humanity and dignity, his views were so profoundly grounded in Christian theology that it was abundantly clear he believed God was the source of human rights, equality, and dignity. This is why there was such vehemence in Walker's condemnation of slavery and his frequent claims that the practice was a sin against God.

The eighth-century prophets were not inducted into the prophetic office because of birth, class, or ability. They were summoned or *called* to it by God. There is clear biblical evidence of the call of Isaiah, Jeremiah, and Ezekiel. There is less clarity regarding the call of Amos, Hosea, and Second Isaiah, although we can easily reconstruct each. Noted previously, there is no call-narrative, as such, for Micah. The passionate and righteous tone of the book, however, as well as its content, are in and of themselves compelling proof of the prophet's call from God.

While virtually anybody might be called to prophecy, there are various means to examine the authenticity of one's claim to that calling. The character of the prophet's message can be evaluated with respect to the highest of Jewish and Christian moral principles. Again, one might try to determine whether the prophet's message has proven true or, if

---

[8] Ibid., 15.

predictive, if it has been fulfilled.[9] Because the call to prophecy is so subjective an experience, it is difficult to apply these criteria fully. Therefore, one may have to appeal to history's lessons as the deciding factor.[10] That is, only by looking back on the work of those who claimed to be prophets in the context of what we take prophecy to mean, can we arrive at some sense of certainty regarding their status as legitimate prophets. But we can be certain of one thing: those who have stood as legitimate representatives of the eighth-century prophetic tradition believed themselves to be called to their appointed tasks by God. Tragically, history is periodically visited by crackpots and lunatics who engage in murderous acts while claiming to be called of God. Consequently, we need trustworthy criteria for authenticating to a reasonable degree the call of God in persons' lives to speak with the special authority of the prophet.

David Walker went to great pains to let us know that he was not just engaged in religious rhetoric, or in an intellectual exercise; that the writing of the *Appeal* and his teaching were not something that he thought up out of the clear blue. Rather, he insisted, the arguments in the *Appeal* were not his own. He was merely being obedient to God's will, i.e., to God's instructions, or to God's call. Walker was careful not only to point this out, but also to clarify his willingness to pay the price of being prophetic, obedient, and faithful to God. Surely this is what Walker meant when he said: "I write without the fear of man, I am writing for my God, and fear none but himself; they may put me to death if they choose."[11] Walker was well aware of the seriousness of his project, and of his role in carrying out what he perceived to be God's call. "I am fully aware, in making this appeal...that I shall not only be assailed by those whose greatest earthly desires are, to keep us in abject ignorance and wretchedness," (59) but also by those who believed that God has ordained that blacks be the slaves of whites. Walker knew full well that for being obedient to what he considered to be God's call, he would also be criticized by many of his own people who, in his words, "are

---

[9] Albert C. Knudson, *The Prophetic Movement in Israel* (New York: The Methodist Book Concern, 1921) 19.

[10] Ibid., 19.

[11] *David Walker's Appeal*, ed. Charles M. Wiltse (New York: Hill and Wang, 1965) 54.

ignorantly in league with slave-holders or tyrants, who acquire their daily bread by the blood and sweat of their more ignorant brethren..." (60).

Like the eighth-century prophets, Walker claimed to be called directly by God. Therefore, the words he spoke were not his own or the words of any other human being. Taking a stance similar to that of the ancient prophets, he virtually equated his speaking and writing to the word or the point of view of God. "His own articulate courage and confident finger-pointing were all intended to reinforce the idea that he was filled with God and spoke for him."[12] The prophet speaks God's words to the people. As Heschel put it, "Prophecy is God's personal communication to man. It deals with what concerns God intimately."[13]

The *Appeal* proffers the sense that David Walker was personally addressed by God when called to his prophetic work. Indeed, he was as confident of his calling to be a champion of the humanity, rights, and dignity of his people as was the shepherd Amos that God had called him to prophesy: "the LORD took me from following the flock, and the LORD said to me, 'Go, prophesy to my people Israel'" (Amos 7:14–15).

Walker recognized the seriousness of his call. In fact, he labored under such conviction that he admonished all alike that he was "in the hand of God" and therefore neither feared anyone nor what may happen to him for proclaiming God's truth. Instead, he was "ready to be offered at any moment" (101). That is, he understood the cost or the price that one must be willing to pay for being faithful to God. Indeed, in his "Brief Sketch of the Life and Character of David Walker," Henry Highland Garnet quoted Walker as saying: "I will stand my ground. *Somebody must die in this cause.* I may be doomed to the stake and the fire, or to the scaffold tree, but it is not in me to falter if I can promote the work of emancipation."[14]

The personal price one might pay as God's prophet is not a matter that either the eighth-century prophets or Walker spent much time deliberating. They understood that when God calls and one answers, "Here am I, send me," she not only proclaims her own readiness but acknowledges that her life is no longer her own. She does not merely enter a profession; nor does she continue to depend solely upon her own

---

[12] Hinks, *To Awaken My Afflicted Brethren*, 228.

[13] Abraham J. Heschel, *The Prophets* (New York: Harper, 1962) 443.

[14] Henry Highland Garnet and David Walker, *Walker's Appeal and Garnet's Address* (1848; Nashville: James C. Winston Publishing, 1994) vii.

resources. When one answers God's call to prophecy, she comes soon to understand, as David Walker did, that she has entered a totally new and revolutionary way of being and living in the world. Prophecy becomes her way of life; her way of thinking, seeing, doing, and relating in the world. Hebrew Bible scholar Gerhard von Rad provides a helpful word on this point: "This was more than simply a new profession: it was a totally new way of life, even at the sociological level, to the extent that a call meant relinquishing normal social life and all the social and economic securities which this offered, and changing over instead to a condition where a man had nothing to depend upon, or, as we may put it, to a condition of dependence upon YAHWEH and upon that security alone."[15]

The prophet puts her trust only in God. She knows that God will provide for her needs, and that in the end the Word of God remains, even if her life must be sacrificed. She believes in the essential goodness in human nature and is keenly aware of the practical inclination to sin. This notwithstanding, she is utterly convinced that it is God in whom she must put her deepest trust and faith.

We do not know the precise time that David Walker sensed and acknowledged God's call to be the voice of his voiceless, enslaved people. We need not be particularly concerned about its chronology. More important is the evidence of Walker's conviction that he was doing God's work rather than his own, or the work of other human beings; that God called and he essentially answered, "Here am I, here am I, I'll go."

In addition, we can be sure that David Walker did not proceed ignorantly on the journey. He prepared himself to do the work of prophetic ministry, and at a time in the history of the United States when it was against the law for blacks to learn the alphabet and to read the Bible. Walker's mother was a "free" woman, and quite possibly knew how to read and write. She likely taught young David all she knew of the fundamentals of reading and writing. For the rest, he was self-taught. Walker understood the importance of education—not only for the sake of one's livelihood and the fostering of a civil and humane society—but for the sake of doing God's work. It was important to prepare himself as best he could in order to respond most adequately to God's call. In this regard, James Turner contends that Walker devoted as much as ten years

---

[15] Gerhard von Rad, *Old Testament Theology* (New York: Harper & Row, 1965) 2:58.

to the study and research of history, theology, philosophy, sociology, and the sordid institution of slavery in preparation for writing what would ultimately become the *Appeal*.[16]

This is a crucial point for any who have aspirations to the ministry. No longer is it appropriate or even intelligible (if it ever was!) to claim that if one is called by God all she need do is open her mouth and God will give her the words to speak. No! In light of the context that the prophet finds herself in, she is obligated to prepare in the most appropriate ways for the work God calls her to do. The divine call has inherent in it a charge, or an obligation to take the necessary steps to do what is required to most effectively and faithfully carry out the requirements of the call. It is in this sense that the one called should understand and heed Saint Paul's words that Christians ought study to show themselves approved of God (2 Tim 2:15). We learn from David Walker that one has to work at preparing for prophetic ministry; that one truly has to study to show herself approved of God.

Divine Justice

The Hebrew prophets were relentless in the "unveiling of injustice and oppression, in their comprehension of social, political, and religious evils."[17] A passage from the Book of Micah is illustrative:

> Alas for those who devise wickedness and evil deeds on their beds! When the morning dawns, they perform it, because it is in their power. They covet fields, and seize them; houses, and take them away; they oppress householder and house, people and their inheritance.... And I said: Listen, you heads of Jacob and rulers of the house of Israel! Should you not know justice?—You who hate the good and love the evil, who tear the skin off their bones; who eat the flesh of my people, flay their skin off them, break their bones in pieces, and chop them up like meat in a kettle, like flesh in a caldron (Mic 2:1–2; 3:1–3).

---

[16] James Turner, introduction to *David Walker's Appeal*, by David Walker (1830; Baltimore: Black Classic Press, 1993) 10.

[17] Heschel, *The Prophets*, 204.

Unlike philosophers, the prophets' deepest concern was not the mere defining justice as such, or developing an aesthetically pleasing theory of justice. Instead, they were concerned with identifying and exposing concrete instances of injustice and oppression, for these were violations of Israel's covenant relationship with God. The prophets were certain that God wanted for justice to be done in a spirit of lovingkindness (Mic 6:8; Amos 5:24). They were concerned about what Heschel refers to as "everydayness," i.e., about the concrete day-to-day matters that affect the humanity and dignity of persons.

The ethical prophet is called to trouble those who have become comfortable at the expense of or through neglecting "the least of these," and to be a remonstrator for the dignity and rights of all persons. It is because of the divine creation of all people that prophets are so concerned about doing justice, rather than simply theorizing about it in some isolated place of peace and comfort. They assume both that God is the author of justice and that every person possesses an inviolable and permanent sacredness because they are called into existence by God. Precisely because of this, we can say that the prophet is called to be an advocate; a champion of the poor, the weak, and the oppressed.[18]

Divine holiness is frequently expressed in the Hebrew Bible by the ancient prophets' reference to God's justice (Isa 5:16) and righteousness (Jer 9:24). Justice (*mispat*) was concerned primarily with "the rights due to every individual in the community, and the upholding of those rights."[19] The prophets' tendency was to speak of God's justice and righteousness in the same breath. Not only was justice to be done, it was to be done in a particular spirit, with a particular attitude. That is, an attitude which reflects righteousness.

Ethical prophecy is concerned not about the unknowable activities of heaven and hell, but about all that transpires on earth. Human beings do not have to guess and hypothesize about this as they would the afterlife. The prophet frequently knows injustice and the cries of the weak and the oppressed firsthand, because he witnesses them in the world in which he lives. On the other hand he cannot know and speak with authority about what happens beyond the grave. Amos knew about economic injustices "at the gate." Hosea knew about a whoring spouse

---

[18] Ibid., 205.

[19] Bruce Birch, *Let Justice Roll Down: The Old Testament, Ethics, and Christian Life* (Louisville KY: Westminster/John Knox Press, 1991) 155.

and the desire to keep pursuing her in the hope that she would repent and return to faithfulness. Because he was a peasant-farmer who lived among the poor and oppressed in the countryside, Micah knew firsthand how the privileged and powerful coveted and seized the land and houses of the powerless. He knew that God required that justice be done in *this* world. The eighth-century prophets had a predilection for knowing about and responding to individual and collective behavior in this world, not in a world beyond the grave. They prophesied of things of the earth, not of heaven and hell. They were concerned that justice be done in this world.

Ethical prophecy "is concerned for concrete realities in the midst of history. God's word was not a theological abstraction but an expression of divine rule in the concreteness of human community."[20] The prophets conveyed the view that, whatever else may be the case with respect to God's cosmic sovereignty, God rules in and over history. The point to be made is that the God of the prophets ruled *in* history, which means that God is always concerned about persons in the world and about all that happens to them. God, as Heschel reminds us, is always concerned about small things, and is indifferent to nothing that affects persons.[21]

God's justice may not always be swift, but according to David Walker, the Africans could count on God's justice, for God's faithfulness and steadfastness had long ago been proven. Time and again, Walker reminded his people of *the certainty of God's justice and mercy*; that white enslavement of the Africans did not go unnoticed by the God of justice and mercy who created all persons only for God's satisfaction. Walker reminded his people that white enslavers

> are so happy to keep in ignorance and degradation, and to receive the homage and the labor of the slaves, they forget that God rules in the armies of heaven and among the inhabitants of the earth, having his ears continually open to the cries, tears, and groans of his oppressed people; and being a just and holy Being will at one day appear fully in behalf of the oppressed, and arrest the progress of the avaricious oppressors; for although the destruction of the oppressors God may not effect by the oppressed, yet the Lord our God will bring other destructions upon them (60–61).

---

[20] Ibid., 258.
[21] Heschel, *The Prophets*, 5–6.

The phrase "God's justice" conveys a dual message. On the one hand it is intended to assure the weak and the oppressed that God cares about them and expects that justice will be done to them. When their needs are persistently unmet, God actively participates in redressing the injustices and inequities they experience.[22] Norman H. Snaith[23] and Stephen Mott[24] both argue convincingly that when the weak cannot on their own achieve justice or depend on human institutions to provide relief, God acts on their behalf. On the other hand, God's justice is intended to convey to wrongdoers God's displeasure with their behavior and God's intention that they be judged, indeed punished. Although God will have the final word, it need not solely be judgment or doom. Nevertheless, those who oppress and treat others unjustly contribute to what the character of God's final word will be.

Some nations thought that Africans were created for the sole purpose of digging and mining precious minerals for whites and working their farms. Not so, rebutted Walker. God, he asserted, was not pleased with whites' treatment of the Africans. "Can the Americans escape God Almighty? If they do, can he be to us a God of Justice?" (71) In both cases, the answer was a resounding "No!" If God is truly the God of justice, as Walker believed, then those who engage in unjust practices and refuse to relent and repent cannot escape God's judgment. Near the end of the *Appeal*, Walker was explicit about his certainty of God's just intentions toward blacks. "Whether you believe it or not," he said to his people, "I tell you that God will dash tyrants, in combination with devils, into atoms, and will bring you out from your wretchedness and miseries, under these *Christian people!!!!!!*" (101) There was no doubt for David Walker that God is the God of justice, and that in the end God's justice would be done.

This raises the issue of divine wrath, an idea whose application by Walker the Christian enslavers found repugnant. But for Walker, as for the Hebrew prophets, it was not possible to talk seriously about the love, compassion, and justice of God without also invoking God's promise of

---

[22] Birch, *Let Justice Roll Down*, 156.

[23] Norman H. Snaith, *The Distinctive Ideas of the Old Testament* (New York: Schocken Books, 1964) 70.

[24] Stephen C. Mott, *Biblical Ethics and Social Change* (New York: Oxford University Press, 1982) 220. Mott actually follows the line of argument presented in Snaith.

divine wrath in the face of continued injustice and violation of the covenant relationship. That God is a holy, just, and merciful being (60, 61), Walker had no doubt. But neither was he doubtful that such a God not only gets angry at injustice and humanly contrived massive suffering and oppression, but ultimately punishes such behavior if it does not cease.

Divine Wrath

L. Susan Bond has rightly characterized Walker's *Appeal* as "an apocalyptic prophetic document, calling white Christians to repentance or judgment."[25] Walker preferred that they repent. He was certain, however, that they would be judged by God and brought to their knees if they did not repent of their very great evil against blacks.

As noted above, we need to remember that David Walker was not the first African American to speak and write of God's wrath and impatience with injustice and slavery. In the eighteenth century, black preachers and others already were describing God as the great liberator and as one who demanded that justice be done. They maintained that those who disobeyed would suffer the wrath of God. In 1788 and 1797 an anonymous black writer and Prince Hall, respectively, warned whites of God's vengeance against those who refused to liberate the enslaved Africans.[26]

While David Walker was not the first African American to announce God's vengeance on the cruel enslavers, he was in a class by himself in terms of the passion and forthrightness with which he uttered such words. During the years of slavery in America it was always dangerous for blacks to publicly agitate against the slavocracy, even when they did so with the least offensive language. Unlike many of his predecessors and successors, Walker was not in the least disposed to softening his language, believing as he did that his were the words of God. His public advocacy against slavery was tantamount to engaging in life-threatening behavior.

---

[25] L. Susan Bond, "To Hear the Angels' Wings: Apocalyptic Language and the Formation of Moral Community in the Sermons of Gardner C. Taylor" (Ph.D. diss., Vanderbilt University, 1996) 144.

[26] Hinks, *To Awaken My Afflicted Brethren*, 174–75.

The eighth-century prophets of Israel considered wrath or anger to be one of the modes of God's pathos. Pathos expresses the idea of God's steadfast, exhaustless love, care, and compassion for persons. The love of God is fundamental, and thus is not only an attribute of the divine nature, but *is* that nature. Anger or wrath, on the other hand, is an expression of divine love, because God is not pleased with injustice. Therefore, according to the Hebrew prophets, divine wrath is an expression of God's eternal, steadfast love and concern for the well being of all persons.[27]

Like those ancient prophets, Walker was relentless in his appeal to words of doom as a result of the injustice and inhumane treatment done to his people. In the Book of Micah, for example, one gets the sense that the first three chapters (the only three of which many contemporary biblical scholars attribute to Micah) are primarily intended to announce divine judgment for the persistent injustice and disobedience of the privileged and powerful. Micah provides a catalog of injustices and misbehaviors by rulers, priests, and officially sanctioned prophets (Mic 3:5, 9–11). He then announces God's judgment: "Therefore because of you Zion shall be plowed as a field; Jerusalem shall become a heap of ruins; and the mountain of the house a wooded height" (Mic 3:12). Because of the peoples' wicked behavior, the prophet declares that when they do call on God, the face of the Divine will be hidden from them.

Walker was both persistent and emphatic in declaring that God will shower fires of wrath on whites for their brutal and unjust treatment of blacks. Although the *Appeal* emphasized the hope of what African Americans could accomplish if they endeavored to throw off all white portrayals of black personhood and rediscovered their lost sense of dignity, Sterling Stuckey tells us that "the burden of the *Appeal* is essentially one of doom for whites."[28] Walker courageously voiced doom-sayings, and stated in clear terms what the avaricious, so-called Christian Americans, i.e., white enslavers, could expect if they continued their enslavement of blacks. As certain as the eighth-century prophets were that God would punish Israel for persistent violation of the covenant agreement, Walker was certain that whites would experience divine wrath if they did not end the treacherous practice of slavery. What

---

[27] Heschel, *The Prophets*, 277.

[28] Sterling Stuckey, *Slave Culture: Nationalist Theory and the Foundations of Black America* (New York: Oxford University Press, 1987) 131.

blacks had to do, he maintained, was to believe and have faith in God's love, compassion, justice, and promise. In addition, they had to look more to themselves than to sympathetic whites for the means to achieve solidarity and liberation.

Contrary to Stuckey's claim, the preponderance of the evidence in the *Appeal* suggests that its "burden" is that of conveying to the Africans a sense of their humanity, sanctity, and dignity, as well as the need to look to themselves and to God for their liberation. This was the positive burden of the *Appeal*. Walker's fundamental concern was for his people, whatever else he may have tried to convey in the *Appeal*. His declarations of doom for whites was a negative burden in the *Appeal*, but not his primary concern.

Although it is true that the promise of divine judgment, i.e. the summoning of Israel before the judgment seat, was the new element that the Hebrew prophets introduced into prophecy,[29] judgment was neither the primary nor the last word from God. God appointed Jeremiah over the nations "to pluck up and to pull down, to destroy and to overthrow…" (Jer 1:10). Note that the four negative verbs in the scriptural phrase refer to destruction or doom. This implied the seriousness and inevitability of God's intention to punish the people for their persistent disobedience. In contrast, however, the last words of the same passage are two positive verbs: "to build and to plant." Implying that a remnant would remain *after* the destruction brought about by judgment, God promised a new day or restoration. God's last word is not one of wrath or destruction, but hope. For God's chief attribute, God's essential nature is love. Love does not—nor does it ever—ultimately prefer to will judgment. God's love is steadfast and unending, which is why the prophets painted a picture of God's unceasing turning toward and searching for disobedient humanity. God's love for humanity is primary. God's judgment is but an aspect or mode of the divine pathos. In this sense, salvation is also present in God's wrath, but only "in the shadow of judgment."[30] God's love for people continues even beyond judgment or wrath. Love is more fundamental than judgment, but in order for love to achieve its purpose, persistent acts of disobedience and injustice must be punished. Salvation will follow in the wake of

---

[29] Gerhard von Rad, *The Message of the Prophets* (New York: Harper & Row Publishers, 1965) 147, 154.

[30] Ibid., 154.

judgment. This is the way we should understand David Walker's prophetic declaration of the judgment awaiting white Christian enslavers.

In the final analysis, God will not be mocked. Because God is the God of justice, the enslavers of the Africans cannot escape God's wrath. The best thing that whites can do, Walker maintained, is to listen to God's Word and change their behavior. If they do not, they will be ruined (86). God will not fail to deliver blacks from enslavement. The only possible way the whites could avoid "the vengeance of God" was to free the enslaved and repent of their sins (86). Consistent with African American religious tradition, and especially in light of social justice issues, Walker was adamant that one cannot do wrong and escape the consequences of God's wrath.

Walker understood, as did the Hebrew prophets, that the biblical doom-sayings were conditioned by the peoples' responses to God's warnings. The Book of Micah reminds: "He does not retain his anger forever, because he delights in showing clemency. He will again have compassion upon us; he will tread our iniquities under foot" (Mic 7:18–19). Accordingly, white enslavers need not necessarily succumb to divine wrath. To avoid God's anger it was required that they repent and change their behavior in accordance with God's requirement that justice and righteousness be done, not tomorrow but today.

One in the eighth-century prophetic tradition does not turn away from the biblical idea of divine wrath, no matter how difficult it may be to reconcile it with divine love. Indeed, in the end it may be that the most we can say about divine wrath is that it is a mode of divine pathos and divine love, and that finally, it is among the strangest of God's works of love.[31]

Hope for Repentance and Salvation

In nearly every case, the warnings of divine judgment that David Walker uttered were conditional and therefore left open the door to the fourth element of prophecy that is prominent in the *Appeal*, viz., *hope for repentance and ultimate reconciliation*. In the writings of classic and more recent scholars on the Hebrew prophets, there is agreement that the

---

[31] Paul Tillich, *Love, Power, and Justice* (New York: Oxford University Press, 1960) 48–51. An instructive discussion, influenced by Martin Luther, on the "proper" and the "strange" work of divine love.

prophets generally began their prophecy with words of doom or judgment, but they always ended with words of hope.[32] Indeed, one student of Hebrew prophecy was impressed by "the almost complete absence of a message of doom" in Deutero-Isaiah,[33] while the other prophets began by preaching doom and judgment but ending with a declaration of hope.

None wrote more poignantly about the Bible being the story of God's relentless search for the people and the hope that they would hear and obey the covenant agreement than Heschel. It is the story of how God turns toward the people, not of their turning toward God. "Indeed, all of human history as seen by the Bible is the history of God *in search of man*. In spite of man's failure, over and over, God does not abandon His hope to find righteous men. Adam, Cain, the generation of the Tower of Babel—it is a story of failure and defiance. And yet, God did not abandon man, hoping against hope to see a righteous world."[34]

This is why after the destruction prophesied by Jeremiah, God announced the establishment of a new covenant. The law would now be etched into the being of persons so that God would be their God, and they would be God's people (Jer 31:31–33). While David Walker began by preaching the divine judgment of doom to white Christians for their role in slavery, he also expressed the hope that whites would repent. At one point Walker admonished:

> I tell you Americans! that unless you speedily alter your course, *you* and your *Country are gone*!!!!!! For God Almighty will tear up the very face of the earth.... I warn you in the name of the Lord, (whether you will hear, or forbear,) to repent and reform, or you are ruined!!!!!! Do you think that our blood is hidden from the Lord, because you can hide it from the rest of the world by sending out missionaries.... O Americans! Americans!! I call God—I call angels—I call men, to witness,

---

[32] See Albert C. Knudson, *The Beacon Lights of Prophecy* (New York: Eaton & Mains, 1914) 87, 121, 191, 228. See also Heschel, *The Prophets*, 37.

[33] Knudson, *The Beacon Lights of Prophecy*, 255–61.

[34] Abraham J. Heschel, "Prophetic Inspiration: An Analysis of Prophetic Consciousness," *Judaism: A Quarterly Journal of Jewish Life and Thought*, 11/1 (1962): 10.

that your destruction *is at hand*, and will be speedily consummated unless you REPENT (83, 85).

The doom sayings Walker directed toward whites were not absolute or final. They were conditional. They were hypothetical imperatives, i.e., *if* the white enslavers did not liberate the Africans, *then* there would be hell to pay. This means that after every such warning, God has yet another word, viz., a word of hope. Indeed, "the destruction of Israel was never the last word of any prophet. Beyond the ruin would rise the new building of God."[35] Despite the doom sayings, there was an ever present hope in the biblical prophet's message that, as Georgia Harkness maintained, was "grounded in the faith that God would not permit His people to be utterly blotted out...."[36] Walker shared this sentiment. White slavers would be doomed only if they continued to hold the Africans in slavery.

At any rate, Walker clearly pointed out that death and destruction needed not occur, *if* enslavers repented of the sin of slavery, and then set at liberty those held in captivity. But as sure as God is a just God, Walker warned, the prophecy of doom would be realized if repentance and appropriate behavior did not immediately follow. What readers of the *Appeal* have not always seen is that despite the fierceness of his words, Walker hoped that white enslavers would repent and liberate their captives in order to avoid God's wrath. To this regard he said:

> *I hope that the Americans may hear*, but I am afraid that they have done so much injury, and are so firm in the belief that our Creator made us to be an inheritance to them forever, that their hearts will be hardened, so that their destruction may be sure. ... I am awfully afraid that pride, prejudice, avarice and blood, will, before long, prove the final ruin of this happy republic, or land of liberty!!! Can any thing be a greater mockery of religion than the way it is conducted by the Americans? (83, 85; emphasis added)

---

[35] Knudson, *The Beacon Lights of Prophecy*, 87.

[36] Georgia Harkness, *The Sources of Western Morality* (New York: Charles Scribner's Sons, 1954) 119.

David Walker *hoped* that the whites would repent. The study of history and his own experience, however, convinced him that *many* whites were so consumed by their prejudice toward the Africans and were so avaricious, selfish, arrogant, and wretched that they would not repent and bow down before God, let alone champion the liberation of the Africans. Instead, Walker believed that such persons would instead hold on tenaciously to the unfounded belief that the Africans were less than human, created only to serve whites and their children (91). It was precisely because of whites' insistence that the Africans were at best subhuman that Walker was so passionate and adamant about insisting on acknowledgement of the humanity and absolute dignity of his people.

Some may wonder whether Walker was serious about the hope that whites would repent and that there might be reconciliation between the two races. It makes sense to assume that he was earnest about these matters since "the search for freedom and the readiness to consider changing realities in the interest of that search were both important to him."[37] According to Walker, God did not will the destruction of whites, for God is love. He knew that to claim that God ever wills the destruction of any person or group would be a claim against God's fundamental holiness, love, justice, and righteousness. Such a God would never will the destruction of human life. In the case of white enslavers, it may be said that God willed that they be saved from destruction, *if* they would hear, repent (99), and change their behavior. Furthermore, although Walker believed there could be a reconciliation between blacks and at least some of the whites, he insisted—anticipating Malcolm X and the Black Liberation Theology Movement of the mid-1960s—that blacks should take the lead role in defining the terms of such reconciliation. In addition, Walker believed both that public national repentance for wrongs done to blacks (100), as well as the need to do justice to the enslaved, were necessary preconditions to reconciliation between the races. Where there is no mutual respect of equals between persons, there can be no satisfactory reconciliation. Free persons and the enslaved cannot be reconciled until they stand on equal ground.

God as Loving and Compassionate

---

[37] Stuckey, *Slave Culture*, 131.

The discussion now turns to a more extensive discussion on the last two principles of ethical prophecy to be considered: *the compassion and love of God*, and the *sacredness of persons*. The first of these focuses on a particular conception or way of thinking about God that was expressed by prophetic persons, such as David Walker. The eighth-century prophets of Israel had a particular way of thinking about God, a radically different God than that depicted in classical Greek and Roman philosophy that found its way into early Christian thought. Based on what many contemporary proponents of Christianity say about God, e.g., that God can choose to be illogical and irrational, or that God has no need for persons, it is clear that remnants of the classical Greek and Roman ideas about God persists even today. But this is a doctrine of God contrary to that of the prophets.

David Walker reflected the ethical tradition of eighth-century Hebrew prophecy. Ethical prophecy must be theocentric, which means that it must be seen that the prophet attributes the source or cause of prophecy to God. It is, therefore, necessary to know something about Walker's understanding of the God in whom ethical prophecy is grounded.

Walker was already a deeply religious person by the time he moved to Boston around 1824. Not much is known about his mother, other than she was a "free" woman who knew the fundamentals of reading and writing and taught these to her son. It is likely that it was she who encouraged and inspired the development of Walker's deep religious faith and convictions, as well as his fierce hatred of slavery and the toll that it took on their people.

In addition to his deep religious convictions, Walker was self-educated, understood the value of knowledge, and that it made people unsuitable as slaves. He knew that one who possesses knowledge is never content to remain the slave of another. One in possession of knowledge tends to be a thinker, and the success of the type of slavery practiced in this country was predicated on insuring that the Africans did as little of their own thinking as possible. Slavery functioned as well as it did for enslavers, and for as long as it did, because whites denied most of the Africans the right to learn and to do their own thinking. Coupled with this, whites were, in too many instances, successful in getting the Africans to believe they lacked the ability to learn and to think for themselves.

As a little boy on the Baltimore plantation of Hugh Auld, Frederick Douglass learned how well slavery functioned as long as blacks were denied the right to learn to read and write. When the wife of Master Auld was found to be teaching little Frederick how to read the Bible, Master Hugh, as he was called by the enslaved, became visibly upset. He scolded his wife in young Frederick's presence, reminding her both that it was against the law to teach blacks to read, and that knowledge made the enslaved unhappy and difficult to manage. Douglass recorded the incident in one of his autobiographies: "Of course he forbade her to give me any further instruction, telling her in the first place that to do so was unlawful as it was also unsafe, 'for,' said he, 'if you give a nigger an inch he will take an ell. *Learning will spoil the best nigger in the world. If he learns to read the Bible it will forever unfit him to be a slave.* He should know nothing but the will of his master, and learn to obey it.'"[38]

Even though a child, Douglass understood from that conversation that "knowledge unfits a child to be a slave," and therefore he knew precisely the most direct route to freedom.[39] Since Master Hugh was of the opinion that Douglass could not possibly comprehend the meaning of what he said to his wife during his tirade, he made no effort to have him removed from the room. But by failing to do so, Douglass heard and understood enough to be even more determined to continue learning, and to plan his escape from slavery.

Sterling Stuckey rightly observes that Walker's "concern for morality was rooted in religion."[40] This is another way of saying that what Walker believed to be important in ethical and moral behavior was grounded in his religious beliefs, in his understanding of the Bible, and especially in his conception of God. His concern for moral behavior was grounded in his theology, or the way he thought about God. Because Walker was several generations removed from his African ancestors, he might not have known that morality is rooted in religion, or in one's conception of God, and that this was a prominent idea in African traditional thought.[41]

---

[38] Douglass, *Life and Times of Frederick Douglass*, 78–79 (emphasis added).

[39] Ibid., 79.

[40] Stuckey, *Slave Culture*, 113.

[41] See John S. Mbiti, chap. 4, 5, 16 in *Introduction to African Religion*, 2nd ed. (Oxford: Heinemann Educational Publishers, 1991).

There are numerous references to God in the *Appeal*. Nearly all of these are either preceded or followed by statements regarding the way persons treat each other, and the way they live together in the world. Furthermore, we get a good sense from the *Appeal* that the way one thinks about God necessarily affects the way he thinks about persons and what is required of them in their relations with each other. Belief in a God who created humankind and all that there is, but never again was involved with creation might lead one to conclude that there is no transcendent value to what was created, whether thing or person. Such a stance might lead people to wonder: "If God does not care, why should we? Why strive to be moral in interpersonal and collective relations, if God does not care or require it?"

On the other hand, belief in a thoroughly immanent God—of whom it may be said "God is everything and everything is God"—seems to promise that God and creation are brought exponentially nearer to each other. This would purportedly have the effect of fostering in persons the sense that God cares about them and the world. The trouble with the idea of a divine immanence that is too thoroughgoing, however, is that it undermines individuality and the moral spirit. That is, in a radicalized theology of God's thoroughgoing immanence there is no room for human individuality, freedom, and responsibility, each of which is necessary if morality is to have any meaning at all. By definition, in order for there to be human moral responsibility, there must be freedom, which presupposes individuality. But freedom is denied if God is immanent in a radically thoroughgoing sense. There is no such thing as individuality if "God is me and I am God." If God is the All, and persons are but rays or emanations from God, then persons cannot, in a moral sense, be held responsible for their misdeeds. This honor (or dishonor) would have to go to God, since persons' individuality would be included in God—for according to the absolute immanentist view, God is all. Therefore, even though persons make and act on choices in the world, they are not really responsible for their choices and actions. God is! So, once again persons may be inclined to wonder *why* they should expend the time, energy, and effort trying to behave morally if God is so close to them that they have no legitimate individuality. In such a case, one cannot be held morally responsible for anything she does.

David Walker was a proponent of neither the idea of a wholly removed God nor a radically thoroughgoing, immanent God. He saw

God as the transcendent "Other," worthy to be worshiped, and yet immanent enough to care for and work co-operatively with persons to actualize God's will that they live together as diverse members of one family. He taught that God and persons are engaged in an ongoing joint venture of striving to achieve justice and community in the world. God was, for Walker, the *liberator* of the enslaved and nominally free blacks. Walker's deepest conviction was that God would deliver his people from oppression under white Christians (91). A too distant, uncaring, uninvolved, impersonal God, even though omnipotent, would not be concerned about blacks' liberation from the bondage of slavery. This was not the God of David Walker, and most assuredly it was not the God of the eighth-century prophets and of Jesus Christ. For God called and sent the prophets precisely because God cares about persons.

Walker had no interest in the intellectual exercise of trying to prove the existence of God. The reality of the atrocious conditions to which his people were subject allowed no time for the luxury of philosophical gymnastics. Instead, Walker sought to determine the character of the God portrayed in the Bible and by Christianity. He therefore *assumed* the existence of the Creator-God, before whom every knee must bow, and to whom *every* person is accountable for their deeds and behavior in the world. In this, Walker recognized *a fundamental equality of all persons in the eyes of God*. He reasoned that God is the God of blacks, whites, and all other persons.

For these reasons, Walker adamantly held that it was, at best, idolatrous for blacks to refer to enslavers as their masters. Addressing blacks, he asked: "Have they [white enslavers] not to make their appearance before the tribunal of heaven, to answer for the deeds done in the body, as well as we? Have we any other master but Jesus Christ alone? Is he not their master as well as ours" (69)? According to Walker's Christian beliefs, there is one God who is Creator and Sustainer of all persons. Walker thereby reasoned that all must answer to that God, for all are equal before God. God is a jealous God, who created persons to serve God only. "God Almighty is the *sole proprietor or master* of the WHOLE human family," said Walker, "and will not on any consideration admit of a colleague, being unwilling to divide his glory with another" (61). God abides no competition. Blacks' loyalty must be to God only, not to their white captors.

Walker wanted to communicate that because they belonged to God only, and consequently were created to serve only God, it was in fact a sin for blacks to passively accept the conditions of slavery imposed on them by whites. God alone is any person's master. God is jealous, permitting none to usurp God's mastery over any part of creation. Enslaved Africans who passively, or even willingly, served whites in slavery were, according to Walker, guilty of idolatry. Therefore, blacks could be obedient to God only by exerting every means to extricate themselves from slavery and any other form of servile humiliation or systemic prejudice.[42]

God, according to Walker, is impartial, and thus is no respecter of persons (81). Since God created all persons first and last for God's enjoyment, none have a right to enslave, exercise coercive power over, or otherwise dehumanize another human being. To do so is a violation of God's will, and therefore effectively puts one in danger of divine judgment. Walker believed this principle of divine impartiality to be grounded in the Bible. Although white enslavers had access to the Bible on a daily basis, Walker was convinced that because of their treatment of the Africans, they did not believe in divine impartiality. Instead, the actions of the enslavers implied their mistaken belief that God was partial to them.

The Gospel of Jesus Christ makes no distinction between the value of persons and groups. That is, no distinction is made as to whether one person or group is more human, valued, or favored by God than any other. God respects no person or group of persons, e.g., whites or blacks, over any other. God is, in this sense, no respecter of persons.

David Walker asked white captors whether they believed the color of their skin somehow made them superior to blacks, and whether they believed that God respects skin color only. He reasoned that if God alone decides on the race and gender of every person, what right has any person or group to disregard and disrespect another solely on the basis of

---

[42] In the most fundamental sense, *all* persons belong to God only. There was no question for David Walker that although whites sought exclusive ownership of the Africans, the latter were in fact the exclusive creations of God (*Appeal*, 88). Indeed, had God not communicated through the prophet Ezekiel that all life, all adults, all children belong to God only (Ezek 18:4)? Therefore, Walker reasoned that for the Africans to willingly submit to enslavement and degradation by the whites is sin before the God of the prophets and of Jesus Christ.

physical characteristics? For if God made persons as they are, only God can make them different from what they are (85). God is impartial. To mistreat persons, to dehumanize them as white enslavers did the Africans, merely incites God's judgment and wrath. Because God does not favor one person or group over another, God did not create whites "to sit in the shade" and enjoy the bounties of God's world at the expense of the Africans (89).

Walker maintained that God is not only loving and compassionate, but also *omniscient* and *omnipresent*. One does not see these terms in the *Appeal*, but their implied consequences are scattered throughout. For example, Walker said that there is nothing that gets past God; nothing that goes unnoticed or undetected by God. God is everywhere present at all times (omnipresent), and knows all that is knowable (omniscient). Walker warned enslavers that neither the brutality to which they subjected blacks nor the spilling of African blood can be hidden from God, no matter how successful they are in hiding it from others (83). God knows and sees all. White enslavers only deceive themselves if they think they can escape "the penetrating and all-seeing eye of God who is continually taking cognizance of the hearts of men" (89–90).

Although Walker taught that God possesses the classically described attributes of omnipotence (for which he often substituted "God Almighty"), omnibenevolence, omniscience, and omnipresence, he did not believe God would do for blacks what they could do—indeed must do!—for themselves. In part, this may have been because of Walker's belief that the good and loving Creator-God imbued all persons with a sense of self-determination. The consequence is that no person, no matter the conditions to which subjected, is ever entirely helpless. In this sense, no oppressed group is ever completely victimized. If nothing else, persons can decide *how* they will manage and respond to their suffering and oppression, and whether and how they will seek their liberation. To be a person is to be imbued with the *power* of self-determination or the power of will. That is, the power to choose this or that, and then to be able to strive toward its achievement. Walker believed—as Malcolm X did after him with respect to lingering racial prejudice in contemporary society—that blacks were not responsible for their condition of oppression in slavery, but that they alone were responsible for the way they responded to it. Blacks' responsibility was not primarily to change the whites' perception of them, but to change their own perceptions of themselves, a view of self largely imposed by whites.[43] This is why Walker was adamant that every black person obtain and read Thomas Jefferson's *Notes on the State of Virginia*, Query 14, where the founding father declared the Africans to be inherently inferior to whites. Walker argued that Blacks themselves must be the ones to refute Jefferson's assertion (67, 75, 76).

Walker possessed a strong, analytical mind. He knew that if God were truly omnipotent, all loving, and created persons with the capacity for self-determination or freedom of will, God would have to always respect this inherent capacity in persons. Although Walker did not say so in the *Appeal*, he seemed aware that the power of self-direction within humans put a limit on God's own exercise of power. Otherwise, why would he contend on the one hand that God would affect blacks' deliverance from slavery (91), and on the other hand that blacks themselves must prepare the way for God's work of liberation (77)? The God of David Walker seemed to need, or at least desire, the cooperation of created persons toward the achievement of God's purposes in the world.[44]

What this comes down to is Walker's belief in the idea of cooperative endeavor between God and persons, as well as the belief—similar to the Hebrew prophets—that not only do people need God, but God needs people in the adventure of the divine-human encounter. The power of both God and persons, especially the power of the enslaved, is needed to conquer slavery. God sides with any who are in favor of and will work for the establishment of justice. Those, like the enslaved Africans who yearned for justice, did not need to worry that they were outnumbered by the whites or that the latter made it illegal for them to obtain education (66). For God, Walker maintained, is ever working with the enslaved Africans to obtain their release. As much as Walker despised slavery, he was just as passionate and determined to convey that as dehumanizing and painful as it is to be under the foot of slavery, even this condition did not render blacks completely helpless. Self-determination was to him a paramount virtue. Even slavery of the

---

[43] See *Malcolm X Speaks*, ed. George Breitman (1965; New York: Pathfinder Press, 1992) 40.

[44] This is also a Jewish view of God's relationship with persons. See Abraham J. Heschel, *Man Is Not Alone* (New York: Farrar, Straus & Young, 1951) 241–44.

most brutal kind did not excuse failure by blacks to do all that was required to recapture and enhance their sense of humanity and dignity.

Walker was thoroughly convinced that God is a just and holy God for all persons (62), inasmuch as God creates, loves, and sustains all. This means that since God is the Creator and is impartial, God will allow no group to live in peace and tranquility at the expense of another group. As both just and merciful, God always comes to the assistance of the underdog, a lesson that even children learn when they read the prophets and the Gospels. This is what white enslavers who professed Christianity frequently forgot. The compassionate, just, holy, and merciful God of the prophets and Jesus Christ is forever the ruler of all creation. God hears and is saddened by the cries, tears, and agony of the oppressed. Because God is just and holy, God will set them at liberty. Walker's conviction about this was firm and unshakable.

It stands to reason that a God who creates out of love, goodness, and justice simply will not allow the dehumanizing treatment of any group of people to continue unabated. Instead, Walker maintained that the God of the Christian apostles and the Hebrew prophets "will at one day appear fully in behalf of the oppressed, and arrest the progress of the avaricious oppressors" (60). Even if God does not bring about liberation through the oppressed themselves, God is always working on their behalf, and therefore they can be assured that eventual deliverance will come. God's liberation of the oppressed will not be without a price to oppressors, which could include their own children rising up against them (61). According to Walker, those who oppress and enslave others can be none other than God's enemies, and therefore should not be protected, but destroyed (74). Walker taught that because God is just, this itself is compelling reason to believe that God did not create the Africans to be enslaved by whites. This is why Walker was willing to die, rather than to passively submit to slavery and tyranny. He reasoned that he and his people are created by and belong to God, as much as any other group of persons. "God has been pleased to give us two eyes, two hands, two feet, and some sense in our heads as well as they."[45] As any group of people, the Africans possess infinite worth to God. If this means anything at all, it means that one is obligated to protect and defend her divinely imbued worth as a person.

---

[45] *David Walker's Appeal*, 11n.

In the presence of the suffering and pain of his people, David Walker found himself looking squarely into the face of the problem of evil. While he sought to defend the doctrine of the goodness and love of God Almighty despite the suffering of blacks, it was not his primary intention to address theodicy. He was not overly concerned with explaining the riddle of evil's presence in a good and just God's creation. His faith was in an all-powerful, all-loving God whom he considered to be the great liberator of the oppressed throughout history. He had neither the desire, nor the patience, to work at trying to solve the dilemma of divine omnipotence and omni-benevolence in the face of black suffering under dehumanizing slavery. The enslaved Africans did not need a theoretical, but a practical, concrete solution to their suffering. Consequently, Walker set out to show how God, blacks, and other concerned persons could work together cooperatively to eradicate slavery. Because he believed God to be both loving and just, he knew that God was not the cause of his peoples' suffering. The cause was humanly contrived. He argued that it was arrogant, avaricious, greedy, tyrannical white people who caused the Africans' enslavement, not the God of the prophets.

Henry J. Young has written that according to Walker, "God, *through his omnipotence*, would one day appear in behalf of the oppressed and eradicate the oppression of slaves."[46] But what Walker actually said was that God "being *a just and holy Being* will at one day appear fully in behalf of the oppressed" and will eradicate their oppression. Walker's emphasis lay elsewhere than on divine omnipotence. Walker emphasized the justice and holiness of God. More often than not, one finds him referring to God's goodness, justice, and holiness rather than to divine omnipotence. He also referred frequently to what his people needed to do for themselves (self-determination) in cooperation with each other and with God. Walker was not talking about the perfect immutable, impassive, impersonal, uncaring God of classical Greek and Roman philosophy. He was talking about the God of the prophets and of Jesus Christ. This is the perfectly personal, loving, caring God, who refuses to give up on persons.

On balance, the ethical attributes of God, i.e., love, goodness, holiness, and justice were more important to Walker when he discussed

---

[46] Henry J. Young, *Major Black Religious Leaders 1755–1940* (Nashville: Abingdon Press, 1977) 46 (emphasis added).

slavery and God's hatred of it. Rather than through God's omnipotence, deliverance will come through God's steadfast love, goodness, and justice, along with blacks' cooperation with each other and with God to that end. Indeed, it is fair to say that for the prophets and for David Walker, the classical Greek and Roman description of a deity who had no need of persons was literally dead. Such a God, Walker implied, is the God of white enslavers, and not the God of Jesus Christ and the Hebrew prophets. The white enslavers' god worked with them to insure that the Africans remain in slavery. This god did nothing life-sustaining for the Africans.[47]

Sacredness and Dignity of Blacks

The chief burden of David Walker's prophecy was to call blacks back to acknowledging their fundamental humanity and inherent sacredness as people of God. This did not by any means undermine the importance of his declarations of judgment on unrepentant white enslavers. Walker's more positive and constructive concern was the saving of his people, not heaping judgment on whites and their degrading system of slavery.

Walker's conception of God provides clues to his theological anthropology or doctrine of the person. Because of the social conditions facing Walker and his people, he was not concerned to put forth an abstract philosophical-psychological portrait of what it means to be a person. He sought, instead, to defend and vindicate his conviction about the humanity and innate dignity of his people. This argument against their enslavement introduces the final element of prophecy to be

---

[47] Walker would have identified with the perception of the white man's god as portrayed by the character Lorenzo in James Baldwin's play, *Blues for Mr. Charlie.* Reacting against those black Christians for whom church attendance and prayer was the answer to the frequent murders of their people by white men, Lorenzo proposed that blacks take it on themselves to lynch the white's characterization of God, with the entire community as witnesses. "It's that damn white God that's been lynching us and burning us and castrating us and raping our women and robbing us of everything that makes a man a man for all these hundreds of years. Now, why we sitting around here, in *His* house? If I could get my hands on Him, I'd pull Him out of heaven and drag Him through this town at the end of a rope." (James Baldwin, *Blues for Mr. Charlie* [New York: Dell, 1964] 15.) In unmistakably clear language, this monologue insists that the god of classical Greek and Roman culture is not the God of the prophets and of Jesus Christ, or of David Walker; nor should this be the God of any thinking being who embraces the Christian faith.

examined by this discussion, viz., the sacredness and dignity of persons in general, and contrary to the dominant white perspectives of the period, of blacks in particular.

It may be argued that the most distinct contribution of eighth-century Hebrew prophecy is the emphasis on God's relentless care and love for persons. So much does God value persons that God constantly searches for them. The prophets took as a matter of course the sacredness of persons in the presence of God. Because persons are created by God, the prophets assumed their infinite worth to God. According to the prophets, so valuable are persons to God that nothing that happens to them is considered by God to be trivial.While the prophet Ezekiel reported that every person belongs to God (Eze 18:4), Isaiah reported that so precious is every person to God that God loves and calls each one by name (Isa 43:1, 4). It is reasonable to say, then, that another test for the presence of ethical prophecy is whether the alleged prophet acts out of a firm conviction and awareness of the sacredness of all persons.

William Lecky, a nineteenth-century historian whose field was the study of European morals, argued that it was the conception of "the sanctity of human life, which led the early Christians to combat and at last to overthrow the gladiatorial games"[48] and to stress the worth of the slave, the "savage," the infant, and even the gladiator. Christianity, according to this view, introduced a new and revolutionary emphasis on the sacredness and value of the person before God.

Indeed, it might well be argued that Christianity, especially in its early stage, was the religion *par excellence* of the person.[49] It is not accurate to say, however, as many in the Christian tradition have said, that Christianity was the only or even the first religion to focus on the dignity and sacredness of the person. Nor would it be accurate to say, with Lecky and Ernest F. Scott, that this is a distinctively Christian contribution.[50] Scott argued that Jesus "discovered the individual." Accordingly, it was Jesus who first recognized "that every man has a

---

[48] William E. H. Lecky, *History of European Morals* (New York: D. Appleton, 1879) 2:38–39.

[49] Teilhard de Chardin made a claim similar to this. See Henri De Lubac, *Teilhard de Chardin: The Man and His Meaning* (New York: Mentor Books, 1965) 26.

[50] Ernest F. Scott, *Man and Society in the New Testament* (New York: Scribner's Sons, 1947) 79, 83, 111, 140, 282.

worth of his own, and is not merely a superfluous unit in the mass."[51] According to this view, the individual person was of little worth before Jesus entered history. The group or community was of greater significance and value. The idea of the worth of every person is, according to Scott, the most distinctive feature of Jesus' teaching and ethic.[52]

The claim that Jesus (or Christianity) was the first to emphasize the dignity or worth of the individual person is historically problematic. Lawrence Hyde has provided a helpful response :

> But this view is rendered plausible only by contrasting the teachings of Jesus with the debased attitude towards human beings which was characteristic of ancient civilizations in their decline. To the disinterested student of these questions it is sufficiently plain that respect for the individual and veneration of the divine life expressed through his being has been a basic element in the ethical teachings of all the great sages, whether we consider Zarathustra, the Buddha, Confucius, Lao-Tzu or Socrates.[53]

It is more accurate to argue that early Christianity emphasized the sacredness of persons in a way and to a degree that many other religions had not. There is, however, no indisputable proof that Christianity was the first or the only religion to acknowledge the value of the individual as opposed to that of the group.

To its credit, early Christianity staunchly rejected the practice of the destruction of human life as a matter of entertainment. Such practices clearly were deemed to be sin. Human life was considered to be of infinite and inviolable worth. Lecky has highlighted the point:

> The first aspect in which Christianity presented itself to the world was as a declaration of the fraternity of men in Christ. Considered as immortal beings, destined for the extremes of

---

[51] Ibid., 77.

[52] Ibid., 283.

[53] Lawrence Hyde, "Radhakrishnan's Contribution to Universal Religion" in *The Philosophy of Sarvepalli Radhakrishnan*, ed. Paul Arthur Schilpp (New York: Tudor Publishing, 1952) 381.

happiness or of misery, and united to one another by a special community of redemption, the first and most manifest duty of a Christian man was to look upon his fellowmen as sacred beings, and from this notion grew up the eminently Christian idea of the sanctity of all life.[54]

It is important to note that the emphasis on the sacredness and dignity of persons was also a chief concern of the Hebrew prophets (Eze 18:4; Isa 43:1, 4). It is therefore an important element of ethical prophecy. Emphasizing the centrality of the dignity of persons is a way of testing the authenticity of presumed prophetic claims. One claiming to be called by God to prophesy, must also exhibit an unequivocal sense of and appreciation for the sacredness of *all* persons.

The sanctity and worth of persons to God was not a point that the prophets had to research or prove. They took it for granted,[55] i.e., accepted it as a matter of course. Nowhere do we see this more clearly than in the Book of Amos. That prophet's denunciations of injustice sent a clear message as to the value and sacredness of every person. Why else would Amos be so emphatic about the need to let justice roll down like waters and righteousness like a mighty stream (Amos 5:24)?

More than anything else, David Walker sought to save his people from slavery, and to convince them that they were whole persons who possessed inherent dignity and deserved all of the rights and privileges pertaining thereto. Because human worth is bestowed by God, Walker argued, it can neither be given nor taken away by mere human beings. It was important to Walker that his people recapture their lost sense of humanity and dignity. He was, therefore, not as concerned as some scholars believe about expending energy and time expressing hatred for whites. To the contrary, Walker's primary *modus operandi* was to express deep love and affection for his people in all that he said and did.

The word "dignity" is derived from the Latin, *dignus*, which means worth or value. At a time when the humanity and dignity of people of

---

[54] Lecky, *History of European Morals*, 2:17–18. The last part of Lecky's statement, i.e., "and from this notion grew up the eminently Christian idea of the sanctity of all human life," is put too strongly, for this was an idea that could be found in African traditional religions long before the appearance of Christianity.

[55] Francis J. McConnell, *The Prophetic Ministry* (New York: Abingdon Press, 1930) 21.

African descent was severely challenged and undermined by barbaric slavery and the laws of the land, David Walker courageously took up their cause as his own. Indeed, it *was* his cause, inasmuch as he so readily and fully identified with his people. Walker had neither the desire nor the energy and time to try to convince enslavers that both they and the enslaved belong to the one God of the universe, and that neither race was the superior or inferior of the other. Walker was primarily concerned to impress upon his people that, like whites, they were of divine parentage and loved by God. Not sub-persons, blacks are whole persons who possess absolute dignity. Blacks are infinitely valuable precisely because they are created, loved, and sustained by God. Walker might well have been the first African American to publicly argue this point so passionately, systematically, and persuasively.

Time and again, David Walker affirmed black humanity or personhood which was, for him, a given. When stressing the humanity of his people, he often reminded them that as persons (who belong only to God!) freedom is their "natural right" (100). Although he generally focused on socio-political freedom in his teaching, his emphasis on self-determination implied that to be free to decide one's direction in life is what it means to be a person. It is not whites alone who are created with the capacity for self-direction and self-determination. On the contrary, all persons possess fundamental, divinely appointed freedom and dignity; thus, all people have inviolable inherent rights as persons.

Walker wanted his people to recapture their lost sense of preciousness. Because every person is infinitely valued by God, no individual may be sacrificed for others,[56] and most assuredly should this not be done as easily and callously as white enslavers sacrificed the Africans. Rather than sacrifice an individual person for the group, this

---

[56] This is a provocative point that has implications for the classical atonement theory. A number of feminist and womanist thinkers have called the longstanding theory into question, and indeed, have rejected it. See Joanne Carlson Braun and Rebecca Parker, "For God So Loved the World?" in *Christianity, Patriarchy, and Abuse: A Feminist Critique*, ed. Joanne Carlson Braun and Carole R. Bohn (Cleveland OH: Pilgrim Press, 1989) 1–30, and Delores S. Williams, *Sisters in the Wilderness: the Challenge of Womanist God-Talk* (Maryknoll NY: Orbis Books, 1993) 161–67, 199–202.

Although the point of my discussion is not to raise the "Christological dilemma," I understand that I have created the opening for it. Although I have some appreciation for the critique of some feminist and womanist theologians, I know at this time only that I find classical atonement theory, i.e., substitutionary theory, to be problematic.

way of thinking in prophecy requires that the group choose instead to sacrifice all rather than allow one individual to be destroyed needlessly, or only for the sake of the group. The message here is that even one individual person is so precious to God that God prefers that she be saved.

Like other nineteenth-century black leaders, and once again in anticipation of Malcolm X, David Walker was preoccupied—indeed obsessed!—with affirming the humanity and dignity of his people. Although many blacks did not know it, this was precisely what they needed. To a large extent, the reason for Walker's emphasis in this regard was that many whites considered the Africans to be less than human, as beings whose value was not intrinsic but only instrumental. That is, what value blacks had was determined by white enslavers. As "property," blacks were deemed to be worth the amount of work that enslavers could get out of them, or the amount of money for which they could be sold.

Walker knew, in a way that many of his black reformer contemporaries did not, that the task of convincing blacks of their own humanity and inherent dignity was one of gargantuan proportion. The primary reason for this was that whites had successfully and systematically convinced many Africans that they were sub-human, and that because of this, their fundamental reason for being was to permanently serve in the capacity of slaves. Many blacks actually internalized whites' conception of them, believing that they were what whites said: theirs was primarily a servant role.

The internalization of this white conception of black personhood was the primary reason so many blacks passively accepted enslavement and would not, even when the odds were well in their favor, overthrow their captors and liberate themselves. This was complicated by the fact that blacks were not a unified community, making it easy for whites to subdue and keep the Africans in check. Blacks would often be found "in league with tyrants, and receive a great portion of their daily bread, of the moneys which they acquire from the blood and tears of their more miserable brethren whom they scandalously delivered into the hands of our *natural enemies*!!!!" (70) The internalization of whites' perception of them is what made it possible for one or two whites to control fifty or more blacks. The experience of slavery severely distorted the personality and self-image of many blacks, thereby making Walker's a monumental task, viz., helping blacks throw off such distorted images of themselves and to regain a broad-based sense of self and dignity.

Walker argued that whites believed "all the inhabitants of the earth," except the Africans, were persons, and therefore should be free. The Africans, however, did not warrant freedom since presumably they were not full persons. They were thought to be "brutes," deserving and worthy only of a life of servitude under whites (62–63). Indeed, had not Thomas Jefferson argued that the Africans were "inferior to the whites in endowments both of body and mind?"[57] Had he not argued that Phyllis Wheatley produced nothing worthy of being considered poetry, and that "compositions published under her name are below the dignity of criticism"?[58] And furthermore, did Jefferson—a paradigm of the dominant white attitude toward blacks in eighteenth and nineteenth-century America—not also claim that any improvement that the Africans made was due solely to their associations with whites?[59]

Accepting and believing what whites said about their sub-human status, many blacks behaved accordingly. This is why it was necessary for persons of African descent, like David Walker, to relentlessly and emphatically assert the full humanity and dignity of blacks. Walker understood that a primary objective was to convince blacks that they were made in the image of God, as much as any other group of people. He was not as concerned about convincing whites of blacks' humanity and dignity. If he could get his people to believe in their inherent humanity and worth, they would behave and act in ways that would enhance community-making among themselves.

Whites assumed their own humanity and dignity. In addition, they had the institution of the law and the political apparatus to affirm their assumption. They needed no one to convince them that they were persons, that they possessed infinite worth and therefore ought to be free. But these same whites did all in their power to convince each other and the Africans that the latter were essentially poor copies or shadows of white personhood.

In *Democracy in America* (1835) Alexis de Tocqueville presented a fascinating analysis of the democratic principle and what it means to live

---

[57] Thomas Jefferson, "Query XIV" in *Notes on the State of Virginia*, ed. William Peden (1982; Chapel Hill: University of North Carolina Press, 1995) 143.

[58] Ibid., 140.

[59] Ibid., 141.

under a democracy. Having visited the United States, he wrote of his perception of how blacks were perceived by Anglo Saxons. He concluded that under any but a dictator who demanded it, whites and blacks would not likely be able to live together on the basis of equality. What he witnessed was basically what Jefferson had written about in *Notes on the State of Virginia*. Tocqueville wrote: "we scarcely acknowledge the common features of humanity in this stranger whom slavery has brought among us. His physiognomy is to our eyes hideous, his understanding weak, his tastes low; and we are almost inclined to look upon him as a being intermediate between man and the brutes."[60]

Is it no wonder that blacks needed powerful, courageous voices to remind them of the sense of personhood and dignity bestowed upon them by the one God of the universe. They needed a voice like David Walker's to press them to rediscover and embrace their lost sense of selfhood and worth. The best way to do this was to look to themselves and to the God of their forebears. There was no need to look to whites for support and approval. They—not whites—must get the point about black humanity and dignity, and once again internalize it as they had done prior to being torn from the African continent.

David Walker was able to affirm black dignity, and to do so with a determination and passion that has seldom been demonstrated in the history of African presence in the United States. He knew that if blacks began to believe in and assert their humanity and dignity, it would no longer matter to them what whites thought. The liberation of their minds would enable them to focus more on their own problems, aspirations, and how best to love, befriend, and live with each other in a spirit of community. For Walker, recapturing the sense of black dignity and self-love was more than half the battle in the struggle for complete liberation. He therefore endeavored to teach his people what was important for their health, survival, and liberation as full persons.

Persons, according to Walker, are not emotionless, impersonal objects or specimens for presumed objective, disinterested, scientific study. Furthermore, persons are not merely potentially rational beings with freedom of will.[61] When colonists such as Jefferson and Henry Clay

---

[60] Alexis de Tocqueville, *Democracy in America* (New York: Vintage Books, 1945) 2:372.

[61] Borden B. Bowne, *Metaphysics*, rev. ed. (New York: Harper and Brothers Publishers, 1898), 404–420. See also Bowne's discussion on the importance of the

talked about and compared white and black persons, it was as if they were totally oblivious of the presence in black persons of sensibility, e.g., emotions and feelings. David Walker could see that by utilizing this approach, i.e., ignoring or pretending that black persons are not, finally, beings who also possess sensibility, whites did not have to consider the reasons that the Africans lagged behind the so-called civilized and Christian whites. That is, they did not have to acknowledge or consider the fact that the Africans lagged behind in education and basic life-chances not because of inherent deficiencies, but because whites denied them the right and the means to learn and to be financially self-sufficient. Walker vehemently contended against this tactic by giving texture and sensibility to African personhood. He refused to deal with Africans abstractly. That is, Walker rejected the cold, calculating, impersonal rationalism of Jefferson and other white men. He preferred a fuller, more romantic approach to discussing the nature and plight of human beings in the world. It was never David Walker's intention to deny the basic humanity and dignity of whites. By focusing on reestablishing in his people their own sense of personhood and worth, Walker was also arguing that to be a person, regardless of race, is to have a clear sense of one's own inherent worth and to grant that as well to others.

"Personhood" is more than the mere sum of intellect and will, a failing of the reasoning characteristic of Jefferson and others who were a product of the European Enlightenment. Persons have many more activity-potentials than reason and will. As a complex unity of a multiplicity of activity-potentials, e.g., thinking, willing, wanting, appreciating, and remembering (in part),[62] a mere examination of the rational and volitional factors will not provide the fullest sense of what it means to be a person. Walker therefore insisted on the need to at least add the elements of feeling and emotion when discussing persons in the world. Short of this, whites would never be convicted of the way they so easily rationalized the enslavement and abuse of the Africans. Walker therefore sought to take away whites' rationalistic crutch in the *Appeal*. Peter Hinks put it this way:

---

sensibility in relation to the intellect and will in *The Principle of Ethics* (New York: American Book Company, 1892) 49–56.

[62] Peter A. Bertocci, "The Psychological Framework for Ethical Reflection," in *Personality and the Good: Psychological and Ethical Perspectives*, by Peter A. Bertocci and Richard M. Millard (New York: David McKay Co., 1963) chap. 7.

To introduce the emotional element was to refute the validity of discussing the issue as a solely intellectual one while asserting the integralness of emotional expression to the life of humans. Part of Walker's strategy for establishing the humanness of blacks was to have them emote vigorously as a way to make clear that they were not dulled, beaten beings and that they did not acquiesce to the charge of inferiority like beasts would in fully accepting their owner's authority. Varied and powerful emotional expression was essential to what was human, proponents of romanticism asserted. Thus the very act of blacks emoting argued for their humanness.[63]

Walker knew how the whites in the original thirteen colonies responded to treatment by the British, i.e., to taxation without political representation. They resented being taxed while being denied basic human rights and a voice in their governance. He reasoned that this was a natural human reaction to such treatment. Moreover, the very fact that the Africans were bitter and angry over being enslaved by whites was argument not against, but in favor of their full humanity. For it is human beings—persons—who *feel* and self-consciously *experience* bitterness and anger when their personhood is in any way assaulted or disregarded. Blacks' response to whites was similar to the latter's reaction to the British.

That the Africans responded with resentment to enslavement and dehumanization was, for Walker, a strong argument for their own full humanity. Indeed, near the end of the *Appeal*, Walker implies that were blacks not in fact full-fledged persons, they would not exhibit hatred toward whites. The fact that blacks are truly persons explains and validates the humanity of their hatred of whites who treated them as something other than fully human. Hatred is a human, not a nonhuman, trait. Hatred is frequently a defense mechanism that emerges when one's personhood is abused or otherwise violated. Blacks' response was the natural response of full-fledged persons. To the whites, Walker said: "You are not astonished at my saying we hate you, for if we are men, we cannot but hate you, while you are treating us like dogs" (100n). If the

---

[63] Hinks, *To Awaken My Afflicted Brethren*, 211.

Africans, treated inhumanely by whites, had failed to respond by hating whites for subjecting them to degrading slavery, one then could reasonably have questioned the humanity of blacks. Blacks' response to the abuses of slavery and race-prejudice was consistent with what full-fledged persons do under such circumstances. Their response was in substance little different from that of the white colonists' to British abuses before the Revolutionary War.

The Africans were persons—period. David Walker repeatedly reminded them of the fact. "Are we MEN!!—I ask you, O my brethren! are we MEN" (68)? Whatever it took, Walker drove home the point about the fundamental humanity and dignity of his people. It was blacks, not whites, who must assert and affirm their humanity. "We are people," said Walker, "notwithstanding many of you doubt it" (84). What God gave to blacks, viz., humanity and dignity, they could not themselves give away nor be stripped of it by others. Affirming the dignity of his people is where Walker's energy and passion lay. He wasted little time preaching to whites about their sin against God and black humanity. He was concerned to uplift his people by helping them to regain their sense of self and dignity.

So deeply did David Walker believe in the humanity and dignity of his people, and that these traits were grounded in a good and loving God, that he urged them to do whatever was necessary—even to kill or be killed!—to remove the feet of oppression and tyranny from their necks. Death, for Walker, was preferable to continuing in slavery. In this regard, he would have had nothing but praise for two slave women: Celia "a Slave," and Margaret Garner. Walker had been dead approximately fifteen years when these women, because of their deep love for self and their people, took their stand against enslavement and rape. Their reaction to their bondage was consistent with the legacy of resistance left by Walker and other black forebears.

Celia, "A Slave"

All that is known about Celia is that she was approximately fourteen years of age when she was purchased by Robert Newsom in 1850 and taken to his farm in Callaway County, Missouri. She had lived in Audrain County, which bordered Callaway County to the north. There was no question as to Newsom's intended relationship with Celia, for when they arrived at his farm, he immediately raped her. It is difficult to imagine the effects of the emotional and psychological trauma and devastation that the rape had on Celia. She was raped repeatedly over a five year period. She bore two children by Newsom. Contrary to what many whites believed, female slaves embraced and sought to live up to positive moral standards. It was uncommon, for example, that female slaves under fifteen years of age willingly engaged in sex.[64]

Celia fell in love with George, a slave on the Newsom farm. Aware that Newsom was forcing sex with Celia, George gave her what proved to be a deadly ultimatum regarding the encounters with the white enslaver. In response, Celia would murder Newsom (if one can really call it murder!), be convicted, and executed by hanging. George's ultimatum put Celia in a moral quandary, notwithstanding the fact that he too was faced with a moral dilemma, although his was not comparable to Celia's. At least, it might be argued, he was not being forcibly raped.

African women were totally vulnerable to sexual exploitation by any white or black male during (and after!) slavery. The difference was that white men had absolute power over the bodies of enslaved women. Since the law in slave states did not recognize rape as a crime against black women, even in the case of black male rapists, there was seldom hope of successful prosecution. The white enslaver considered the enslaved to be unencumbered property. Enslavers therefore reasoned—and the law supported their rationale—that one could not trespass or otherwise violate his own property. In the case of white males, enslaved females had very little choice other than to submit, although there are numerous accounts of enslaved women who fought white rapists. Such resistance was, however, a very dangerous thing for these women to do.

Because of George's ultimatum, Celia told Newsom that she would not be forced into sexual activity with him again, and that if he tried she would hurt him. When he next tried to rape her in the cabin he provided for her on the farm, she gave him two solid blows to the head with a stick, inadvertently killing him. She then cremated his body in her fireplace. When Newsom's family missed him at breakfast the next morning, and he did not turn up after an extensive search, they questioned George, who fairly quickly implicated Celia. To save his own skin, he gave her up. Celia was interrogated for hours at a time, and despite her deteriorating physical condition, she never once implicated

---

[64] Melton A. McLaurin, *Celia A Slave* (Athens GA: The University of Georgia Press, 1991) 21.

George. Circumstantial evidence implied that she had help in committing and-or covering up the "murder." To the end, Celia neither implicated George nor any other slave who might have assisted her. [65]

David Walker would have cheered and applauded Celia's stance. But it might also be said that he would not have appreciated George's cowardly behavior. He would have concluded that George was one who could be trusted only to betray his people if his own life and interests were at stake.

It is important to note that Celia exhibited no remorse or pangs of conscience after she killed the rapist. This was not uncommon for blacks who either killed their owner or who, when he or his wife died, did not hesitate to strike their dead body and declare that they would not see heaven. Harriet Jacobs told of the slave woman who, upon the death of her mistress, slipped unobserved into the room where the dead woman lay, slapped her twice, and said: "The devil is got you now!"[66] So much for the myth that the enslaved believed their enslavers were going to heaven.

Inasmuch as Celia was brutally violated by Newsom from the time she was but a fourteen year old child, it should not be difficult to understand why she might not experience pangs of conscience after taking his life. This was not first and foremost about revenge or indiscriminate violence against a white man. It was about Celia's sense of her own humanity and dignity, and the fact that he violated these at whim. In short, Celia took the life of the rapist who, each time he raped her, took her life.

Although Celia might well have killed Newsom even if George had not given her that terrible ultimatum, that he gave it at all is nevertheless

---

[65] The state of Missouri allowed that slaves charged with a capital crime could have a court appointed attorney. Celia's attorney was John Jameson, who was also an ordained Disciples of Christ minister. Disciples followed Alexander Campbell's suggestion that slavery was not a theological or faith issue, but a political one. Indeed, Campbell's stance itself was political, which meant that members could decide individually for themselves which side of the slave issue to take. However, I beg to differ with this stance. Because it has to do with human beings it cannot, for the theist, be political and not theological and ethical. Whatever affects human beings has to do with God. This makes it theological. Whatever goes to the issue of how persons are treated has to do with conduct or ethics. The Disciple leader and his followers do not get off the moral hook that easily.

[66] Harriet A. Jacobs, *Incidents in the Life of a Slave Girl*, ed. Jean Fagan Yellin (Cambridge MA: Harvard University Press, 1987) 48.

troubling. Quite possibly this happened to many more black women than we know. Much of what Melton A. McLaurin said in the conclusion of his book on Celia should not soon be forgotten:

> George was unable to prevent Newsom's sexual abuse of Celia, yet he was also unable to deal with it emotionally. It was George's male ego that placed Celia in the quandary that led to Newsom's death and her arrest, conviction, and execution. Yet when faced with a choice between protecting Celia or protecting his own life, George unhesitatingly chose the latter. What the case of Celia documents is the powerlessness of a male slave to protect a loved one, a male slave's smoldering resentment toward his loved one when she was forced into a sexual relationship with her master, and the male slave's natural and understandable act of self-preservation brought about by his equally natural and understandable jealously. If the conditions that produced the case of Celia were common on the small farms and plantations on which most slaves lived, then tension between black men and women was an inevitable product of slavery.[67]

Most of what McLaurin says about George is reasonable. However, he goes too far when he contends that it was a "natural and understandable act of self-preservation" for George to give up Celia to save himself. We have to weigh this against the fact that Celia was abandoned by George, and yet she did not come close to implicating him in the "crime." Celia was a person too, but she did not seek to save herself at George's expense, thinking perhaps that as a people they were to rise or fall together.

Was it not also "natural and understandable" that Celia should seek to preserve her own life? She too was powerless, not allowed to choose her own mate, and had no legal control over her body. But like George, like any person, she at least retained the power of choice, despite the severely limited field of alternatives before her. Celia *chose* not to give George up to the white authorities, just as George *chose* to implicate her and to save himself. Perhaps in part, Celia did not give up George or any other slave who might have helped her because she knew that not only

---

[67] McLaurin, *Celia A Slave*, 118.

would she be executed, but that they would be likewise punished. It might also be the case that she had too much sense of pride of self, too much respect for the dignity of her people, and possessed so much love for them that she could not risk the possibility of yet another black person being executed for what circumstances beyond her control forced her to do. Celia took action against the man who violated her humanity and dignity, preferring to risk her own death than to allow the violations to continue. Celia was a hero,[68] a witness to her own sense of humanity and preciousness before God.

Margaret Garner

In the winter of 1856, Margaret Garner, a Kentucky slave, successfully escaped to Cincinnati, Ohio, with her four children, her husband, his parents, and five other enslaved Africans. Garner was determined that rather than remain in slavery and have her children grow up under that cruel institution, she would rather take their lives and her own. As the white captors were breaking in the door to the house they hid in, Garner slashed the throat of one of her daughters with a butcher knife. The daughter died. Although she was prevented from killing the other three children, she tried her best to succeed. She said that slavery was hell for the black woman, and it pleased her that her daughter would not have to endure it.

As the white captors returned her to Kentucky for trial, she attempted to drown herself in the river.[69] Her infant daughter was in fact drowned. Her husband and his parents made it clear that their desire was to be free, but that they would not attempt suicide if returned to slavery. But Margaret Garner was made of tougher moral fiber. Her stance was, freedom or death—now![70] When she appeared in court "she begged the judge to kill her; she said she would 'go singing to the gallows rather than be returned to slavery.'"[71] So deeply did Garner prize freedom for herself and her children, that she preferred death to slavery.

---

[68] I once heard Maya Angelou use the term "shero." I frankly prefer it when referring to women.

[69] Peter M. Bergman, *The Chronological History of the Negro in America* (New York: Harper & Row Publishers, 1969) 210.

[70] See the account of the Garner incident in *Black Women in White America: A Documentary History*, ed. Gerda Lerner (New York: Vintage Books, 1973) 60–63.

[71] Lerone Bennett, Jr., *Before the Mayflower: A History of Black America* (Chicago:

David Walker would have viewed this as the quintessential example of morally appropriate black self-love, love of freedom, and love of black children. Garner was willing to take her own life and the lives of her children precisely because she so seriously embraced the African, Jewish, and Christian belief in the inherent worth of persons. Her judgment was that if she could not live and be treated as one who possesses inviolable worth, then life itself was not worth living. Garner took the life of one child, rejoiced that another drowned, wanted to take the lives of the other two, and attempted suicide, not because of a lack of love for self and for her children. She did so because her love for self and her children was so deep and so wide that she could not bear living in a society wherein their humanity and dignity were denied.

It is important to point out that what Margaret Garner did was for reasons opposite than those of contemporary young African American males who either take their own lives or the lives of other blacks. It was not a matter of self-hatred and lack of pride of race for Garner and other slaves who engaged in similar behavior, as is so often the case among many young African American males today. The latter tend to lack self-respect, self-esteem, self-love, and sense of dignity. Much of their behavior is spurred by self-hatred, and a near total absence of *any* sense of the value of human life, not least their own! This is different from the healthy self-love exhibited by Celia, Garner, and other African American ancestors. Indeed, many were the cases of black lovers who committed murder-suicides when it was found that one or the other was going to be sold. So deep was their love and commitment to each other that rather than be separated by the white enslavers, they decided in favor of death.[72] But the key is that the decision was based not on self-hatred and hatred for the other, but on self-love and love for each other.

David Walker held that those who will not fight for their dignity and freedom deserve, along with their children, spouse, and other family members, to be kept in slavery and to be brutalized and "butchered" in the worst imaginable ways (66). Celia fought for her dignity, as did Margaret Garner. Both did so in the only way available to them. Even though Garner took the life of one of her children, applauded the

---

Johnson Publishing, 1969) 156. See the longer account of the Garner incident in *Black Women in America*, 60–63.

[72] Herbert G. Gutman, *The Black Family in Slavery & Freedom, 1750–1925* (New York: Pantheon Books, 1976) 349.

drowning of another, and preferred to commit suicide rather than be returned to slavery, it was in fact her deep sense of humanity and dignity that spurred her to action. It was her way of saying that as a human being she had the right to live a full life on her own terms and not as the slave of another. David Walker would have understood Garner's actions to be those of resistance to injustice and the defense of life that is worth living.

For Walker, the defense of black dignity and humanity was nothing short of a moral obligation. The woman with good sense would never easily submit to rape and other aspects of the dehumanizing slavery of white Christians, which is why—had he known of them—Walker would have applauded the actions of Celia and Margaret Garner. The slave who was in control of her faculties "would cut the [slaveholder's] throat from ear to ear"(78), said Walker. As for himself, Walker declared his preference to die or be put to death rather than to live as a slave. His sense and conviction of the dignity of persons necessitated such a stance. Clearly, this was the stance taken by Garner. That is, if one is serious about conceptions like the inherent dignity of persons, it stands to reason that he would be willing to do whatever it takes to at least protect his dignity and that of his family.

Affirmation of Black Humanity and Dignity

For David Walker, if human dignity and preciousness are values to be respected, they are values to be defended. Lest one is merely waxing eloquent when she speaks of the dignity of persons, she must be willing to go to any lengths to protect and enhance it. Walker would have agreed with Joseph W. Browne's view of the lengths to which one should be willing to go in order to defend human dignity: "It seems to me that respect for the personal dignity of the human sometimes demands the use of force in the defense of that dignity. Should a people permit another people to enslave it? Should we permit drug peddlers to destroy our children? Should I stand by idly while my fellow human being is attacked?"[73] If one truly believes that blacks possess innate dignity, it would be necessary to be willing to take steps to defend that dignity. One cannot read the *Appeal* and fail to conclude that David Walker believed blacks not only to possess infinite inviolable worth, but that he was

---

[73] Joseph W. Browne, *Personal Dignity* (New York: Philosophical Library, 1983) 105.

willing to defend that worth by any means necessary. Walker preferred means short of violence, but if all else failed, he did not rule it out.

David Walker believed and declared that God called him to do what he was doing. This is why he was so confident that God would take care of him. Walker valued his own life highly. He was not hesitant, however, to say that he would sacrifice that life in a heartbeat for God and for the liberation of his people. Walker said he would rather die than remain under the heel of whites. He was diligent in his efforts to impress upon his people this same perspective.

Walker was adamant that the behavior of white Christian enslavers did not determine the humanity and worth of Africans. Therefore, blacks should not look to them for approval or permission to rediscover and affirm their full humanity and inviolable sacredness. Walker grounded the personhood and dignity of his people in the God of his faith. He taught that, "it pleased [God] to make us black"(65), despite what whites like Thomas Jefferson believed—that blackness was "unfortunate," and that blacks were less human than whites. Walker was certain that God makes no distinction between persons on the basis of color. "Did not God make us as it seemed best to himself" (85), he asked? Blackness, indeed all shades of humanity, have divine approval. God willed the color of Africans, Asians, Europeans, etc. Therefore, no individual or group has a right to mistreat and disrespect another on the basis of color, "which none but the God who made it can alter." It followed for Walker that any who abuses another on the basis of color is in danger of divine judgment.

In the most fundamental sense, humanity is the same the world over. The God who creates all persons, implants in each the divine image. Indeed, every person *is* the image of God. In part, then, white enslavers' fear resulted from their own innate sense that the Africans were not beasts or brutes, but as much persons as they. If this was true, it was conceivable that blacks would—if they were truly persons—despise the whites to the point of retaliating against them. The reason for their retaliation, however, would have less to do with black hatred of whites than with black's rediscovered self-love.

Walker was convinced that there was in whites "a secret monitor," telling them the Africans were, as much as whites, persons; and because of this, white enslavers must have known that blacks could have nothing in their hearts for them but contempt and the hope for their oppressors' eventual deaths (95). Even Thomas Jefferson experienced some apprehension about his claim that blacks were inferior to whites, not warranting treatment appropriate to those who enjoyed full personhood. In Query 18 of *Notes on the State of Virginia*, he nervously pondered the fate of a nation that denied basic rights to any of its citizens:

> And can the liberties of a nation be thought secure when we have removed their only firm basis, a conviction in the minds of the people that these liberties are of the gift of God? That they are not to be violated but with his wrath? Indeed I tremble for my country when I reflect that God is just: that his justice cannot sleep for ever: that considering numbers, nature and natural means only, a revolution of the wheel of fortune, an exchange of situation, is among possible events: that it may become probable by supernatural interference! The Almighty has no attribute which can take side with us in such a contest.[74]

To be sure, Jefferson did not explicitly name the enslaved Africans as persons, and therefore as citizens deserving of the same basic rights as whites. But he implied his doubt as to the status of the Africans as citizens. He seemed to be second guessing himself. Was it possible that the Africans were full-fledged persons after all? Even in the infamous Query 14 of *Notes on the State of Virginia* there appears to be some vacillation as to whether the Africans were fully human or not. At least it appears that Jefferson did not completely close the door on the possibility. For Jefferson, the very possibility that the Africans might be full human beings was even more reason for the anxiety he experienced in the previously cited passage from Query 18.

Not only was Walker convinced of the presence of the image of God in his people, but he believed whites themselves suspected this to be the case, although very many of them could not bring themselves to admit it and to treat blacks like full human beings. Because of this, many whites could not help but be suspicious of the enslaved Africans' every move. They were therefore compelled to deny them access to biblical knowledge and other types of educational learning. According to Walker, the fear among whites was that if blacks ever came to the knowledge and

---

[74] Jefferson, *Notes on the State of Virginia*, 163.

realization that they were endowed with the image of God and were as fully persons as were whites, they would do what whites themselves would do were they enslaved. They would kill or be killed, in order to recapture, protect, and enhance their dignity as persons. The whites knew, as Walker insisted his people must learn, that the image of God having been implanted in persons cannot be removed by even the most drastic of human actions. Therefore, whites were acutely aware that the educated slave could never be fit for slavery, and would always pose a threat to the system of slavery. Despite the brutality enslavers may unleash on the subjects of their abuse, persons always have in them a sense of its wrongness. This is because of their awareness, however faint, of the image of God in them, and thus their inherent sense of their own sacredness. Walker had a word on the matter:

> Man, in all ages and all nations of the earth, is the same. Man is a peculiar creature—*he is the image of his God*, though he may be subjected to the most wretched condition upon earth, yet that spirit and feeling which constitute the creature man, can never be entirely erased from his breast, because the God who made him after his own image, planted it in his heart; he cannot get rid of it. The whites knowing this, they do not know what to do; *they are afraid that we, being men, and not brutes, will retaliate*, and woe will be to them... (95, emphasis added).

It is significant that Walker characterized the person as "the image of God," for this means that the image of God is to be equated not only with the spiritual, mental, or rational aspect of human beings, but with the whole person. This implies not only the sacredness of the mind, intellect, and will, but of the sensibility and the body as well. Inasmuch as God calls into being whole persons, it is the whole person—mind and body—that is the image of God. Therefore, the whole person is sacred and warrants salvation or liberation. David Walker would not think of saving the souls of his people without also freeing and saving their bodies from dehumanizing, body-destroying slavery.

The Africans were not, by nature, slaves. They were human beings, created in and as the image of the Creator God. Contrary to the beliefs and teachings of many whites, Africans' value had much less to do with their ability to labor in the fields or to produce more persons for slaveholders, than with the image of God permanently etched into their being. Because Walker believed there was one God, who is loving and just, he concluded that it was a travesty for whites to imply, by their treatment of blacks, that God implanted the image of God in whites only, or implanted more of the divine image in whites than in Africans. Furthermore, Walker maintained that deep down inside, many white slaveholders also believed the Africans were not slaves by nature, or less human than whites. This is why he declared that if whites did not end slavery, it would literally destroy the country. A major part of the war he envisioned and predicted would be an internal moral struggle.

Because of his belief in the love, justice and holiness of God, and his conviction that the image of God inheres equally in all persons, David Walker had no doubt that his people would eventually gain their freedom. He was convinced that as persons under a just and loving God, they *ought* to be free. Freedom is not only the essence of their being as persons, it is also God's will that they and all persons be free to live fully human lives, individually and communally. To be free is what it means to be a person,[75] and conversely, to be a person is what it means to be free. This fundamental freedom is abused if the laws and practices of a nation denies select groups of persons the right to be politically and socially free. Neither David Walker nor the Hebrew prophets were concerned with merely affirming an abstract form of metaphysical freedom. Proclaiming such freedom under God was not sufficient. Their desire was to actualize that freedom for all persons.

In the *Appeal*, we find significant emphasis on the need for blacks to recapture their lost sense of humanity and dignity. Although he recognized the need for individual blacks to come to terms with this, Walker was never concerned merely with the well being of the individual. He realized that no person can be a full person in isolation; that no person can be all she can be apart from a loving, nurturing, supportive family; and that every person grows or develops to full personhood only in community with other persons.

The goal of David Walker's liberation project was not simply the freeing of individual Africans in order that they could achieve what they might for their own self-enhancement, self-aggrandizement, or that of those close to them. Walker's chief hope was that individual Africans in

---

[75] See Paul Tillich, *The Protestant Era*, trans. James L. Adams (Chicago: University of Chicago Press, 1948) 115.

possession of the truth, a modicum of freedom, and other resources would feel a sense of obligation to apply what they owned and enjoyed to the service of the entire community of blacks, both in the United States and throughout the world. His concern was not that an African here and there be liberated, but that Africans all over the world be set free. In this sense, it may be argued that Walker was the first Pan-Africanist in this country. He reminded his people—"free" blacks and slaves—that none of them could ever be truly free until they and blacks all over the world shared that same blessed estate. This line of reasoning points to two additional aspects of Walker's theology and anthropology. Both of these have been implied throughout this discussion, but need now to be expressly stated.

Numerous times, Walker listed some of the varieties of people in the world: Asians, Africans, Europeans, Indians, and so forth. Sometimes he did this as a way of supporting his belief that no other group of people in history had been subjected to a form of slavery as brutal as that experienced by the Africans under whites of European descent. In this he argued against Jefferson, who maintained that the Africans were not treated as badly as the enslaved in more ancient times.[76] In other cases Walker cited the variety of people-groups as a reminder that the same God who created one group created the others. Walker espoused the view that there is one God who is Creator of all persons regardless of their race, gender, and class. Precisely because God instills in persons the divine image, all belong to the same God, who desires that persons the world over live together as a family, or in community. This is possible only if every person, every group, recognizes and respects the humanity and dignity of self and of others. From this, there follows yet another important element of Walker's theology and anthropology.

Since all persons derive from the same divine Source, and are called into existence not merely as individuals, but as individuals-in-community, it is reasonable to say that God creates them for community with God and other persons. No person is created to live in solitude. Is it not the case that at birth every baby enters the world with at least two personalities already present, that is, the mother and God? Both greet the newborn, i.e., the third person. It is therefore reasonable to say that *every person is born in and for community*. By definition, God is the only self-

---

[76] Jefferson, *Notes on the State of Virginia*, 141–43.

existent being, and thus has always been present to greet each person called into existence, even if the mother died while giving birth and was not able to share in the greeting. God knew well the relational nature of the first person in whom the divine image was implanted (Gen 2:18–24). Therefore, God quickly created a second person, lest the first be lonely and miserable amid the bounties of God's world.

Consistent with his African ancestors, David Walker's ethic was more communal than individualistic. But since he recognized the worth of the individual and the need for his autonomy in relation to the community—that it is the individual who ultimately must decide how to respond to outside forces that may depersonalize him—it may be more accurate to say that Walker's was a personal-communal ethic. That is, Walker recognized and stressed the absolute dignity of the individual because she is imbued with God's image, indeed *is,* God's image. Walker, however, was committed to the principle of the interrelatedness of all persons because of his conviction that God creates persons in and for community, i.e., to live together in a human familial relationship. Since Walker's primary audience was his own people, here again his focus on the interdependence of persons was essentially directed to blacks—enslaved and free.

Understanding the fundamental interrelatedness between all persons everywhere, Walker was especially concerned to awaken his people to this truth. He could therefore proclaim to them: "We are all in the world together" (96). Or, he could remind "free" blacks who claimed to be both happy and free, that no African could be either of these in the truest sense, until all are. "For I believe it is the will of the Lord that our greatest happiness should consist in working for the salvation of our whole body" (77), he said. Persons, then, can be all they can be only within a community that enjoys and guarantees the freedom of all people. This also suggests that persons must dedicate themselves to doing the work of establishing such a community. Whatever individual blacks accomplished must be done not for self only, but for the enhancement of the entire community of blacks. This points to yet another element of Walker's thought that has important implications for African Americans today, viz., the significance of black self-determination.

Conclusion

This chapter has presented a discussion of six principles of ethical prophecy which were identified in David Walker's *Appeal*: sense of call and the cost of prophecy, divine justice, divine wrath, hope for repentance, love and compassion of God, and the sacredness of all persons. This chapter established that David Walker had a better sense of the extent of slavery's damage to the psyche of his people than most. Subjection to this most degrading, inhumane form of slavery was bad enough. Its adverse effects were exacerbated by the tendency of many blacks themselves to internalize and believe whites' perceptions of them. To some extent, this had the effect of causing many of the Africans to lose touch with the sense of their innate humanity and worth. This in turn contributed to the loss of self-determination, especially regarding the willingness to take advantage of opportunities to take their freedom by participating in escape plans, or even spur of the moment opportunities to escape to freedom.

Walker told of one despicable case that makes the point very well. A group of sixty Africans had been purchased by "a negro driver." They were chained together, and were being herded to the Mississippi River. Successful in filing through their shackles, the Africans finally charged and overtook their captors. A number of the Africans successfully escaped to the woods. Because the "negro driver" was not killed, but only slightly injured, one of the captive women actually helped him mount his horse in order to go for help at a nearby plantation. As a result of the woman's aid, all of the escapees were captured. This woman was a person who, in Walker's view, was the epitome of what he called "servile deceit." She was deceived about the reality of her own humanity and dignity, and was bound by the interpretations that whites had of her as less than a full person. She believed what they said about her, and therefore had no sense of the need to escape from captivity, or to allow others to escape.

David Walker was of the mind that he and his people were as human, and possessed as much dignity, as whites. It was therefore blacks' responsibility to shed and denounce whites' interpretations of them, formulate their own, and find their own means that would give them the best chance of obtaining eventual freedom. This would require self-determination, as well as an indomitable will to be full persons and accept the risks and responsibilities that entails. Self-determination, the desire and the capacity to take one's own life and destiny into his hands, is what many more Africans needed during the years of slavery. Indeed, they need it as much, if not more, today! David Walker's emphasis on black self-determination and what he believed his people were capable of accomplishing is the subject of the next chapter.

Chapter 4

Walker's Call for
Black Self-Determination

A number of references have been made to David Walker's insistence that his people take their destiny into their own hands; that they look to themselves, individually and collectively, and to their God, for liberation from slavery. Convinced that God is always present and desirous that justice and righteousness be done, Walker was equally convinced that persons have been created in such a way that they can do much in the way of determining their fate in the world. Because persons are created in freedom to be free, Walker always believed that a key to his people's liberation was their inherent sense of self-determination. His greatest challenge was that of finding the means to awaken his people to their lost sense of self-worth and self-determination. Walker was convinced that until blacks recaptured their sense of these, there was little hope that liberation would come.

David Walker did not pretend to believe that if blacks would only pray and worship God more, this would somehow shatter the shackles around their necks and ankles. Although he lived by the conviction that God would have the last say, and that white enslavers and acquiescent blacks would someday have to contend with God's wrath, he was always mindful of the role of the enslaved, as well as that of "well meaning" white people in the eradication of slavery and the establishment of justice. The fate of victims of injustice is never solely in the hands of oppressors. Few of his contemporaries knew this better than David Walker. He knew that if nothing else, his people retained within themselves the power to choose how they would respond to their enslavement. This, he maintained, is fundamental to what it means to be a person. The inherent freedom and the right to choose how to respond to practices that undermine one's humanity and dignity can neither be taken nor given away. It is this inner freedom to which those experiencing excruciating oppression can appeal at those moments when it seems that there is simply no way out, or that the life good to live is no longer possible. If nothing else, they still retain the capacity to decide how to respond to their situation. The reference here is to an innate spiritual power, controlled only by the individual moral agent. It is this power of choice, this freedom to decide, that makes it possible for one to retain a sense of dignity and hope in even the most devastating circumstances.

In Walker's insistence on the need for his people to invoke self-determination and to direct their own destiny, he was actually anticipating key ideas popularized by the Viennese logotherapist, Viktor Frankl (1905–1997), and by the atheistic existentialist, Jean-Paul Sartre (1905–1980). Key elements of Frankl's logotherapy (existential analysis, or meaning therapy) developed during his confinement in a Nazi concentration camp during World War II. Frankl discovered that the human being can transcend and survive the most cruel mistreatment if he has a reason or meaning for which to live. If one has a *why* to live for he can generally find within himself the resources to withstand almost any obstacle. The point is not that such a one—or group!—suffers willingly, but that he does so with dignity, and in the hope that he will be able to overcome it through his will to live for his most significant meaning in life. Such a one must be committed to resisting annihilation by every means at his disposal. This makes it possible for one to retain a sense of dignity, even in a concentration camp. Such a one never gives in to the inhumane treatment to which he is subjected. If nothing else, his stance makes him "worthy of his suffering." One always has the power to decide how he will respond to what is being done to him. Frankl writes that how one "accepts his fate and all the suffering it entails, the way in which he takes up his cross, gives him ample opportunity—even under the most difficult circumstances—to add a deeper meaning to his life."[1]

No matter the outward circumstances or conditions, the person always retains the power or freedom to decide how to respond. Conditions are sometimes so despairing and dehumanizing that what is important is not what we expect from life, but what life expects for and from us. Reflecting on the concentration camp experience Frankl put it this way: "We needed to stop asking about the meaning of life, and instead to think of ourselves as those who were being questioned by life—daily and hourly. Our answer must consist, not in talk and meditation, but in right action and in right conduct. Life ultimately means taking the responsibility to find the right answer to its problems and to fulfill the tasks which it constantly sets for each individual."[2]

Persons do not exist and live in a vacuum. Even if one chooses to live in isolation, she still owes a great debt to those who have preceded her and those who will succeed her, i.e., to ancestors and to posterity. This has particular importance in the case of the African enslaved, who believed that they lived not only for self and immediate family, but for their posterity and the "living dead," or ancestors. They felt as much obligation to these as to self and family. The ancestors expected the enslaved to stride consistently toward freedom. If nothing else, this could serve as their reason, their *why* to go on living, even under the cruel conditions of slavery.

Viktor Frankl's theory can be summed up in a famous line from the philosopher Friedrich Nietzsche: "He who has a *why* to live for can bear with almost any *how*."[3] If one has a reason, a why to live for, she will likely find, indeed make, a way to cope until liberation comes. In order to survive and to live into the new day, one has to find the wherewithal to transcend self in the immediate situation. Commenting on this point, Frankl wrote: "I thereby understand the primordial anthropological fact that being human is being always directed, and pointing, to something or someone other than oneself: to a meaning to fulfill or another human being to encounter, a cause to serve or a person to love."[4]

---

[1] Viktor E. Frankl, *Man's Search for Meaning: An Introduction to Logotherapy* (1959; New York:Pocket Books, 1973) 106–107.

[2] Ibid., 122.

[3] Friedrich Nietzsche quoted in ibid., 121.

[4] Viktor E. Frankl, *The Unheard Cry for Meaning* (New York: Touchstone Book,

David Walker was particularly sensitive to the fact that many of his people had been brainwashed by whites about their status as human beings, and that they believed whites' estimate of their humanity. Walker therefore understood perfectly the need to reverse this trend; to awaken in his people their lost sense of humanity and dignity, and challenge them to take steps to free themselves from slavery. To a large extent, this meant awakening their sense of self-determination, the will to be fully human and all that that implies. Walker's was no small task. At stake was the survival, not only of individual Africans, but of black communities as well.

Much of Frankl's focus was on the will to meaning in individuals, as when he wrote: "Man's intrinsically human capacity to take a stand to whatever may confront him includes his capacity to choose his attitude toward himself, more specifically, to take a stand to his own somatic and psychic conditions and determinants."[5] Walker was concerned about the will to meaning *and* the survival-liberation of individual Africans. He was, however, also clearly concerned about the survival-liberation and the will to meaning of the entire African American community. One cannot miss this emphasis in the *Appeal*. Integrally related to this concern is Walker's strong focus on the fundamental freedom of persons to make of themselves what they will. In this regard, he anticipated Jean-Paul Sartre's emphasis on human freedom and responsibility, another central element in David Walker's prophecy to his people.

What Sartre did was essentially to take away from persons all excuses for failure to do this or that. As an atheistic existentialist, Sartre maintained that God has no place in his philosophy and ethics. Because God does not exist, human beings exist before their essence. That is, they first exist and only later, as they develop and experience themselves, do they define themselves. Initially the human being is "indefinable," for at the beginning she is "nothing." She becomes something only later, but even then, she will be only what *she*—not God or some other being—makes of her. She has not God to depend on, for God, according to Sartre, does not exist. She has only herself on which to depend. According to Sartre: "Man is nothing else but that which he makes of

---

1978) 35.

[5] Viktor E. Frankl, "Logotherapy Approach to Personality," in *Psychology of Personality: Readings in Theory*, 2nd ed., ed. Willaim S. Sahakian (1965; Chicago: Rand McNally College Publishing, 1974) 186.

himself. That is the first principle of existentialism.... If, however, it is true that existence is prior to essence, man is responsible for what he is. Thus, the first effect of existentialism is that it puts every man in possession of himself as he is, and places the entire responsibility for his existence squarely upon his own shoulders."[6]

Sartre's existential principle is both individual *and* social, for he makes it clear that no individual ever chooses merely for self. To say that one chooses self, Sartre does not mean that she chooses only self, but that in choosing self, she also chooses for all humanity. "If, moreover, existence precedes essence and we will to exist at the same time as we fashion our image, that image is valid for all and for the entire epoch in which we find ourselves. Our responsibility is thus much greater than we had supposed, for it concerns mankind as a whole."[7] This means that the individual is never merely responsible to and for self, but to and for all persons. When any individual chooses, she is creating an image of human being not only for self, but for all humanity.[8] Therefore, one must always wonder about the effects of her decisions and actions on others, and what type of world it would be if others did the things that she does. Sartre was convinced that there is no way of escaping from this responsibility. What one person decides and does, implicates all humanity. This, according to Sartre, is as good a reason to choose and behave responsibly as to do so out of the conviction that a higher being requires it.

Without God, everything is permitted. This, Sartre contends, is precisely the point of departure of existentialism. Human beings cannot depend on excuses. They and they alone are responsible for all that happens in the world. Persons cannot blame God, the devil, the passions and emotions, or any other such thing. Persons have only themselves to look to—to blame or to praise. Sartre rejects determinism, and proclaims humans to be free through and through, and thus liable for all that

---

[6] Jean-Paul Sartre, "Existentialism is a Humanism," in *The Existentialist Tradition: Selected Writings*, ed. Nino Langiulli (New York: Anchor Books, 1971) 395.

[7] Ibid., 396.

[8] We can hear the influence of the first form of Immanuel Kant's categorical imperative in this stance: "Act only on that maxim through which you can at the same time will that it should become a universal law." See Kant, *Groundwork of the Metaphysic of Morals*, trans. and analysis H. J. Paton (New York: Harper Torchbooks, 1956) 88.

happens in the world. Persons are, fundamentally, free, whether we like it or not.

> We are left alone, without excuse. That is what I mean when I say that *man is condemned to be free.* Condemned, because he did not create himself, yet is nevertheless at liberty, and from the moment that he is thrown into this world he is responsible for everything he does. The existentialist does not believe in the power of passion. He will never regard a grand passion as a destructive torrent upon which a man is swept into certain actions as by fate, and which, therefore, is an excuse for them. He thinks that man is responsible for his passion.[9]

Condemned to freedom! Persons do not have the option not to choose, for even when we opt against making a decision, we in fact choose! The decision not to choose is also a choice.

In choosing, one implicates or involves the whole of humanity, for one is saying through his choice what he thinks the world should look like, and how persons should relate with each other. Furthermore, one only engages in "bad faith" when he claims to have been forced by some other being, circumstances, passions, etc., to choose or behave in a particular way. To be in bad faith is to lie to oneself; to be guilty of "hiding a displeasing truth or presenting as truth a pleasing untruth."[10] Sartre contends that the first act of bad faith is "to flee what it can not flee, to flee what it is."[11] There is no escaping the fact that one makes one's own choices, if only to decide how to respond to a cruel, inhumane practice, e.g., American slavery.

There is no determinism and no excuse-making, for persons are condemned to be free, i.e., to choose. This means that persons make of the world what they want, when they want. These are all ideas to which David Walker would have resonated, although he would have reacted passionately against Sartre's atheism. Walker did not know the language of Frankl and Sartre, but he knew well the basic principles that each

---

[9] Sartre, "Existentialism is a Humanism," 399 (emphasis added).

[10] Jean-Paul Sartre, *Existential Psychoanalysis*, trans. Hazel E. Barnes (Chicago: Gateway, 1962) 157.

[11] Jean-Paul Sartre, *Being and Nothingness: An Essay on Phenomenological Ontoloty* trans. Hazel E. Barnes (New York: Philosophical Library, 1956) 70.

developed and applied in attempts to spur persons to liberation and a fuller, more humane living in the world. Freedom and self-determination are key ethical principles in the prophetic ethics of David Walker.

Meaning of Self-Determination

Self-determination is the inherent potential power in persons to decide a particular course of action on their own, and to generate the power of intellect and will to carry it out. Self-determination is the freedom that a person has from outside or external control to choose a particular course of action, even if socio-political, economic, and other circumstances are such that one's adamant resolve to achieve an intended action is defeated. The point of self-determination is that it is an innate potential power in persons. The possession and use of such potential power is no guarantee, however, that there will be a successful outcome when it is invoked. What is important is that one is inherently endowed with the power of determined effort to achieve some stated goal, or die trying.

Persons are self-determining beings, even though self-determination as such does not guarantee an intended outcome. But self-determination enables the person to make the decision to try, and to bring to bear other resources to increase the possibility of success. Regardless of one's social condition, she has complete authority or power to decide how to respond to her condition, i.e., to accept it, or not.

Self-determination also implies freedom, inasmuch as it has very much to do both with intentional actions, as well as the level of development of one's intellect. By definition, it is assumed that the moral agent is not only free, but has the capacity to reason through a moral decision making process and to understand the implications and the most foreseeable consequences of the choice made. For one to decide, i.e., to determine within oneself to do something, means that he has some intended action in mind. With this freedom, the capacity to decide and to act enters.

As person, one is at least a candidate for this freedom to decide or choose, even if she is subjected to American slavery and daily rape, even if she finds herself in a Nazi death camp. Her field of choices in such cases would obviously be drastically limited, but inasmuch as she is a self-determining being, she always retains *some* power of choice. This is asserted knowing that most of the alternatives for one in such dire straits make no sense at all. And yet as person, she is forced, indeed condemned, to decide between the available dreadful alternatives before her. Does she, like Celia (above, chapter 3), allow the enslaver to continue to rape her? Or does she choose to stop him, which leads to killing him, the consequence of which is her own execution? Either alternative meant death for Celia. On the one hand, she was murdered each time she was raped. But she would also be hanged for killing the rapist.

Celia's was a perfect instance where not one of the immediate alternatives available to her made sense. Whichever alternative she selected would have devastating consequences for her. Hers was truly what Helmut Thielicke characterizes as a borderline situation. This is an ethical situation that is so devastating, heinous, and devoid of value that no available alternative seems capable of extricating one from the moral quandary she is in.[12] Whatever choice one makes when confronted with such a situation will likely have horrendous consequences, as in Celia's case. And yet, as a self-determining being, and thus a person, one is condemned to choose. This condition ought to be an important point to consider when meting out merit or demerit for one's chosen course of action. Ultimately, there is no escaping the fact that one is responsible for the choices made. Indeed, to be a person is what it means to be free, and thus, responsible.[13]

Although legally responsible for her enslaver's death, from a moral standpoint Celia was not completely and solely responsible. For her freedom in deciding—one way or the other—was severely limited by virtue of the few and deadly choices before her; choices forced on her by the immoral system of slavery. Morally, then, this implicated white enslavers—not merely Newsom—in a major way. In the field of morality there can be no perfect responsibility for one's actions if there is not also perfect, unimpeded freedom, perfect knowledge, sharpened intellect, and a wide variety of sensible and humane alternatives from which to choose. When a person such as Celia is forced by uncontrollable and drastic conditions to choose one way or the other, the degree of her moral

---

[12] See Helmut Thielicke, chap. 29–30 in *Foundations*, vol. 1 of *Theological Ethics* (Philadelphia: Fortress Press, 1966); and chap. 17–28 in *Politics*, vol. 2 of *Theological Ethics* (Philadelphia: Fortress Press, 1969) 226–30.

[13] See Abraham J. Heschel, "The Moral Outrage of Vietnam" in *Vietnam: Crisis of Conscience*, Abraham J. Heschel, Robert McAfee Brown, and Michael Novak (New York: Association Press, 1967) 59.

responsibility necessarily varies according to the circumstances that shaped her choices.[14]

When one is being intentionally self-determined, he is consciously putting forth effort of will to accomplish something he has decided upon. Even if he fails to achieve the desired end, he will have put his entire self into trying; will have determined to make the effort with or without external influence. Indeed, that one applies the full power of his will to accomplish a goal is no guarantee that he will succeed. He might well fail in his efforts. But the fact that he was able and willing to try is what makes him a person, and therefore worthy of reverence and respect by any person anywhere in the world.

Self-determination may be equated with "decided agency," i.e., doing or acting in a resolute manner for the purpose of accomplishing some end or goal. This implies that persons also possess the capacity for intelligent thought or reason and have received training for these through formal education. In the most minimal sense, a person is by definition a being who has the capacity for thought or rationality, self-determination or will, and self-conscious awareness.[15] A person at least has the capacity to decide a course of action, think up a plan for achieving the goal, ponder its most foreseeable consequences, carry out the plan with decided determination, reflect on the results, and consider what they may mean for future actions.

Those persons who find themselves in situations like slavery, which intend to crush or deny their humanity and dignity, may find it difficult to get in touch with their innate sense of self-determination, let alone to develop an indomitable resolve to free themselves from enslavement. Such was one of the most devastating consequences of American slavery. Few understood the effects of this person-destroying institution on the Africans as did David Walker.

It was slavery that led so many of the Africans to resort to the dreaded "servile deceit" that Walker detested. Slavery was at the root of

---

[14] See Borden P. Bowne, *Principles of Ethics* (New York: Harper & Brothers, 1892) 168–70.

[15] This is the view of Personalists from Borden P. Bowne to Martin Luther King, Jr. (who studied under Bowne's student, Edgar S. Brightman). See Bowne, *Metaphysics*, rev. ed. (New York: Harper & Brothers, 1898) 116. King gives a similar minimal definition of person in his *Strength to Love* (New York: Harper & Row Publishers, 1963) 141.

the blacks' inability to get in touch with their own humanity and right to be treated like beings who were the image of God, and loved perfectly and steadfastly by God. Walker understood that the slavocracy was both intentional and systematic in its efforts to destroy the psyche of the Africans. The aftermath of such destruction caused blacks to question their humanity, sense of civilization, and sense of culture. Part of David Walker's greatest contribution as a radical black Christian liberationist was his uncanny ability to understand the extent of the damage that slavery did to the psyche of many Africans. In addition, Walker was without peer in his indomitable determination to help his people to recapture their lost sense of humanity, dignity, and determination to be free and whole.

David Walker sometimes referred to enslaved blacks as "helpless" in their condition of oppression. They were victims, and therefore were unable to contribute anything at all to their own deliverance. Historically, that is precisely what it meant to be a victim, i.e., one who was able to do absolutely nothing to help either self or one's group. Unquestionably, white enslavers wanted the enslaved to feel helpless and otherwise completely dependent on them for their livelihood, existence, and eventual freedom. But confident in blacks' essential humanity, dignity, capacity for self-direction, and the presence in them of God's image, Walker declared that despite the brutal conditions to which they were subjected, they were in fact not helpless. In fact, the enslaved Africans themselves possessed the key to their eventual liberation.

One can be "victimized" without being rendered helpless or incapacitated. Although many blacks possessed talents and gifts that could not be fully developed and utilized under slavery, Walker passionately asserted that they should not allow this to be either hindrance or excuse for not devoting themselves to achieving all that they could (67–68).[16] Because blacks' condition could not be worse than it was during slavery, Walker argued that they had nothing to lose by acting to transform their situation. He reasoned that any change would be preferable to passively accepting enslavement, being defined by whites, and waiting for God to name and send a liberator. Walker counseled his people to look to themselves, i.e., to the power within, which made it possible for them to act in their own behalf.

---

[16] This is a point that looms large for the African American community today, especially regarding young black males.

"Some Are Guilty, All Are Responsible"

Walker's stance foreshadowed that of Abraham J. Heschel (quoted in this section's subtitle). For although Walker realized that his people were not guilty of causing their enslavement, he nonetheless believed that both they and their white sympathizers were at least responsible for the way they responded to it. The Africans did not enslave themselves. Nor did they make themselves the chattel property of whites. Walker believed, however, that blacks were responsible as moral beings for either passively accepting bondage or aggressively resisting it.

Is the difference readily noticeable? The Africans were not guilty of causing their enslavement. They were, however, morally responsible for how they responded to the despicable condition that had been forced upon them. And of course, as beings who are the image of God, there was only one reasonable response to slavery if we accept Walker's line of thought. Resistance! Resistance! Resistance!

Heschel conveyed the same principle in his addage: "Few are guilty, all are responsible."[17] This essentially means that no one gets off the moral hook. As human beings created by the one God to live in community, whatever happens in the world affects all persons directly or indirectly. By implication, this means that every person is responsible in some way for all that happens in the world, even if they are not themselves guilty of causing the problem. In fact, as noted previously, we may say that being a person necessarily implies the capacity to reflect that wholeness and the burden to bear its responsibilities.

In the mind of David Walker, his people were morally responsible for how they responded to their forced enslavement. As beings created by God and imbued with the divine image, persons are always morally obligated and responsible for defending and enhancing their humanity and dignity. The hope is that this can be done without severe violations of the common good of the community or human family. This means that no matter what efforts are made to dehumanize and degrade a people, it is their moral responsibility to resist such treatment in the name of the God of the Hebrew prophets.

---

[17] Abraham J. Heschel, *The Prophets* (New York: Harper, 1962) 16.

Well Meaning White People

It is not often acknowledged that David Walker thoroughly appreciated the support and outspokenness of well-meaning, sensitive whites in the struggle to free the enslaved Africans. Some of these were abolitionists who supported the colonization of nominally free blacks back to Africa. Walker concluded that on the whole the American Colonization Society's scheme to send nominally free blacks to an African colony was "not for the glory of God," but for the further anchoring and continuation of slavery. By removing the nominally free, educated blacks from the country, whites would be able to better control those enslaved. They would have less worry about uprisings among the enslaved. But Walker was just as adamant that not all colonizationists should be condemned, since some were in fact "friends" of the Africans. Unfortunately, many of these were naive regarding the full implications of efforts to remove nominally free blacks from the vicinity of the masses of enslaved Africans.

Walker was especially appreciative of Jehudi Ashmun, who died in Africa while helping nominally free blacks establish a settlement in Liberia. He surely had Ashmun and Granville Sharp (the English philanthropist who helped establish the movement to create Sierra Leone) in mind when he said: "Those philanthropists and lovers of the human family, who have volunteered their services for our redemption from wretchedness, have a high claim on our gratitude, and we should always view them as our greatest benefactors" (101; Wiltse, 71).

Although it is not known whether Walker and Sarah and Angelina Grimké (who were contemporaries in South Carolina) were acquainted, there can be no doubt that he would have approved of their emphatic stance against colonization plans. For the Grimkés, the problem was not the Africans, but the racial prejudice of whites and their unwillingness to declare slavery a sin before God and humanity. What Angelina Grimké said in a letter on colonization in which she unmasked the pretentiousness of otherwise well meaning whites makes the point well.

> Every true friend of the oppressed American has great cause to rejoice, that the cloak of benevolence has been torn off from the monster Prejudice, which could love the colored man *after* he got to Africa, but seemed to delight to pour contumely upon him whilst he remained in the land of his birth. I confess it would be

very hard for me to believe that any association of men and women loved me or my family, if, because we had become obnoxious to them, they were to meet together, and concentrate their energies and pour out their money for the purpose of transporting us back to France, whence our Hugenot fathers fled to this country to escape the storm of persecutions. Why not let us live in America, if you really *love* us? Surely you never want to "*get rid*" of people whom you *love. I* like to have such near me; and it is because I love the colored Americans, that I want them to stay in this country; and in order to make it a happy home to them, I am trying to talk down, and write down, and live down this horrible prejudice. Sending a few to Africa cannot destroy it. No—we must dig up the weed by the roots out of each of our hearts. *It is a sin*, and we must repent of it and forsake it—and then we shall no longer be so anxious to "*be clear of them*," "*to get rid of them*."[18]

Although Walker appreciated the sentiments of well meaning whites, he also understood the importance of his people taking their destiny into their own hands. It was necessary to look to their God *and* to themselves first and foremost.

Walker did not conceal his desire that the enslaved blacks should do all in their power to free themselves. He insisted, however, that they should use good judgment, and move in this regard only when they could see their way to do so. In no sense did he mean either that they should wait for divine intervention or for whites to take the initiative in the struggle for liberation. Instead, blacks needed to look to themselves, i.e., decide among themselves and determine their own means to freedom, for they were as much persons as the whites: "It is not to be understood here, that I mean for us to wait until God shall take us by the hair of our heads and drag us out of abject wretchedness and slavery, nor do I mean to convey the idea for us to wait until our enemies shall make preparations, and call us to seize those preparations, take it away from them, and put every thing before us to death, in order to gain our freedom which God

---

[18] Angelina E. Grimké, "Colonization" (Letter VI) in *The Public Years of Sarah and Angelina Grimké: Selected Writings 1835–1839*, ed. Larry Ceplair (New York: Columbia University Press, 1989) 167–68.

has given us."[19] Freedom would come to blacks not by waiting for God Almighty to force the hands of the enslavers, nor by waiting for well meaning whites to determine the optimum time and the best, least threatening, means to seek liberation.

It was necessary for blacks to look to themselves first and foremost. By all means, *they* must resist slavery and injustice. In this regard Walker would have welcomed Robert Alexander Young's *Ethiopian Manifesto* published early in 1829 (just before the *Appeal*), where he lambasted slavery and insisted on black solidarity and unity. But, he would have vehemently rejected Young's counsel that blacks not proceed to actively resist slavery until God actually sent them a leader.[20] It is not clear, however, that Walker was actually acquainted with Young's book. There is no question, however, as to the response he would have given the book.

Liberation and Self-Determination

On the subject of black liberation, Walker was a straightforward self-determinist. He was also action-oriented. We need to remember, however, that he wanted his people to engage in serious deliberations and planning before proceeding with any scheme for liberation. This might well have been a lesson he carried over from his likely participation in the planning of the Denmark Vesey conspiracy. As persons, in any case, the Africans had minds, i.e., the capacity to think their way through schemes for liberation. They needed merely to consider all options, the foreseeable consequences of each, and commit themselves to silence and secrecy. Failure to adhere to the latter led to the demise of the Vesey plans.

To be sure, David Walker was not interested in mere intellectual exercises when he urged his people to think about the best means of liberation, and to be observant for the best times in which to launch their strategies. No, they were to determine the best means of liberation for the purpose of implementing them at the best time. Walker considered deliberating and observing to be types of actions, and not merely

---

[19] *David Walker's Appeal*, ed. Charles M. Wiltse (New York: Hill and Wang, 1965) 11n.

[20] Peter P. Hinks, *To Awaken My Afflicted Brethren: David Walker and the Problem of Antebellum Resistance* (University Park PA.: Pennsylvania State University Press, 1997) 180.

reflection (which is itself a type of action!). Blacks did not have the luxury of engaging in calm, peaceful, uninterrupted reflection merely for the sake of intellectual exercise. Walker had already revealed his dislike for rationalist approaches like that of Thomas Jefferson's and other white intellectuals. In this, Walker's was an anticipation of the action-reflection models that would be introduced in the liberation theologies of the 1970s.

One of the reasons that David Walker was so adamant about impressing on his people the need for self-determination was the tendency of the white intellectual class to develop arguments or rationalizations for the alleged inherent inferiority of the Africans. Jefferson had characterized the Africans' blackness as "unfortunate." When Walker read this he was infuriated, and urged blacks who were aware of and willing to acknowledge their humanity, to buy a copy of Jefferson's book and to craft their own refutation. Once again, Walker modeled what it meant to be a prophet. Before him, no African American took Jefferson's thesis of black inferiority to task as forcefully and with as much vigor and anger. It is true that other nominally free, literate blacks, e.g., William Hamilton, addressed Jefferson's claim, but without the force of Walker's rebuke, and without naming the venerable Jefferson, as Walker had done.

Like most early black nationalists, Walker did not mind the help of well meaning whites in refuting Jefferson's views about blacks. As a self-determinist who believed in his people's fundamental humanity and dignity, however, he declared that blacks themselves needed to rebut Jefferson's claims. "For let no one of us suppose that the refutations which have been written by our white friends are enough—they are *whites*—we are *blacks*," he said. "We, and the world wish to see the charges of Mr. Jefferson refuted by the blacks themselves..." (67). In yet another instance, then, Walker was calling for self-determination among his people.

Consequences of "Servile Deceit"

Like Frederick Douglass[21] and Malcolm X[22] after him, David Walker had no patience with blacks who believed that God ordained that they passively accept enslavement. Walker was utterly disgusted with the practice of those blacks whom he considered traitors because they said or did something that would prolong, secure, or even guarantee their bondage. He resented the idea of blacks seeking to protect enslavers. To Walker, such persons were little more than "blockheads" or "a gang of desperate wretches, who go *sneaking about the country like robbers…*," and whose purpose is to spy on other blacks and report back to white enslavers (74). There was no sympathy—but only complete disgust—for those like the black woman who assisted the "Negro" slave driver and whites in the recapturing of sixteen escaped slaves (73).

Walker could only conclude, sadly, that blacks who behaved as such were casualties of "servile deceit." This term conveys the idea that the Africans' sense of personhood was so deformed and desecrated by white enslavers that it was impossible for many blacks to overcome the psychological battery in order to demand and exercise the right to be their own persons. Those who were overcome by servile deceit therefore lied to themselves about their status, giving license to whites to continue to define who they were. They actually believed themselves to be precisely who whites said they were. They behaved according to the deceit that had been perpetrated on them, even to the extent of betraying other enslaved Africans. The power of such psychological and spiritual abuse is readily seen from instances when blacks betrayed other blacks plotting to throw off the shackles of slavery, as in the case of the Gabriel Prosser (1800) and Denmark Vesey (1822) conspiracies.[23] In other

---

[21] Frederick Douglass, *Life and Times of Frederick Douglass* (1892; New York: Bonanza Books, 1962) 85.

[22] See *Malcolm X Speaks*, ed. George Breitman (1965; New York: Pathfinder Press, 1992) 10–11. Here Malcolm distinguished between the "house nigger" and the "field nigger." The former loved his white master and was totally content with his condition. The latter, on the other hand, hated the slavemaster and would just as soon slit his throat from ear to ear.

[23] See Herbert Aptheker, "Negro Slave Revolts in the United States, 1526–1860," in *Essays in the History of the American Negro* (New York: International Publishers, 1945) 27–27, 40–42. See also Aptheker, *American Negro Slave Revolts* (1943; New York: International Publishers, 1970) 219–24.

instances, slaves refused opportunities to escape to freedom. Many former slaves, even when clearly with the advantage, seemed unwilling to take revenge upon the ones who had been their slave masters.[24]

Peter Hinks' commentary on the concept of servile deceit reveals its insidious nature. The concept had essentially to do with "an internal process that led individual blacks not only to deceive themselves about who they were and what the reality of their environment was, but also to deny their responsibility for gaining self-knowledge and crafting identity. This deceit led them almost ineluctably to being servile, given the specific world in which they existed, and to their belief that they owed certain duties to whites."[25] This is what irritated Walker and other black reformers of his day. Many blacks simply could not help their servile behavior, and seemed incapable of striking out for freedom even when opportunistic moments arose. Such was the thoroughness of the insipid indoctrination enslavers imposed on the enslaved, that many Africans could not get a clear sense of their own humanity and their divinely given right to be treated as beings of infinite worth.

Taking Their Destiny into Their Own Hands

David Walker called for black self-determination, even though he did not use this term. He believed the nature of persons (especially black personhood!) to be such that his people *could,* and *must,* assert their own humanity, dignity, and determination to be free. No matter how difficult things were for them, Walker still placed much of the onus on his people. It was the responsibility of the relatively liberated-minded Africans to awaken in their people their lost sense of humanity and self-determination. Generally, the Africans were not responsible for the causes that led to their enslavement. Walker conceded this. He was, however, adamant that they were responsible for determining *how* they would respond to their enslavement. He also sought to help them to understand that even no response was a response! What he wanted was a more intentional, thoughtful response from his people to their circumstances.

---

[24] See Manning Marable's provocative and instructive discussion in "The Military in the Black Experience: Towards a Theory of the Racist/Capitalist State," in *Blackwater: Historical Studies in Race, Class Consciousness and Revolution* (Dayton OH: Black Praxis Press, 1981) 82–83.

[25] Hinks, *To Awaken My Afflicted Brethren,* 219.

Blacks themselves would have to decide whether to believe characterizations made of them by the likes of Thomas Jefferson. This was their moral obligation. Their freedom would not come if they sat back passively and waited, either for divine intervention or for the pretenders of Christianity to liberate them. Freedom would come only if blacks took their lives into their own hands, and working cooperatively with each other and with God, asserted an indomitable will and persistent actions against slavery. Hinks makes a similar and instructive point in his exegesis of the *Appeal*:

> *Nothing God promised would come to pass without an unprecedented exertion of African American wills.* Walker circumvented the doubt that even he had about God's promises by making their fulfillment totally contingent on human action. The problem was not proving God's existence, but rather motivating blacks to use the powers God had given them—thus the great need to awaken in them, to shock them into recognition of, their "unconquerable disposition."[26]

The theme of black self-determination was a recurring one among nineteenth-century black reformers, even when they did not actually invoke the term. No one emphasized the theme more or to the degree as did David Walker. The theme of black self-determination would reappear in a dramatic way during the Black Consciousness Movement of the 1960s and the early 1970s.

From Those Who Have Much, Much Is Required

As part of his strategy to awaken the sense of self-determination in his people, Walker admonished "free" blacks "who are also of sense" to be intentional and aggressive about enlightening other Africans, especially those who were enslaved and not allowed access to reading and writing. The work of the nominally free blacks was crucial for a number of reasons, not least of which was Walker's dependence on them to read his message to non-literate blacks, or tell them about it.[27] It should be

---

[26] Ibid., 229 (emphasis added).

[27] Ibid., chap. 5 for an excellent discussion on the means of circulating the *Appeal* (especially throughout the South) and the important part Walker hoped that literate "free"

remembered that during this period blacks' primary culture was oral, not literate. The *Appeal* itself had to be addressed primarily to the relatively few literate Africans in America during that time. Walker's hope was that the more fortunate, literate blacks would accept the responsibility of informing, educating, and uplifting the vast number of illiterate blacks, both enslaved and nominally free. His hope was that literate blacks would read the *Appeal* to those who could not read. Walker maintained that blacks who are better educated and possessed more material goods than their sisters and brothers were obligated to do more than the less fortunate to free them from slavery and degradation. One's personal freedom meant little as long as vast numbers of her people remain enslaved and are denied even the right to learn to read and write, or to go and come, or to serve God the way they chose.

Walker's own practice was consistent with this idea. As a "free" black who earned a decent income as the owner of a secondhand clothing shop, he could have lived a comfortable life, and not concern himself with the plight of the masses of his people. Instead, he admonished "free" blacks: "You must go to work and *prepare the way* of the Lord" (77), which was his way of saying that blacks could not (nor should they!) count on even the most friendly and devoted whites to effect their liberation. They should not expect God to do what they could do for themselves in the liberation struggle. However, he firmly believed that God was working on their behalf. Walker admonished blacks to be aggressive in the determination to decide their own destinies, to initiate and lead their own fight for deliverance. Well meaning whites could help in the struggle, but blacks themselves had to take the initiative and provide the leadership liberation required. By doing so, they in fact would participate significantly with God in working toward the goal of full and dignified freedom. Walker believed that the self-determining efforts of blacks contributed to a great work—the work of justice, liberation, and reconciliation.

That he and other black reformers of the period, e.g., Maria W. Stewart, appealed so frequently to self-determinist principles, implies that their converts may have been few. That is, Walker's own faith in racial uplift principles and values "far surpassed the faith that the mass of blacks had in them."[28] This was due, partially, to the fact that the black

---

blacks would play.

[28] Ibid., 88.

masses were more concerned about day-to-day survival than attending
lectures or classes on how to behave. It was also the case that on very
short notice "free" blacks could organize to protect an enslaved African,
and to prevent those who chased him from sending him back to the
enslaver. Frederick Douglass described one such case in *Life and Times
of Frederick Douglass*.[29]

Walker's concern that whites had authored most, if not all, of what
had been written about blacks anticipated a similar concern in Black
Liberation Theology of the late 1960s. Because of whites' own selfish
vested interests, and the fact that they benefited generously from the
system of slavery, blacks were never presented as subjects of history, but
only as objects to be used and manipulated. As far as their positive
contributions to the building of this country was concerned, blacks were
virtually invisible in history books written with white hands. When
blacks were included, they were frequently depicted as docile, content,
ignorant, and totally dependent on whites. Consequently, Walker looked
to the day when God would raise up historians among his own people
who would essentially tell the rest of the story, i.e., tell of the crimes that
this nation, its churches and other institutions committed against blacks.
Walker's hope was that these same scholars would also write about black
self-determination in the struggle to regain blacks' sense of humanity and
worth. He hoped that these historians of color would document the many
contributions of blacks to building this nation (93). Having been much
influenced by the example and witness of Richard Allen, Walker
declared that it would be black historians who would one day do justice
to Allen's name and his contributions to both the church and this country
(93). In this, Walker was not wrong.

Blacks Can Be Free, If They Will

If liberation was to come, blacks had to exert themselves to the fullest in
the struggle. As noted above, Walker rejected all claims that his people
were helpless, despite the fact that they were forced into a most
degrading form of slavery. Near the end of the *Appeal,* Walker declared:
"*We can help ourselves...* if we lay aside abject servility, and *be
determined* to act like men, and not brutes..." (96, emphasis added).
Blacks needed no prodding in this direction by whites, but they did need

---

[29] Douglass, *Life and Times*, 209.

such encouragement from blacks who were at least nominally free, or already liberated enough in their own minds to know the importance of initiating steps toward actualized freedom. No matter how desperate their plight under slavery, David Walker believed his people had in them what was necessary to overcome their involuntary and debasing conscription. In order to do so, they would need to throw off the chain of white conceptions of black selfhood, stop depending solely on outside forces—human or divine—to liberate them, and put their entire being into the struggle (96).[30] In a word, they needed to look to themselves.

For Walker the principle of self-determination meant that by sheer power of determined will and diligent action, and without outside prompting, blacks could accomplish anything humanly possible. Liberation from slavery was within the realm of human possibility. Blacks had to get up from their knees, reject limiting white images and portrayals of their personhood and capacities, and declare once and for all their own sense of humanity and dignity. The Africans were quite capable of determining the means to their liberation, and David Walker was vigorous in reminding them of it.

One thing that has been implicit in the discussion to this point is the importance of renewed and enhanced self-love among the enslaved Africans. To be guilty in such large numbers of servile deceit, and to fail to take advantage of opportunities to escape or to help others escape from slavery, were clear signs that far too many blacks lacked sufficient love of self and possessed low self-esteem. This was alarming to Walker, who read, studied, and understood the Bible as well as most educated people of his day. He therefore understood that God loves persons as such, and that God required that they love God, and their neighbor as themselves. It is the last part of this commandment, spoken by Jesus to his disciples (Luke 10:27), that has frequently been downplayed, ignored, or conveniently forgotten throughout Christian history.

Love of self was germane to the ethic of Jesus, who had a good sense of the importance of appropriate self-love for healthy humanity. Nevertheless, no less a Christian thinker than John Calvin characterized self-love as a "most deadly pestilence."[31] It was something that the Christian was to avoid. Several centuries later, Bishop Anders Nygren

---

[30] See also *David Walker's Appeal*, 62.

[31] John Calvin, *Institutes of the Christian Religion*, vol. 1, book 3, para. 4, ed. John T. McNeill (Philadelphia: The Westminster Press, 1960), 694.

wrote the massive *Agape and Eros,* in which he systematically argued that *agapé* is the virtue and the true Christian love, while *eros* is essentially self-love, and sinful. According to that outlook, true Christian love (*agapé*), has nothing whatever to do with self-love (*eros*). Nygren claimed: "Christianity does not recognize self-love as a legitimate form of love."[32] True Christian love is sacrificial and other-regarding, not self-regarding. Nygren refers to self-love as "a devilish perversion."[33]

The tragedy is that these negative depictions of self-love have been embraced by countless numbers of Christians—including those who, like the Africans in America, were enslaved and dehumanized. Many wrongly seem to think that it is possible to love others without giving a thought to loving self. Even the Bible implies that in order to love the other as one should, one must first love self appropriately. We are told to love God with all our heart, mind, and soul, and our neighbor as ourselves. This injunction implies that there would be difficulty loving the other properly if one did not first have a healthy love of self. One's own self is as worthy an object of one's love as is the neighbor. This is what Erich Fromm meant when he wrote that "my own self must be as much an object of my love as another person. *The affirmation of one's own life, happiness, growth, freedom is rooted in one's capacity to love....* If an individual is able to love productively, he loves himself, too; if he can love *only* others, he cannot love at all."[34] Love of neighbor and love of self are not, according to this line of reasoning, unrelated and separate. Love of self and love of neighbor are interconnected. Love of self is a necessary precondition to rightful and healthy love of others, a point also developed by none other than Immanuel Kant.[35]

David Walker knew that much self-hatred existed among his people. He also knew that to take their destiny into their hands, Africans would first have to recapture their sense of love of self, which itself implied the need for self-determination. Self-determination and self-love went hand in hand for the enslaved. It would not be easy to bring many of the slaves

---

[32] Anders Nygren, *Agape and Eros* trans. Philip S. Watson (Philadelphia: The Westminster Press, 1953) 217.

[33] Ibid., 740.

[34] Erich Fromm, *The Art of Loving* (New York: Bantam Book, 1967) 50.

[35] Immanuel Kant, "Duties to Oneself," in *Lectures on Ethics*, trans. Louis Infield (New York: Harper & Row Publishers, 1963), 116-26.

to this point. Nevertheless, in light of his sense of divine calling, Walker gave himself fully to this task.

Need for Black Leadership

In addition, it was necessary for blacks themselves to take the lead roles in their freedom and processes toward reconciliation. Only if they assume the primary responsibility for determining their own destiny as human beings, and their own roles in the socio-political direction of the country, can it be expected that America will some day be one nation rather than two. When the Scottish bookseller and publisher William Chambers (1800–1883), published his impressions of his visit to the United States, he commented on this. "We see, in effect, *t w o nations*—one white and another black—growing up together within the same political circle, *but never mingling on a principle of equality.*"[36]

In order for America to be one nation, it would have to cease being a "whites only" nation. David Walker saw this level of integration as the only solution to the dilemma of slavery and prejucie, especially since he was opposed to colonization. He wanted whites and blacks eventually to work together cooperatively. He was aware, however, that initially blacks had much work to do among themselves. That is, they needed to work toward the liberation of blacks in and beyond the United States, for they were all one African people. That, more than all else, was their responsibility. Black unity was needed before there could be legitimate hope for unity between blacks and whites. Despite the issues that so divisively separated whites and blacks in his day, Walker maintained a fundamental sense of the unity of the human family under God.

Excursus
David Walker and Malcolm X

David Walker's prophecy includes a strong emphasis on black self-determination. In this, he can be seen as the spiritual father of the one-time black separatist, Malcolm X. The reader might well wonder whether, because of his primary focus on the well being of his people,

---

[36] William Chambers, "We See, In Effect, Two Nations—One White and Another Black" in *Antebellum American Culture*, ed. David Brion Davis (Lexington MA: D.C. Heath, 1979) 281 (emphasis added).

Walker ever taught the literal separation of the races. He did not. Yet, he did call for the establishment of a black nation. Like Black Nationalists who came after him, Walker insisted on the need for black unity and solidarity.[37] Had he called for a separation of the races, he would likely have been supportive of colonization plans of his day—perhaps especially after his discovery that racism existed in Boston and other places in the "free" North. Because Walker did not argue for the separation of the races, he was different from those, e.g., Malcolm X, who succeeded him in the Black Nationalist tradition a century later.[38]

Walker believed that God willed that blacks and whites work things out and be reconciled to each other. After all, had not God created *one* human family, the members of which are to be in relationship with each other, rather than exist in isolation from each other? Furthermore, Walker himself believed it was possible for whites and blacks to be reconciled, provided that certain criteria were met. These included, among other things, the need for blacks to learn to care for and respect self and other blacks, and for whites to make a public national confession of the wrongs, i.e., sins, they committed against the Africans. Clearly, for Walker the spirit of love and friendship among blacks was deemed to be the absolute precondition for black-white cooperative endeavors toward racial reconciliation. Blacks also needed to develop the spirit of self-determination, which would enable them to be their own voice, to tell and write their own stories, and to refute earlier charges of black inferiority. In this way, blacks could become their own best spokespersons and protectors of their humanity.

David Walker appreciated the efforts of sincere and sensitive whites who sought to defend the humanity and dignity of blacks. Like Malcolm X after him, however, he knew it was essential for blacks themselves to acknowledge, assert, and defend their humanity and dignity. They needed to do this when it was popular to do so, as well as when it was not.

---

[37] Sterling Stuckey, *Going Through the Storm: The Influence of African American Art in History* (New York: Oxford University Press, 1994) 89. Stuckey writes that Walker "had recognized the need for the creation of black infrastructures in an earlier piece in *Freedom's Journal*."

[38] Malcolm X himself rejected separatism shortly after his break from Elijah Muhammad and the Nation of Islam.

There are a number of similarities to be noted between Walker and Malcolm X. Some of these include:

1.Although Walker and Malcolm were considered by many of their contemporaries to be irresponsible revolutionaries, a close reading of their writings and speeches reveals that they were more concerned about teaching their people to recapture their lost sense of humanity and dignity than declaring indiscriminate violence and hatred against whites. Their basic concern was not the violent overthrow of white-controlled structures that dehumanized black people. Although neither man was opposed to such violent overthrow if nonviolent methods of correction continued to fail, the point is that this was not at the top of either man's liberation agenda. Both insisted on the need for black liberation, but not necessarily by violent means. Each was more concerned about teaching his people the primacy of black humanity and dignity.

2.In a related sense, neither man was a proponent of random violence against whites, although both were clear supporters of self-defensive violence.

3.Whenever they addressed the issue of violence as means to freedom, it was never their first nor their final word. Each held out the hope that whites would repent of their sins relative to the treatment of blacks. Yet, because of their experiences and their reading of history, neither man believed that most whites would in fact repent. This realization caused them to conclude that violence, as a means to black liberation, was inevitable.

4.Both men offered a scathing critique of white and black Christianity. Walker did so as an inside-outsider, i.e., as a Christian, but not a "mainstreamer." Malcolm's critique was that of a non-Christian and outsider (having grown up a Christian, but converted to Islam while in prison). Both men essentially made a categorical indictment of Christianity. Malcolm failed to acknowledge the element of "blackwater" (Manning Marable's term) or radicalism inherent in black Christianity. Closer inspection reveals that his criticism was really of the otherworldly, compensatory type of black Christianity. Malcolm paid no attention to the protest tradition of black Christianity. This was a strange omission, since he was familiar with the revolutionary agitation of Nat Turner[39] and old John Brown,[40] both of whom were militant Christians.

---

[39] Malcolm X, *Autobiography of Malcolm X*, with Alex Haley (1965; New York: Ballantine Books, 1992) 191–92.

5.Each man vowed never to betray his people. In this sense, each was absolutely *for* his people, for their survival, liberation, and empowerment. This vow was in part the price that each paid in order to earn his community's trust.

6.Each came to terms with the possibility that he might have to give his life for the struggle. Indeed, it is reasonable to say that for both Walker and Malcolm, the struggle was his life. As noted above, Henry Highland Garnet quoted Walker as saying: "It is not in me to falter if I can promote the work of emancipation."[41] In light of his commitment to his people and his awareness of detractors within Elijah Muhammad's camp, Malcolm also expected to die a violent death.[42] Neither man saw life as worth living if he and his people had to live under any form of bondage to whites.

7.Both believed there were *some* sincere whites, and that the true work of these was among their own people, not among blacks.

8.Both decried "servile deceit" among their people. This was a devastating psychological malady, the cause of which was the viciousness of American slavery. So destructive was slavery to the psyche of many Africans that they found it nearly impossible to resist white perceptions of their humanity. The very nature of servile deceit was that the Africans often were not even aware of their consequent mental or psychological enslavement under that pernicious system. In practical terms this frequently meant that they would betray members of their own race. In his *Autobiography*, Malcolm lamented the fact that they had in the Nation of Islam the best organization for black people in the history of their presence in this country, only to have it stymied by "niggers."[43]

9.Each was convinced that a major part of his call was to tell the white man about himself, and no African Americans have succeeded as well at this, and more forcefully, than Walker and Malcolm.

10.Both men were unrelenting in the call for the fostering of black unity and open to some degree to the creation of a black nation. Walker differed from Malcolm in that he never called for an absolute separation

---

[40] Ibid., 192.

[41] Quoted in Henry Highland Garnet, "A Brief Sketch of the Life and Character of David Walker" in *Walker's Appeal/Garnet's Address*, preface by William Loren Katz (New York: Arno Press and the *New York Times*, 1969) 9.

[42] Malcolm X, *The Autobiography of Malcolm X*, 150, 417, 447.

[43] Ibid., 448.

between the races, as the latter had done while a follower of Elijah Muhammad. Malcolm rejected this idea after his liberation from the race-based, separatist, and exclusionary ideology of the Nation of Islam.

11.Walker and Malcolm were each insistent about the need for education among blacks, and the importance of knowing about Africa's contributions to progress in world history. Much of what Walker learned about Africa came through reading articles in the *African Repository*, published by the American Colonization Society, many of which focused on Africa's contributions to civilization.[44] In addition, a number of these were reprinted in *Freedom's Journal*. Walker, it will be recalled, was the Boston agent for this first black journal in America. What he learned from these articles convinced him that the Africans were not merely docile participants in developing Western civilization. They were actually the chief sources of it. But considering the time period, and the fact that there was not much archeological, anthropological, and historical data available in print about Africa, it would be reasonable to conclude that many of the articles about Africa were informed more by what the writers knew about ancient Africa and Egypt from biblical texts.[45] It should also be noted that Walker depended heavily on the black oral tradition, as well as extemporaneous black preaching, from which he probably gleaned information about Africa.

Malcolm X, on the other hand, had access to more reliable sources on African contributions. He also had firsthand experience in African countries, having made a number of trips to the African Continent toward the end of his life. He was clear in pointing out that one cannot hate her place of origin, without ultimately hating herself.[46] Both Malcolm and Walker sought to convince their people that they were Africans, pure and simple. This fact, they maintained, linked them to Africans all over the world. It is also the case that Walker impressed upon his people that they were American citizens as well, and as such should be recipients of the guarantees of the Declaration and the Constitution.

12. Both were Pan-Africanists, believing that blacks the world over are one people, and that what happened to any group of blacks anywhere in the world also affected other blacks.

---

[44] Hinks, *To Awaken My Afflicted Brethren*, 181.

[45] Ibid., 192.

[46] Malcolm X, *Malcolm X on Afro-American History* (New York: Pathfinder Press, 1982) 73.

Conclusion

David Walker was without peer in terms of his ability to forcefully articulate his dismay over the way his people were treated by white proponents of Christianity. But as much as this unsettled him, he issued a scathing rebuke to his people for their failure to take their destiny into their own hands. He believed God was on the side of the oppressed Africans, but that they should not make the mistake of expecting God to do everything for them. Their eventual liberation and freedom would not roll in on the wheels of inevitability (as Martin Luther King, Jr. was also fond of saying to his black contemporaries). Sterling Stuckey was not wrong when he wrote: "There was no greater believer than [Walker] in the inherent worth, the redeeming power, of black humanity. Though he thought God on the Africans' side, he urged them to make a determined effort of their own to overthrow their oppressors."[47] Blacks had what it took to liberate themselves, and also to help make the world worthy of being redeemed by God. No one believed this more than David Walker.

The next chapter addresses more explicitly the moral preten-tiousness of white proponents of the Christian faith. As an ethical prophet, David Walker was not only critical of his own people for their failure to be intentionally and persistently self-determined in seeking to liberate themselves, he also saw it as his moral obligation to take white Christians to task for their hypocrisy of claiming to be followers of Jesus Christ on the one hand, and enslaving and brutally mistreating the Africans on the other. In either case, whether criticizing his people's lack of self-determination and urging them to take up their own fight, or criticizing white "pretend" Christians and declaring the wrath and judgment of God, David Walker was engaging in dangerous, life-threatening behavior, characteristic of the life and work of the ethical prophet. David Walker was a clear threat to the slavocracy. It is no wonder that part of the lore surrounding his life and work is the longstanding belief that he was murdered not long after the publication and distribution of the *Appeal*.

---

[47] Stuckey, *Going Through the Storm*, 90.

Chapter 5

Moral Pretentiousness of White Christianity

Like a number of nineteenth-century blacks, such as Maria W. Stewart, Frederick Douglass, Douglas Dorsey, Lunsford Lane, Harriet Jacobs, and Henry Bibb, David Walker wrote and spoke with passion about the difference between genuine or "proper" religion and the religion lived and taught by white enslavers and others given to prejudicial attitudes toward blacks. These Africans generally were not fooled by the version of Christianity taught them by whites. Frequently they pretended—as a survival technique—to believe what white ministers preached and taught. Very deep within themselves, however, many of the Africans believed that such teachings were from the devil—not from God or Jesus Christ. Nothing in their cultural and religious heritage from Africa would allow blacks such as David Walker, to accept as truth the idea that they were less human than whites, and that it was God's intention that they be enslaved.

The religion of the white enslaver was to the more enlightened enslaved Africans "hypocritical religion," in comparison to "true Christianity." Many Africans "rejected the slaveholder's gospel of obedience to master and mistress. ... Nowhere is the slaves' rejection of the master's religion clearer than in their refusal to obey moral precepts held up to them by whites, especially commands against stealing."[1] Many of these enslaved had enough sense to know that it was not possible for them to steal what actually belonged to them, inasmuch as it was produced by their uncompensated labor. This was the case of both the enslaved and those who escaped to freedom, e.g., Harriet Jacobs, Henry Bibb, Frederick Douglass, and Mattie J. Jackson. For example, when Mattie Jackson was ready to make her escape from slavery, she discovered that she needed money. She therefore *took* it from her owner. Jackson wrote about this incident: "When I made my escape from slavery I was in a query how I was to raise funds to bear my expenses. I finally came to the conclusion that as the laborer was worthy of his hire, I thought my wages should come from my master's pocket. Accordingly I *took* twenty-five dollars. After I was safe and had learned to write, I sent him a nice letter, thanking him for the kindness his pocket bestowed to me in time of need."[2] Notice that Jackson did not say that she "stole," but that she "took," twenty-five dollars from the enslaver's pocket. The enslaved were very clear about the distinction between stealing from enslavers and taking back from them that that was rightfully theirs anyway. For the enslaved, it was merely taking back what their stolen labor produced. Indeed, many understood that they themselves were actually stolen from their homeland by the white man, and then herded like cattle into the holds of stinking, tightly cramped slave ships for the miserable journey through the Middle Passage and to a life of devastatingly cruel slavery. Nobody, save the God of the Hebrew prophets, knows how many millions of Africans were lost during those voyages.

Once the Africans arrived and were sold into slavery, numerous steps were taken to dehumanize them. They were forced to work from sunup to sundown in the sweltering heat of the sun in order to make a life of ease and comfort for the white thieves who had stolen and enslaved them. They were not allowed to speak the languages of their villages, to retain their own names, or to worship in ways consistent with their African backgrounds. The Africans' labor was literally stolen from them,

---

[1] Albert J. Raboteau, *Slave Religion* (New York: Oxford University Press, 1978) 294–95.

[2] Mattie J. Jackson, "The Story of Mattie J. Jackson as told to L. S. Thompson" in *Six Women's Salve Narratives* (New York: Oxford University Press, 1988) 38 (emphasis added).

meaning that they were given no compensation for services rendered for over two hundred years. Essentially then, much of present-day white American wealth are the gains of theft. In addition, the Africans were denied literacy and other skills needed to function in the strange, hostile culture in which they were forced to live.

Non-Liberating Christianity

The more enlightened enslaved had no doubt that the religion preached and taught by the white enslaver and his preachers was inconsistent with their understanding of religion in general, and the gospel in particular. The religion of the enslaver was also a far cry from the moral requirements of African traditional religions. The latter required that persons be respected as persons-in-community. Many of the Africans accepted the white man's teaching of Christianity, but not without filtering it through the grid of their own experiences and religious beliefs. In this way, they were able to develop a conception of the Christian faith that was unlike any that previously existed.

In general, the enslaved knew that there was no good-news about being enslaved and systematically dehumanized by otherwise religious people. Nor was there for the Africans anything that was good news about those who claimed to be bearers of the gospel, but who enslaved and treated them like non-persons. Many of the Africans could see that the whites held the Bible in their hands, while simultaneously subjecting them to what Walker, who examined the system of slavery among the ancient Greeks, believed to be the most abject form of slavery and degradation in the history of civilization.

When David Walker examined what historians said about the slave systems of the Romans and the Greeks, he concluded against Thomas Jefferson's claim that slavery in ancient times was more vicious and inhumane than that in the United States. Furthermore, Walker concluded not only that slavery was a primary reason for the Romans' destruction, but that by comparison it paled in severity to the enslavement and treatment of the Africans in this country.[3] The Romans, unlike the Americans, did not declare that their enslaved were not members of the human family. Neither did they deny them the right to have legally

---

[3] *David Walker's Appeal*, ed. Charles M. Wiltse (New York: Hill and Wang, 1965) 14.

recognized and protected families. Because they acknowledged the fundamental humanity of those they enslaved, the Romans did not deny them basic necessities of life. Moreover, since the Romans did not base slavery on race, it was much easier for escapees to blend in with the wider population. The Africans did not have this luxury in the United States. Because of the color of their skin, theirs was always a conspicuous presence, unless the complexion of their skin was light enough for them to pass for white. Walker did not deny that slavery was immoral for any group of people, including the Romans. His point was that its ancient practice in Greek and Roman history was not as vile and degrading as slavery had become in the Americas.

The same whites who proclaimed the gospel of Jesus Christ would beat the Africans unmercifully. Often, such beatings would be administered for no reason than being found on their knees praying to the same God that whites claimed to serve (81). These same men frequently violated the bodies of enslaved females, while exhibiting no pangs of conscience or sense of having violated them. They had absolutely no sense that by so doing they also violated the God of the prophets and of Jesus Christ. David Walker believed that the "pure and undefiled religion, such as was preached by Jesus Christ and his apostles, is hard to be found in all the earth" (80). There was no doubt in his mind that the religion of white enslavers did not come close, to either the word, or the spirit, of Jesus Christ.

Walker was convinced that most whites internalized what intellectuals like Thomas Jefferson said about the Africans, namely that they were in all significant areas—intellectual and moral ability—of direly diminished capacity in comparison to whites. The Africans were at best deemed imperfect replicas of whites. Since whites were completely human, and blacks were not, they had no rights that the whites were bound to respect by the application of civil law, religion, or morality. Considering blacks to be sub-humans, it was reasonable to the whites that the Africans should live a life of servitude and service to them.

Therefore, the good news of the gospel only applied to whites, spiritually and substantively. The good news for the Africans, presumably, was that they were allowed by the whites to serve them through forced labor and unrestrained sexual abuse. White enslavers believed Africans were enjoying a privilege to serve in these ways. After all, the whites maintained that they themselves were responsible for any signs of culture and civilization among the enslaved and nominally free Africans. Indeed, had not Jefferson stated as much in the infamous Query XIV in *Notes on the State of Virginia*?[4] Early twentieth-century white historians such as Ulrich Bonnell Phillips agreed wholeheartedly with Jefferson on this point: "This progress of the Negroes has been in very large measure the result of their association with civilized white people."[5]

The Christianity of white enslavers required that the Africans always obey them. White Christianity was, for all intents and purposes, foisted on the Africans as a "gospel of unquestioned obedience." If the Africans chose not to be obedient to their white enslavers, the religion of the latter permitted that they be beaten in the most brutal fashion. Harriet Jacobs told of white preachers who preached such nonsense to blacks.[6] David Walker also cited such incidents. One of these occurred when he went to Charleston, South Carolina, in the hope of hearing the gospel truth preached. He was not at all surprised when "our Reverend gentleman got up and told us (colored people) that slaves must be obedient to their masters—must do their duty to their masters or be whipped" (82). Walker's great consternation about this was that such foolishness was preached by one who claimed to be a minister of Jesus Christ, "whose very gospel is that of peace and not of blood and whips, as this *pretended preacher* tried to make us believe" (82, emphasis added). For Walker, those who preached such a nonsensical doctrine mocked the God of Jesus Christ.

The Africans knew that of all the things white ministers preached against, it was a rare white clergyman who preached against slavery and their brutal mistreatment and depersonalization. It was also rare to find a white minister who preached the true gospel of Jesus Christ to white Christians, and challenged them to live by its principles. Very much like many of their present day successors, white ministers and their constituents during slavery had a predilection against prophecy. Had they

---

[4] Thomas Jefferson, *Notes on the State of Virginia*, ed. William Peden (1982;Chapel Hill: University of North Carolina Press, 1995), 141.

[5] Ulrich B. Phillips, "The Plantation as a Civilizing Factor" in *The Slave Economy of the Old South: Selected Essays in Economic and Social History*, ed. Eugene D. Genovese (Baton Rouge: Louisiana State University Press, 1968) 83.

[6] Harriet A. Jacobs, *Incidents in the Life of a Slave Girl*, ed. Jean Fagan Yellin (Cambridge MA: Harvard University Press, 1987). See chap. 13, especially p. 74.

acknowledged and taken seriously the tradition of Hebrew prophecy, with its emphasis on righteousness and justice, they would have been forced to preach, teach, and act against the entire system of slavery, rather than to make their peace with it and do all in their power to perpetuate it.

Christianity without Morality

Christianity without morality! This sounds like an oxymoron. It is! Based on the principle of *agapé* love, Christianity might in principle be the moral religion *par excellence*. Because God is considered to be love, as well as the author of love, proponents of the Christian faith are expected to live lives that are commensurate with the ethic of *agapé* love. This means that their lives should reflect the highest morality or life good to live; a life grounded in the love of God. Therefore, a phrase such as the one at the beginning of this section must look and sound odd to one who knows anything about Christianity.

Christianity is a supremely moral religion in theory, if not in practice. Many whites who claimed to be Christians also participated in the sin of slavery. If the ownership of human beings is considered sinful, as David Walker maintained, and if proponents of Christianity were also enslavers, it follows that theirs is a religion without morality. Furthermore, it follows that such religion cannot be Christian, for proponents of Christianity at its best consider the ownership of human beings to be immoral, and therefore sinful.

At best, most white enslavers only pretended to be moral in light of the Christian faith, and David Walker took them to task for it. He detested their moral pretentiousness, and did not mince words about his total disrespect and disregard for their brand of Christianity. For theirs was not the Christianity of the apostles of Jesus, nor was it the religion of the prophets. Indeed, it was Walker's view that one is involved in a serious contradiction if he thinks it possible to be an enslaver and a Christian at the same time. For, he believed, all persons are created in the divine image. Consequently, God requires that each person serve God and God only, for every person belongs to and is accountable only to God.

The Christianity of Henry Clay and other white Christian colonizationists was not grounded in the gospel. David Walker was too intelligent and too much of a student of the Bible to allow himself to believe that the God of Jesus Christ would take seriously the petitions of these phony proponents of the Christian faith. Clay maintained that ample provision might be made for the colonization of blacks—especially for "free" blacks!—in some area of the African coast, and that the white Christian enslavers could then transmit to them "the blessings of our arts, our civilization, and our religion." He had only the best interests of whites in mind. Walker must have found Clay's proposal rather humorous, in light of his belief that it was Africa that actually civilized the West. In response, Walker said he would ask Clay: "What kind of Christianity? Did he mean such as they have among the Americans—distinction [i.e., between the races], whip, blood and oppression? I pray the Lord Jesus Christ to forbid it" (86). Clay made reference to "a peculiar, a moral fitness, in restoring them [i.e., "free" blacks] to the land of their fathers." By removing the nominally free Africans, he said, the Africans would no longer be subjected to "the evils and sufferings which we had been the *innocent* cause of *inflicting* upon the inhabitants of Africa" (86). One can imagine Walker's outrage over Clay's claim to white innocence in this regard.

Walker easily unmasked Clay's moral pretentiousness and deception. For as noted previously, it became clear in the speeches given by Clay and other members of the enslavers' class, that the real aim of the colonizationists was to separate once and for all, the nominally free blacks from their enslaved sisters and brothers. Cutting through their moral and religious pretense, Walker could see that the fear of most white enslavers who advocated colonization was that the "free" blacks were always seeking to instruct the enslaved on their humanity— reminding them that they were full-fledged persons, with an inborn preciousness, and as such ought to be free (87). Remember, to most white enslavers, education unfits a person for slavery. If we grant this, it is not difficult to understand why most of the white colonizationists wanted to separate the nominally free blacks from those who were enslaved.

The purpose of most white Christian colonizationists, therefore, was not to liberate the Africans from slavery. The enslaved were to remain under the feet of white Christians, and with no change in the way they were treated. The real goal was to get rid of nominally free blacks like Walker, who were believed to put unsettling ideas into the heads of the enslaved Africans about humanity, human dignity, and freedom. Such teachings, enslavers declared, were not conducive to maintaining the system of slavery. The enslaved who were taught by free blacks that authentic or proper Christianity was a religion of freedom—including socio-political freedom—became restive and agitated. In addition, many who were taught by free blacks to read and write were less fit to be duped and enslaved. Of course, David Walker himself intentionally urged free blacks who were literate, and those with more resources, to teach and provide for their enslaved sisters and brothers. For Walker, those blacks who had much, in comparison to the enslaved, were more obligated to those who were worse off. In this, he was adherent of the principle that from those who have much, much is expected. Such persons are therefore more heavily obligated to stand and fight with the least of God's people.

Slave and ex-slave narratives, letters, and autobiographies compel the belief that most Africans already knew that (before they were forced into slavery) they were human beings imbued with the image and fragrance of God, and therefore ought to be free. This was not something they had to be taught, either by nominally free blacks, or by well meaning whites. David Walker's point about the moral pretentiousness of many white Christian colonizationists was well put. Whatever else one may say, the purpose of colonization was not for anything as noble as abolishing slavery. Rather, the true purpose was to separate the nominally free blacks from their enslaved sisters and brothers; to insure that the enslaved remain in a state of perpetual ignorance and vulnerability to the slavocracy.

By colonizing and depriving "free" blacks of the opportunity to educate and otherwise assist enslaved blacks, colonizationists hoped that the enslaved would remain servile and docile in their wretched condition. Enslaved black forebears craved, but were denied the right to education. In the minds of many enslavers, the most dangerous impediment to the system of slavery was widespread education among the slaves. Therefore, no effort, no resource, was spared in attempts to deny education to the enslaved Africans.[7]

---

[7] It is ironic indeed, although not in the least surprising, that presently massive numbers of young African Americans do not take advantage of the educational opportunities available, because many are aware that even with a formal education, their future is as suspect as it is without it. They know this because of what they have seen happen to countless numbers of their own peers, parents and other relatives.

Moral Pretentiousness of White Christian Colonizationists

White enslavers must have known that resistance to enslavement was as old as the institution of slavery itself, and that American slavery was no different. Indeed, it is known that the Africans' resistance to enslavement by the Europeans began even before they were forcibly loaded onto the slave ships.[8] The Africans did not go willingly with their European captors. There were fights to the death during the forced marches from the villages to the slave ships on the shores of the Atlantic Ocean. Furthermore, there were many reports of suicides and attempted suicides once the captives arrived at the beaches and were put into holding cages. Some gulped down sand, tried to slash their wrists, and otherwise attempted to take their lives, rather than be forced to leave the African shorelines. During the Middle Passage, some even jumped overboard, preferring to be devoured by sharks, than to be taken from their beloved Africa.

We have already seen that Walker did not believe all colonizationists to be the enemies of blacks, and therefore did not condemn all who were involved in colonization plans. Instead, he considered some to be "friends" of blacks. However, he felt that these white "friends" had themselves been duped or misled about the real purpose of colonization. He therefore encouraged them to withdraw their support from such schemes(98).

Unlike these supporters, however, Walker saw through the colonizationists' real reason for wanting to send free blacks to Africa. Most of the colonizationists were guilty of moral pretension in this regard. Walker had observed the treatment of both the enslaved and the nominally free blacks in his home state of North Carolina and in other parts of the country. He was therefore not only experienced in the ways of white enslavers and their frequent deceptions, but was an incisive analyst and critic whose critique of slavery was radically religio-moral in tone and content. Commenting on a speech given by colonizationist Elias B. Caldwell, Walker said: "The real sense and meaning of the last part of Mr. Caldwell's speech is, get the free people of colour away to Africa, from among the slaves, where they may at once be blessed and happy, and our slaves will be contented to rest in ignorance and wretchedness, to

---

[8] Rufus Burrow, Jr., "The Origins of Black Theology," chap.1 in *James H. Cone and Black Liberation Theology* (Jefferson NC: McFarland Publishers, 1994).

dig up gold and silver for us and our children. Men have indeed, got to
be so cunning, these days, that it would take the eye of a Solomon to
penetrate and find them out (90)."

Fortunately, most free blacks did not abandon their enslaved sisters
and brothers. Walker said the whites mistakenly believed that free blacks
did not care what happened to those who remained in chains. Walker was
himself intentional about urging free blacks to unite around the issue of
the emancipation of all enslaved Africans.

Any concern voiced about the well being of blacks by most white
Christian colonizationists was essentially a pretense, and therefore could
not be taken seriously. Walker was unceasing in his efforts to unmask
such pretenses. It was too often the case that even when whites did the
right thing regarding issues pertaining to slavery, they did so as a matter
of convenience or of socio-political and economic expediency, rather
than for sound religious and moral reasons. For example, Henry Clay
might well comply with a law prohibiting the importation of slaves, but
would do so "more through apprehension than humanity" (89), through
fear of detection and punishment by law (insofar as whites were actually
punished by the courts in those days!). This is yet another instance in
which David Walker anticipated Malcolm X and the Black Liberation
Theology movement. Malcolm would insist, for example, that when the
white man did right by blacks, he did not often do so out of a sense of
morality, but out of political or economic self-interest.[9] The white man
seldom did what he did on the basis of anything as honorable as the
recognition of and respect for the full humanity of people of African
descent.

The other side of the issue of the moral pretentiousness of white
Christian colonizationists is revealed in how Walker thought about the
moral sense of his own people, and whether he believed them to be
morally superior to whites. After all, Walker was convinced that most
white proponents of the Christian faith were engaged in the devil's
activity of the enslavement of his people. There was no question that
slavery was a sin against God and humanity. Walker was also convinced
that God would use blacks to bring whites to their knees *if* they did not
put an end to slavery. But does this mean that for Walker his people were

---

[9] *Malcolm X Speaks*, ed. George Breitman (1965; New York: Pathfinder Press, 1992)
40.

morally superior to whites? Would one who stood in the tradition of Hebrew prophecy, as Walker did, hold such a view?

Are Blacks Morally Superior to Whites?

Several times in his enlightening discussion on David Walker, Sterling Stuckey makes the claim that Walker believed blacks to be superior to whites in both character and morality.[10] Indeed, it is the case that Walker himself made claims to this affect a number of times in the *Appeal*. But what is not easily apparent is whether this was for him a metaphysical claim, or whether it was one that he based primarily on history and experience. That is, did Walker believe blacks to be inherently morally superior to whites, or was it his belief that they were morally superior to whites because they had not subjected other groups to degrading slavery in the Americas? Stuckey implies that Walker's was indeed a fundamental claim about human nature relative to blacks, which means, in his view, that blacks were the moral superiors of whites. Inasmuch as Walker possessed a keen mind, was an incisive analyst, and was much more serious about the moral quality of Christianity than were enslavers, it is important to clarify whether he actually believed the Africans to be inherently superior to whites in character and moral sense, as Stuckey claims. Or, was the claim of black moral superiority by Walker primarily a rhetorical device.

It should come as no surprise, that Walker's concept of God had much to do with his stance regarding the moral capability of blacks and whites. For example, if he believed God to be essentially partial to one group over others, or to be selective about who should enjoy the bounties of God's creation, one might reasonably argue that Walker's claim that blacks were morally superior to whites was a metaphysical one, and thus was not a rhetorical ploy of some sort. If Walker intended his claim to be a metaphysical one, it would then be possible to argue that God created blacks as morally superior to whites. As we saw in chapter three, however, Walker did not believe that God was selective in this way. Instead, he believed that God endows all persons equally with the divine image, which means that all have equal worth before God. This means

---

[10] Sterling Stuckey, *Slave Culture: Nationalist Theory and the Foundations of Black America* (New York: Oxford University Press, 1987) 122, 132.

that God at least *intends* that all persons possess equally the potential or capacity for morality of the highest type.

What specifically did David Walker say regarding the moral superiority of blacks over whites? What did this man, situated in the tradition of ethical prophecy, really mean when he declared the moral superiority of his people?

Although he did not believe that it was in the intended nature of things as instituted by God, Walker repeatedly made the claim that whites were the "natural enemies" of blacks (94). This conclusion was a necessary consequence of the role they played in the dehumanizing practice of slavery. That is, it was a result of whites' claims and accompanying practices that Africans were less human than they, and therefore were not fully members of the human family. Whites accused the Africans of being the seed of Cain, and therefore as deserving only to be condemned to a life of slavery. This was a claim that Walker insisted could not be verified in the Bible. It forced him to make the observation that white Christian enslavers themselves acted more like the seed of Cain, brutalizing and murdering God's people for no reason than the color of their skin. Who, he wondered, really thought and behaved like they were the offspring of the murderous Cain? Walker asked: "How many vessel loads of human beings have the blacks thrown into the seas? How many thousand souls have the blacks murdered in cold blood to make them work in wretchedness and ignorance, to support them and their families" (95)? Was it the Africans who outright denied to whites their divine birthright of full humanity and dignity through the way they treated them?

Moreover—based on observation, experience, and history—blacks, according to Walker, were not as hard of heart, unmerciful, and unforgiving as whites. He maintained further that where blacks are seen to exhibit such traits toward whites, these are based on reactions or responses to dehumanizing slavery and other types of abusive treatment. Whites, on the other hand, "have always been an unjust, jealous, unmerciful, avaricious and blood thirsty set of beings," (69), especially regarding the Africans. In addition, Walker's study of history and his own experiences led him to conclude that whites were "always seeking after power and authority" (69). All one need do, therefore, is to examine the historical record. Look anywhere in the Western world: Greece,

Rome, Gaul, Spain, Britain, and the Americas and one finds whites "acting more like devils than accountable men" (69).

But this was not the case with blacks, who, "never were half so avaricious, deceitful and unmerciful as the whites" (69). It is, however, important to remember that for Walker this was not a theological or metaphysical claim about fundamental human nature. It was a claim based on history, observation, and experience. If it had been a fundamental claim about human nature, it would have been inconsistent with Walker's conception of God. He believed there is one God, who calls all persons into existence, and who intends that each be equally endowed with humanity and dignity. This means that no person, no group, is inherently more or less human, more or less moral, than any other.

This point cannot be emphasized enough. For one to understand David Walker's claim about human nature relative to blacks and whites, it is first necessary to understand that he was fundamentally theocentric in outlook. Therefore, most of what he said about human nature was grounded in his conception of God. And God, for Walker, is the ground or cause of all persons' being in the world. Since God is no respecter of persons, no person or group is inherently and necessarily morally superior to any other.

It is important to remember that Walker criticized both white non-Christian and Christian enslavers. He concluded that as Christians, "we see them as cruel, if not more so than ever. In fact, take them as a body, white Christians are ten times more cruel, avaricious and unmerciful than ever" were the European heathens (69). "But being Christians, enlightened and sensible, they are completely prepared for such hellish cruelties" (69) as they perpetuate against blacks. Africans, even when half as enlightened and with less intelligence, surpass even the "most enlightened and refined" whites in the treatment of other groups, Walker maintained. It was on the basis of behavior such as this that Walker concluded blacks were far superior to whites in character and moral behavior. The empirical evidence confirmed his belief that the moral sense of many whites was not as developed as they pretended.

It is true that Walker was suspicious of any claim that whites were "as good by nature" as blacks (69). The weight of the support for his position falls on experience and history, not on some inherent theological truth about human nature. All one had to do, according to Walker, was to observe the behavior of many whites and that of blacks, and one could not help being convinced that whites more than blacks tended to be consistently devilish in their attitudes and behavior regarding race, and on a much grander scale. There is no question that David Walker was on target in this regard. Remember, however, that his conclusion was based not on metaphysical or theological claims, but on empirical observations and a careful examination of sociology and history.

David Walker did not contend that blacks were inherently superior to whites in character and morality. When he did refer to such superiority in his people, he said it was based on empirical observation of the behavior of whites and that of his people. Walker declared: "*Natural observations have taught me these things*." (73, emphasis added). Therefore, to reiterate, Walker's claim that blacks were inherently morally superior to whites was not a metaphysical or theological claim, but one based upon observation, experience, and history. He arrived at his conclusion on the basis of what he witnessed and experienced first hand. Although Walker referred to "a solemn awe in the hearts of the blacks, as it respects murdering men," (73) while whites tend to resort quickly to murder if they anticipate some gain, he did not mean that blacks possessed this awe innately, while whites did not. Rather, he believed that this was a result of socialization, selfish vested interest, and differences in value systems.

Walker was quite clear that this "solemn awe" blacks possessed regarding the murdering of persons was one of the reasons that whites were able to take advantage of them (73n.). This is yet another reason that even when blacks had opportunities to kill their white captors and escape to freedom, they frequently did not. Moreover, when they tried, they often failed because they were betrayed by other blacks. Indeed, this observation is also evidence that Walker did not believe blacks to be inherently superior to whites in character and moral behavior. Such superiority would mean that there was no need for blacks to learn not to betray each other. Instead, they would necessarily come to the age of maturity and responsibility with the full knowledge and awareness that they are not to do such things. The truth was that some enslaved Africans engaged in just such practices. Few acts were for Walker more morally repugnant, for example, than blacks conspiring against and betraying other blacks to white enslavers.

Walker was surely aware of instances in which blacks would bully their own people, both in the slave quarters, and in communities of nominally free blacks. What Eugene Genovese wrote about the "bad nigger" who terrorized and inflicted violence on other blacks[11] must be a phenomenon familiar to Walker. Awareness of such behaviors would have been sufficient to deter Walker from claiming that blacks are innately morally superior to whites. Walker was a careful observer of human beings and was not disposed to pretending that any group was, by virtue of race, class, or gender alone, superior to any other. He knew full well that as human beings, his people could be every bit as vicious and cunning—if only toward each other!—as whites.

The most that David Walker would have conceded regarding the question of whether blacks were innately morally superior to whites is that by virtue of being persons, both blacks and whites came into being with an inherent moral nature. But his own experience, observations, and reading of history convinced Walker that the presence in persons of a moral nature meant only that they have the internal equipment for moral experience. It did not mean that they would necessarily behave morally in their interpersonal and collective relations. The presence in persons of a moral nature means only that they meet the minimum requirement for moral experience. Essentially, this means that persons are "candidates" for morality, which implies the need for socio-cultural and intellectual maturation and training. Moral experience itself has to be intentionally sought, and will always be informed and influenced to some extent by how one was socialized and by the educational, cultural, and other opportunities to which one has been exposed. Persons do the choosing. But in addition to this, their choosing has to be based on some degree of intelligence, at least to the degree that they know what they are doing, even if they have not thought sufficiently about the most foreseeable consequences of their decision and action.

To be a person is to have the innate capacity for moral experience. David Walker *assumed* the humanity of blacks and whites alike, and thus was of the view that both had the capacity for moral experience and the potential to behave morally. Walker did not, however, assume that any particular race was inherently morally superior to any other, a position that was consistent with the Hebrew prophets and Jesus Christ. For in

---

[11] Eugene Genovese, *Roll Jordan Roll: The World the Slaves Made* (New York: Vintage Books, 1974) 625–30.

Jesus, all human beings—regardless of gender and race—have equal worth before God, and equal opportunity to live morally. Therefore, the conclusion is that when David Walker talked about the moral superiority of his people, he was not making metaphysical claims about human nature. He was merely acknowledging what he witnessed and experienced regarding the behavior of blacks and whites.

Angelina Grimke and Christianity

It is not known whether Sarah and Angelina Grimké, who conducted most of their public ministry from roughly 1835 through 1839, knew of David Walker, or whether he knew of them. It is known, however, that the Grimké sisters were still living on their father's plantation in Charleston, South Carolina, when the Denmark Vesey conspiracy was uncovered in 1822. It is also known that David Walker was in Charleston during that period.

The Grimké sisters were eventually banned for life from their hometown because of their staunch militancy and determined outspokenness regarding the abolition of slavery. They were also the first Anglo women to campaign fearlessly and forthrightly for the rights of *all* women. It is important to underscore "all," for unlike most nineteenth- and many twentieth- and twenty-first-century white feminists, the Grimké sisters were careful to point out that white women also held black women, men, and children as property, and were often as tyrannical in their treatment of them as their white male counterparts. In "An Appeal to the Women of the Nominally Free States," Angelina wrote of the plight and status of black women. "They are our country women—*they are our sisters*; and to us, as women, they have a right to look for sympathy with their sorrows, and effort and prayer for their rescue. Upon those of us especially who have named the name of Christ, they have peculiar claims."[12] White women who claimed to be Christians were, by virtue of this claim, morally obligated to take steps to abolish the practice of the enslavement of black women, even as they worked diligently to establish the socio-political rights of all women. Grimké would not allow her white sisters off the moral hook; would not allow

---

[12] Angelina Grimké, "An Appeal to the Women of the Nominally Free States" in *Root of Bitterness: Documents of the Social History of American Women*, ed. Nancy F. Cott et. al. (Boston: Northeastern University Press, 1996) 248.

them to easily claim a position of moral neutrality regarding the issue of slavery. In addition, Angelina did not hesitate to point out that "our *colored sisters* are dreadfully oppressed," and as persons, are made to bear diminished rights. Grimké was bold and courageous in using her voice and privileged social position on behalf of enslaved women.

Both Walker and Angelina Grimké cast their argument against slavery more in moral-religious, than in political and sociological terms.[13] It was frequently the practice of even religious leaders of the period, e.g., Alexander Campbell, leader of the Disciples of Christ, to deny that slavery was a theological, moral, or faith issue. They claimed that this was solely a political or social issue. Unfortunately, this left the door open for Disciples to choose which side of the slavery issue they would come down on, without fear even of moral retribution.[14] Indeed, why would there be such fear on the part of people for whom slavery was not a moral, but a political issue?

Like David Walker, Grimké argued vehemently against African colonization plans. Unlike colonizationists who were unwilling to take on the issue of the emancipation of the Africans, Grimké addressed this directly. By doing so, she was able to detect the moral pretentiousness of proponents of colonization. On moral-religious grounds she pointed out that the fundamental principle is that "*no circumstances can ever justify* a man in holding his fellow man as *property*; it matters not what *motive* he may give for such a monstrous violation of the laws of God." The whites' claim that the African is property "is an annihilation of his right to himself, which is the foundation upon which all his other rights are built. It is high-handed robbery of Jehovah; for He has declared, 'All souls are *mine*.'"[15] By implication, this means that blacks too belong only to God, and therefore are obligated to serve God only. It will be recalled from earlier discussions that this was also Walker's view. Slavery, for Grimké, was also a violation of the Constitution. More fundamentally, however, it violated the laws of the God of Jesus Christ.

---

[13] Angelina Grimké, "Appeal to the Christian Women of the South" in *The Public Years of Sarah and Angelina Grimké: Selected Writings 1835–1839*, ed. Larry Ceplair (New York: Columbia University Press, 1989) 66.

[14] For a discussion of this issue see Melton A. McLaurin, *Celia A Slave* (Athens GA: The University of Georgia Press, 1991) 76–77.

[15] Angelina Grimké, *Letters to Catherine E. Beecher* (Boston: Isaac Knapp, 1838) 8.

Unlike most white abolitionists, Grimké was not a gradualist. That is, she argued not for the gradual emancipation of the Africans, but for their immediate freedom. In addition, she saw nothing benevolent in colonization plans. Instead, the benevolence of most colonizationists was little more than a cloak for their "monster Prejudice."[16] Grimké was very likely the first white woman in the United States to declare racial prejudice and the enslavement of the Africans to be a sin. She did not mince words regarding this. Slavery, she declared, was a sin against God and humanity.[17] She saw it as a theological and moral problem of the first magnitude. In this regard, she was similar to Walker, Harriet Jacobs, and other nineteenth-century black reformers. Grimké was clearly a giant among nineteenth-century Anglo abolitionists-feminists. Who knows how much more progress might have been made in matters of race and gender in this country had Walker, Maria Stewart, and the Grimké sisters known each other and been able to do the work of liberation together.

Having discussed David Walker's background, given an overview of the nature of ethical prophecy, named and examined six principles of prophecy that one finds in the *Appeal*, discussed the significance of self-determination, and considered the pretentiousness of white Christianity, it is appropriate to consider socio-ethical implications of this study for the African American community today. This is the subject of chapter six.

---

[16] Ibid., 40–41.

[17] Grimké, "Appeal to the Christian Women of the South," 56.

Chapter 6

The Relevance of
Ethical Prophecy for Today

In the ethical prophecy of David Walker we can see that the God of the Hebrew prophets is the ground or cause, as well as the sustainer of persons in the world. Inasmuch as Walker believed God to be the source of persons' existence, he also seemed to know that in the most fundamental sense God is responsible for all that happens in the world. From a moral standpoint, this makes God the most heavily obligated being in the universe. It is important to draw distinctions here regarding the nature of divine responsibility in the world.

It is reasonable to say that as the creator and sustainer of persons, God is *causally* responsible for all that happens in the world. This is a metaphysical claim. Since God, however, creates persons in freedom to be and to live free in the world, it would be unreasonable to say that God is morally responsible for what persons choose to do or not to do. American slavery, for example, came about not because of moral decisions made by God, but as a result of immoral human decision-making.

David Walker understood this difference in human and divine responsibility in the world. He did not blame God for the cruel, inhumane slavery to which the Africans were subjected. He knew that by definition, and in light of the message of the eighth-century prophets, God eternally works toward and hopes for the return of persons to covenant relationship with God and with each other. Despite human stubbornness and hardheartedness, God cares about persons unendingly. God is responsible for what happens in the world only to the degree that God creates persons in freedom to be and to live free in the world. God is responsible for creating the type of world that persons live in, and for creating them as they are. Therefore, only in this extended causal sense is God responsible for what happens in the world.

David Walker, much like the Hebrew prophets, names persons as the supreme culprits for what happens in God's world from a moral standpoint. He therefore stressed human responsibility for both the existence of social evils and sins such as slavery, and for the eradication of such practices and the implementation of steps calculated to lead to democratic, just, and righteous living. In this sense, Walker anticipated later existentialist thought, although in outlook he was himself thoroughly theistic. He was convinced that while persons are morally responsible for what happens in the world, the enormity of problems such as slavery will also require divine-human cooperative endeavor for their positive resolutions. Persons could not solve the problem alone, no matter how hard they try. There is much that persons can and cannot do, but they will unquestionably need the assistance of God, e.g., the power of God's grace that enables them to do what they otherwise could not. Yet, much of Walker's focus was on human responsibility for what happens or does not happen in the world. With this same sentiment in mind, it is time to consider the socio-ethical implications of Walker's ethical prophecy for African Americans in the twenty-first century.

What is the relevance of ethical prophecy today? More pointedly, since the argument of this book is that ethical prophecy is what one *does* and *lives*, what can be learned from the ethical prophecy of David Walker that could jump-start and energize ministry in local black churches and other areas of the African American community? In light of the devastatingly tragic phenomenon of intra-community violence and murder among young African American males, for example, what would a ministry based on principles of ethical prophecy require of pastors, lay leaders, church executives, and church members? This, at a time when the number one cause of death to African American males between

15–24 years of age continues to be homicide at the hands of other African American males in the same age groups. This is a "disease" that especially strikes young black males, regardless of class, quicker than speeding bullets from semi-automatic and automatic weapons. Too, too many black boys have already, and will, either succumb to homicide disease themselves, or they will pass the disease on to one of their peers, or to innocent bystanders in their community. They will do so easily and with few, if any, pangs of conscience. There are many things important to the health of the black community that would be good to pass on, but homicide disease, which long ago surpassed epidemic proportion, is not one of them.

Some Final Reflections On Ethical Prophecy

Contemporary ministry is missing a necessary ingredient. Without this ingredient, churches and their members do little more than "play church." That is, they do nothing that even remotely resembles the real work of ministry, i.e., serving God and ministering to the least of the sisters and brothers. They do little or nothing to contribute to the establishment of justice, equality, and a genuine spirit and practice of sharing and communal living. In short, ministry is missing the spirit of the prophecy that was exhibited in the life and witness of Amos, Micah, Isaiah, Jeremiah, Hosea, and those few personalities imbued with prophetic inspiration who have appeared from time to time. Only in those times does it appear that churches become alive and energized about the divine call to do justice in the spirit of righteousness. Without the presence of the divinely inspired prophet, either in or outside the churches, the least of the sisters and brothers are without a clear voice; without a spokesperson to declare God's infinite compassion, as well as God's judgment. Too much of contemporary ministry has no sense of the significance of ethical prophecy.

In the absence of this ingredient, ministries tend to be self-serving. That is, ministry is done as if it is an end in itself, or as if it should be done with only the members of a particular local church in mind. Such churches fail on every turn even to serve the communities in which they are located. Failure such as this is a predictable tendency since the churches are essentially self-serving. What happens outside the walls of such a church is of no concern to those inside.

Historically, at least, the missing ingredient was present in the experience of many African American Christians. Among contemporary black persons of faith, however, there has been a shameful amount of slippage regarding this most precious ingredient for ministry. That is, its presence is less evident in ministries today than in times past.

The necessary and too often missing ingredient is the protest tradition of African American Christianity that was linked to the Hebrew prophets' emphasis on the divine imperative to *do* justice in the world. Today we only see remnants of this tradition in the ministries of some black churches. Much like their white counterparts, black churches tend on the whole to be fairly priestly in outlook, and do ministry primarily with their faithful members. One can find a prophetic black church in America today, but she has to look mighty hard. In this sense, many black churches, whether the historically black denominations or black churches in white denominations, have become as American as white churches, which means that ethical prophecy is virtually absent. But for an occasional reference to the Hebrew prophets and to Jesus' concern that the poor and the oppressed be liberated and empowered, most churches—white and black—fail to provide ministry in ways that address the socio-political and economic plight of the masses of the people. What Howard Thurman said about the sermons preached during his day is equally true of most sermons preached today. They lack the energy and passion of ethical prophecy, seemingly more concerned about "saving the souls" of congregants, while paying scant attention to the injustices that crush and destroy their day-to-day lives. The question is: What does the preached word have to say about both the victims and the perpetrators of injustice? Howard Thurman expressed his view in 1949:

> I can count on the fingers of one hand the number of times that I have heard a sermon on the meaning of religion, of Christianity, to the man who stands with his back against the wall. It is urgent that my meaning be crystal clear. The masses of men live with their backs constantly against the wall. They are the poor, the disinherited, the dispossessed. What does our religion say to them? The issue is not what it counsels them to do for others whose need may be greater, but what religion offers to

meet their own needs. The search for an answer to this question is perhaps the most important religious quest of modern life.[1]

White churches tend to uphold the *status quo*, and generally conform to the pervasive ethic of society, rather than to hold up and promote the counter-*status quo* ethic of the prophets and Jesus Christ. When it comes to the socio-political and economic orders, many white churches are more concerned to know what business executives, politicians, and economists think, rather than what God expects. Rather than challenge corrupt social and political institutions in light of the gospel, these white churches essentially remain silent. They do not challenge the corrupt practices of the powerful and their institutions as did Amos, Isaiah, and Micah.

To a large extent, many black churches today are little different from white churches. Yet it must also be said that, on the whole, they tend to be more disposed to lodge a prophetic critique and to do what ethical prophecy requires than white churches. It also must be admitted that, at this hour in history, very few African American churches can boast of having bragging rights regarding the place of ethical prophecy in their ministries. Indeed, the tragedy of intra-community violence among young black males alone has reached such epidemic proportions that it is not very helpful to assert that by comparison with white churches, black ones are more disposed to being prophetic. In light of the non-prophetic ministries in most white churches, it is not saying very much; nor is it complimentary to say that by comparison black churches tend to be more prophetic.

There are moments in history when all we can say about neutrality or indifference is that it is a crime against humanity and the universe. Indeed, those who are theistic can go much further and say that there are times in history when the behavior of individuals, groups, and institutions is so heinous and life-threatening that neutrality is not only a crime, but a sin against humanity, the rest of creation, *and* the God who loves and sustains them. One need only recall the tragedy of American slavery. Only God knows how many tens of millions of Africans died or were killed during the cruel journey of the Middle Passage, and after their arrival in the Americas to be sold into slavery. The reason for the

---

[1] Howard Thurman, *Jesus and the Disinherited* (Nashville: Abingdon-Cokesbury Press, 1949) 13.

unspeakable tragedy these unknown lost suffered is directly linked to the greed, sin, pride, and the attitude of white enslavers. They held that Africans were so far inferior to whites that they had absolutely no rights. Nothing therefore bound the slavocracy by law, conscience, or in God's name to acknowledge and respect the humanity of the enslaved. What value the Africans had was thought to be solely dependent on their use to whites as servants. None who is honest and in touch with their own humanity can deny that this was one of those moments in history when *indifference* was entirely unacceptable on the moral-spiritual plane; was a crime, indeed a sin of gargantuan proportion against all humanity and God.

In more recent times, other particularly heinous acts against humanity and God have cast neutrality and inaction as moral and spiritual crimes. The Jewish holocaust during the twentieth century was one of those periods when neutrality was in fact a monstrous crime and sin. There are also the tragedies in South Africa, Rwanda, Bosnia, Tiennamin Square, Northern Ireland, and the Middle East. There is the horror of black against black violence and murder among young African American males in urban battle zones; violence on a massive scale that boggles the imagination and kills the spirit. Then there is the tragedy of the United States government devoting a tremendous amount of human, economic, and other resources in the war and post-war involvement in Iraq.

It is really quite simple. There are moments in history, such as those named above, when it is cowardice, criminal, and sinful to be indifferent or to pretend to be neutral. The Hebrew prophets differed from all others in that they declared indifference to moral scandals to be both evil and sin. Amos, Isaiah, Micah, Hosea, and Jeremiah declared God's utter detestation of indifference to what was happening to the poor and the oppressed. They also proclaimed in the most unequivocal terms that God cares about everything that happens to persons in the world; that God cares in special ways for the poor and the oppressed, and that where these are concerned, God will not be mocked. Moreover, God will not permit injustice and its perpetrators to have the last word.

Persons matter to God. Because God cares about everything that happens to human beings, there is nothing that happens to them that God perceives as trivial. In this sense, there are no small or large injustices that anger God to varying degrees. God is angered by injustice, whatever its content. Any and all injustice, no matter its scale, diminishes the worth of all persons in the world. This does not mean that persons are diminished in the most fundamental sense, for the trace or image of God in every person is placed there by God. Even though God gets angry and is poised to judge those who engage in dehumanizing practices against others, the ones dehumanized are just as valuable to God as they were before being subjected to such practices. No matter how degrading our behavior toward others, their worth before God is not diminished in the least. God gives human worth, and it cannot be taken away. God expects that the faithful, the morally sensitive ones, will know when it is time to literally scream a YES or a NO, depending on what is happening in the social order. That is, God expects that the faithful will know when to stand and audibly declare: "I am for," or "I am against." Having declared one's moral stance, it is then necessary to exhibit the strength and courage to engage in appropriate, bold actions as one's best witness against behavior that would be deemed unacceptable by the God of the prophets.

Ethical prophecy or prophetic ethics requires that the faithful be unashamedly partisan in favor of the socio-politically least of God's people. But it also requires that they take an unqualified stance against the interests of the mighty and powerful few, if it seems that these are against the well being and the welfare of the poor and oppressed in the world. Prophetic ethics, like theological social ethics, exists not as an end in itself, nor primarily as simply one more occasion or opening for rational reflection. It is no mere risk-free intellectual exercise. Prophetic ethics exists primarily as a means to the social betterment of those forced to the outer boundaries of church and world. While claiming to take prophetic ethics seriously, if what a person engages as a theological social ethicist does not have the potential to have a meaningful impact on the predicament of the least of the sisters and brothers, then there is no reason for him to be a theological social ethicist. The work of the seminary professor, regardless of the discipline he teaches in, for example, must be to enhance the well being of persons-in-community and to make the world a gentler, sweeter place to live. If not, we work for a paycheck, which is no different from what most people do. Yet, most seminary professors claim that what they do is their vocation, which means that they believe themselves to be *called* by God to do what they do. If this is so, for what purpose can God be calling other than to help make persons better than they are, and to help make the world a place for all to live with dignity?

The religion of the Hebrew prophets and all who have taken them seriously, such as David Walker, is a religion of energy, risk, excitement, justice, and liberation. Such religion declares God's anger and impatience with indifference toward social evil and injustice. It also requires adherents to speak the truth for its own sake, without concern for the political fallout or other consequences for having done so. In addition, prophetic religion requires its members to adhere to a particular set of standards and practices, e.g., respect for persons as persons, and insistence that all be recipients of justice. Prophetic religion and ministry requires that proponents of the faith give up any and all beliefs and practices that alienate them from each other, from God, and other persons. Those who adhere to the religion of ethical prophecy realize that they cannot continue their racist, sexist, heterosexist, abusive ways. This is what was behind David Walker's scathing and persistent criticism of white enslavers who professed to be adherents of the Christian faith. For Walker, his black reformer contemporaries, and courageous people like the Grimke sisters, God was against the enslavement of the Africans. The reformers expected all who professed Jesus Christ to be against slavery and racial prejudice. God is against anything that demeans and undermines the value of persons.

Too many Christian ministers have not yet learned that the God of the prophets does not call them to "tickle the ears" of their hearers, i.e., to make them feel good in their indifference and wrongdoing. They somehow have not learned that one called by God cannot be a keeper of the *status quo*; that to be a Christian is to be against all that is inconsistent with God's expectation that justice be done. The primary spokesperson for the white "social gospel" in the late nineteenth and early twentieth century, Walter Rauschenbusch, put it nicely: "If a man wants to be a Christian, he must stand over against things as they are and condemn them in the name of that higher conception of life which Jesus revealed. If a man is satisfied with things as they are, he belongs to the other side."[2] The Christian walk is not an easy walk. Few have known this better than David Walker. He knew—and believers must learn

---

[2] Walter Rauschenbusch, *Christianity and the Social Crisis* (New York: Macmillan, 1907) 90.

today—that as a religion, Christianity is itself counter-cultural, as is its ethic of *agapé* love.

The ethical prophet is courageous and dependent first and foremost on God to see her through. Like William Augustus Jones, she recognizes: "Timid souls cannot preach to a wicked world."[3] One who would do God's work in the world today must be made of tougher skin and possess the courage of a lion.

David Walker was committed to the language of the Hebrew prophets. There were no timid fibers in his soul. He was nurtured in the black church as a boy, and doubtless heard prophetic sermons delivered by nominally free black preachers. From boyhood to adulthood, Walker saw with his own eyes the contradiction between the Christian gospel and the enslavement of his people. He concluded early in life that one cannot be Christian while simultaneously and insistently claiming to be innately superior to other persons because of race. Walker and other black reformers of his era were clear in their minds about where God stood on the issue of slavery. God was against it. And because God was against the enslavement of the Africans, every God-fearing person, regardless of race, gender, or class should be against it. If one was a Christian, and understood what that meant, he had to be against slavery.

In addition, Walker was in frequent attendance at the socio-politically active A.M.E. Church during the period he lived in Charleston, South Carolina. There can be little doubt that he frequently heard prophetic sermons delivered at that church by Reverend Morris Brown and others. We have learned in previous chapters that a number of the leaders and founders of this church, e.g., Morris Brown, Henry Drayton, and Charles Corr were active participants in the Denmark Vesey conspiracy. They were convinced that the gospel and the spirit of the Bible were against slavery. Indeed, this church has been aptly described as "a glaring symbol of black resistance" to white oppression, and "the center of the Vesey conspiracy."[4] When the conspiracy was discovered, Brown and others had to escape to the North to preserve their

---

[3] William A. Jones, Jr., *God in the Ghetto* (Elgin IL: Progressive Baptist Publishing House, 1979) 155.

[4] Peter P. Hinks, *To Awaken My Afflicted Brethren: David Walker and the Problem of Antebellum Resistance* (University Park PA.: Pennsylvania State University Press, 1997) 28, 38.

lives. Talk about excitement in ministry! It certainly kept David Walker on fire for God's work against the enslavement of his people.

How many churches—black or white—meet on a regular basis today to discuss how the ministry they are involved in can halt black against black violence and murder among young African American males? Any church that is thoroughly committed to being involved in solving such major social issues will surely receive divine approval. For such a church would be involved in the present day social crisis, not by accident, but because this is how its leaders understand their faith commitment and their call. That is precisely where much of the excitement in ministry comes from, that is, through the engaging of the pressing issues that affect the daily lives of the people, particularly the least of these. Trying to determine, collectively with the people, how best to concretize the prophetic tradition of the church and the gospel—now that is exciting stuff!

Foregoing chapters have argued that David Walker stood squarely in the tradition of ethical prophecy. The most cursory reading of the *Appeal* would reveal all of the elements of the type of prophecy discussed above: divine call and cost of prophecy; divine justice; divine wrath; hope for repentance and salvation; love and compassion of God; and the sacredness of persons. What message might these principles communicate to pastors and church members in general, but to African American pastors and church members in particular? There are, of course, a number of things one can glean from Walker's prophetic ethics for ministry in black churches and communities today. In what follows, I suggest seven of these. This is not an exhaustive list. It is, however, a list that provides clues to what should be involved in any ministry that takes ethical prophecy seriously. These observations are not considered in a particular order of priority.

Model Divine Pathos

There is an important reason for God's relentless pursuit of persons. God's hope is that persons will return to covenant relationship. In the very first book of the Bible we learn that it is unquestionably the case that all of creation is important to God, and that God is not just concerned about the well being of Israel but of all humanity.[5]

---

[5] See Bruce C. Birch et al., *A Theological Introduction to the Old Testament*

Throughout this discussion the emphasis has been placed on God's care and compassion for persons. God cares about persons and what happens to them in the world; cares because persons have a special place of importance to God. This emphasis does not preclude God's care and concern for the entire creation. It is a reminder, however, that the Hebrew prophets and Jesus Christ focused on the dignity of persons. David Walker did as well.

It is important to remember that for the theist-creationist, which is the stance of most Christians, persons do not just happen into existence accidentally. Instead, the Christian conviction is that a loving and caring God thoughtfully and willfully summons each person into existence. Each person is here because God called that individual into existence. Each person must be important, must matter to God, inasmuch as God thought and willed each one into existence. So precious is each person to God that God calls each by name, and declares that each belongs to the Creator.

Unlike the indifferent, distant god of classical Greek and Roman philosophy, the God of the prophets and of David Walker is the God of infinite and steadfast love and concern for all persons. This God is "too merciful to remain aloof to His creation. He not only rules the world in the majesty of His might; He is personally concerned and even stirred by the conduct and fate of man."[6]

This is clearly an implicit message in David Walker's *Appeal*. So important and valuable are persons to God that God refuses to give up on any person, despite persistent disobedience and unfaithfulness. Even when God allows judgment to come, this too is but a mode of divine pathos and love. The hope, the salvation, may lie on the other side of the doom or judgment, but it is quite real. Walker could prophesy divine wrath to white enslavers on the one hand, and stress God's care and concern for his people on the other. He could do this because he had no doubt that persons in general were of inestimable value to God, and therefore mattered to God. Consequently, he was certain that God cared enough about what happens to persons not to ever give up on them. Walker could speak words of doom to white enslaves precisely because of his conviction that God cares even about them, and that God's word of

---

(Nashville: Abingdon Press, 1999) 44–53.

[6] Abraham J. Heschel, *Man Is Not Alone* (New York: Farrar, Straus & Young, 1951) 244.

doom is never the last word; that there is always another word—a word
of hope—just waiting to be preached or taught to God's people. Finally,
of course, all people are God's people. God's expectation is that persons
will hear that word of hope and respond accordingly.

Although David Walker did not use the term "divine pathos," he
modeled its meaning. Anybody who takes ethical prophecy seriously
today must do the same. In all that pastors, church leaders, and
committed lay people do, they must model God's love, care, and concern
for persons, as well as God's hope that they will return to covenant
relation. It will never be enough to simply tell the people about God's
concern for them. Those engaged in prophetic ministry must model this
in every area of their lives, in the big as well as the small things. In this
sense, divine pathos has to become not merely an important doctrine. It
must become a way of life, a way of understanding and living. This
means that one has to stay the course, and not deviate merely because the
going gets tough.

God cares! Always! This is the message of ethical prophecy. It has
never been the case that persons first turned toward and sought out God.
Before persons even knew who they were, or began to develop theories
about the existence of God, God was acting and caring for them and the
world.[7] From Genesis to Revelation, we see God taking the initiative and
turning toward persons, seeking them out even as they run and try to hide
themselves from God. History, as seen through the Bible, is one long,
uninterrupted story about God's relentless search for persons[8] to return to
covenant relation with God and with each other. So much does God love
and care for persons that despite having fallen short of the mark time and
time again, God continues to pursue them, in the hope that they will hear
and heed God's Word.

That God so unceasingly searches for persons emphasizes that they
are of special significance to God. Persons are of inestimable value to
God. No scholar on ethical prophecy has expressed this point more
poignantly and adamantly than the late Rabbi Abraham Joshua Heschel.
Generation after generation, God has been waiting, searching for a
people who will live both justly and compassionately. It is not merely

---

[7] Birch, *A Theological Introduction*, 44–45.

[8] Abraham J. Heschel, "Prophetic Inspiration: An Analysis of Prophetic
Consciousness," *Judaism: A Quarterly Journal of Jewish Life and Thought*, 11/1 (1962):
10.

that we humans need God, but according to Heschel, God also needs persons. The human person is a divine need, said Heschel.[9] God needs us to help do the work that God expects to be done in the world; to help make the world redeemable, or worthy of being redeemed. This means that we humans not only possess inviolable worth, but we also have major moral responsibilities for the care of self, others, and the rest of God's creation. In this sense, no one ever gets off the moral hook. If nothing else, we are each responsible for the way we respond to what is done to others and the rest of the created order. According to prophetic ethics, we should cease pretending that what happens in God's world does not in some way implicate us.

Divine pathos should be modeled first and foremost today for those counted among the weak and the poor, or the least of the sisters and brothers. It simply must be modeled for children, for women of all races, and for young African American males. Too many of the latter can identify no reason for being and living, at least no such reason that is life-saving rather than life-destroying. In the United States, however, children, women, and young African American males are among the most vulnerable groups who need to know that God is, that God is Personal, and that God's grace is immediately available. They must also be assured that God not only cares about them, but brings to bear all of the divine resources to those problems that make their lives so miserable. The best, most concrete way for them to know this is, without question, for divine pathos, divine care, concern, and love to be modeled for them by those who claim to do ministry in accordance with the basic principles of prophetic ethics. Living God's concern for such persons is the best way to model it. And the best way to live divine pathos is to put one's body, soul, and mind—everything that is oneself—on the line for those counted among the least of these. Prophecy requires that one get involved in the blood and guts affairs of persons in their world, which means that it is not enough to just write, speak, or reflect about such matters. At some point one really does have to involve himself in the dangerous, deadly affairs of those persons and groups who are most vulnerable. One has to be willing and have the courage to go out on that moral limb, risking everything for the salvation and the well being of

---

[9] See Carl Stern's interview with Heschel in *Moral Grandeur and Spiritual Audacity,* ed. Susannah Heschel (New York: Farrar, Straus, Giroux, 1996) 397.

those children, women, and men who have been traditionally forced into the gutters of life.

The prophets came to say that God is involved in the affairs of persons in the world, that God is not an uninvolved spectator. What does this mean in the most concrete sense? In cases of the abuse of women and children, for example, those involved in prophetic ministries, those who know about such cruelties, need to declare both the sin of such abuse and God's infinite care and concern for the abused. Such persons need to declare the divine expectation that such abhorrent practices cease, not over time, but immediately. This means that Christians who are aware of the prophetic nature of their faith should be committed to assisting in the eradication of practices that undermine the worth of persons.

If an abuser happens to be a member of a particular church, he should be named, and if necessary, called out from the pulpit some Sunday morning. That is right; you have read it correctly! Call the abuser out some Sunday morning before the entire congregation. To be sure, in this day and age, that can be a dangerous practice. The pastor should plan well her strategy for this public confrontation. She should be sure, for example, that she spoke beforehand with two large, Christian, but otherwise tough persons in the congregation, persuading them to sit on either side of the one to be called out, prepared to restrain him if necessary.

Prophetic ministry is not a ministry for the timid. It is dangerous ministry, to say the least. It is always, always counter-*status quo*. This means it is always up against it, as it were. And to be up against it means that one—or the ministry one is involved with—is always susceptible to retaliation in one form or another.

In all candor, it is naive to expect that most pastors, male or female, black, red, white, brown, or gold will call out a parishioner from the pulpit (especially one who the pastor knows very well), and publicly expose the sin of brutal abuse. But if one takes ethical prophecy as seriously as did David Walker, and if one really believes that God is neither indifferent to, nor pleased with, the male abuse of women and children, then something as drastic as what was proposed above should not seem too drastic at all. The boundary situation frequently calls for a boundary response, which might well mean getting one's hands both dirty and bloodied in the attempt to resolve the problem. In fact, in light of the sin of abuse against a woman or child, to call the perpetrator out during worship service is rather tame by comparison. The more dignified members of a church might well feel that it is uncouth for a pastor to do in a Sunday morning service what is proposed. It is, however, no more undignified and sinful than the abuse of women and children.

There is a powerful illustration regarding just such a daring act from the pulpit that merits review. One of the twentieth century's most brilliant and prophetic pastors, and arguably one of the ten best preachers of his day, was the late Vernon Johns. Johns was Martin Luther King, Jr.'s predecessor at the Dexter Avenue Baptist Church in Montgomery, Alabama, and served as senior pastor for approximately four years (1947–1952). The ministry that Johns embarked on uniquely prepared the way for King.[10] Not one for sugarcoating what he believed to be God's truth, the word that Johns preached from the pulpit to his middle-class, black congregation caused many members to literally cringe in embarrassment and caused some to stop attending. He was not disturbed in the least by the discomfort experienced by some of the members. Johns clearly understood his to be the voice of God. It was his calling to speak God's truth, nothing but the truth, and to "let the chips fall where they may."

There was, according to Johns, no hiding place for those who commit violent crimes against persons. Johns was quite clear that just because one could commit a violent crime and not be prosecuted by the law did not mean he was home free in the eyes of God; or, if that one happened to be a member of Dexter Avenue Baptist Church. One such person was a medical doctor by the name of R.T. Adair, who shot and killed his wife on suspicion of adultery. Adair did not spend a single night in jail for this violent crime. After all, his wife *belonged* to him—as many men, regardless of race, have believed—and he could damn well do to her what pleased him, without fear of legal retribution. A man's home is, after all, his castle, and what he does there is his business!

Johns was outraged, and the next time that Adair came to church he let the entire congregation know it. Taylor Branch has recorded the incident:

---

[10] Lewis V. Baldwin, *There Is a Balm in Gilead: The Cultural Roots of Martin Luther King, Jr.* (Minneapolis MN: Fortress Press, 1991) 183.

But when Adair next took his customary seat at Dexter, Johns sprang quickly to the pulpit. "There is a murderer in the house," he announced to a stunned congregation. "God said, 'Thou shalt not kill.' Dr. Adair, you have committed a sin, and may God have mercy on your soul." Johns stared down at Adair in solemn judgment, with one eye in a menacing twitch caused by a childhood kick from a mule. Then he sat down. Although his public rebuke carried no further sanction, it was a shockingly bold fulfillment of another special role of the Negro preacher; substitute judge and jury in place of disinterested white authorities.[11]

That legal authorities were not concerned about the violation and death of Mrs. Adair was, in Johns' judgment, no excuse for the pastor of the perpetrator to remain silent about it. Inasmuch as the church sanctuary is no more sacred than any other space in God's world, addressing the matter from the pulpit was as good a place as any. Mrs. Adair mattered to God, and what matters to God must matter to those who are called to be God's ministers. Therefore, Johns called Dr. Adair out, right there in the worship service. Vernon Johns would not have understood most pastors' predilection today for being politically correct; nor would the Hebrew prophets and David Walker. There comes a time when a pastor has to speak the truth for its own sake, and not worry about the outcome, e.g., how many members will leave the church, or how much reduction occurs in the offering.

Others have modeled divine pathos differently than Vernon Johns, but few have done it better. Johns put it all on the line, in more than one instance. This explains, at least in part, why his tenure as senior minister at Dexter was so brief. Indeed, remembering Johns' stormy tenure, Ralph Abernathy's advice to Martin Luther King, Jr., was that if he wanted to remain at Dexter, he should endeavor to be a pastor more than a prophet.[12] It is true that pastors who would be prophets wear out their welcome, and consequently are often without a church. Yet, the prophetic way was the way of Vernon Johns.

---

[11] Taylor Branch, *Parting the Waters: America in the King Years 1954–63* (New York: Simon and Schuster, 1988) 15.

[12] Ibid., 109.

In Johns, the word and the voice of God were truly raging. The prophet is one who "feels fiercely," said Heschel. "God has thrust a burden upon his soul…. Prophecy is the voice that God has lent to the silent agony, a voice to the plundered poor, to the profaned riches of the world."[13] Even if one has neither the courage nor the personality to do it as Johns did it, he should at least have the good sense to know that this is what prophetic ministry is all about. It is about modeling divine pathos, and putting one's entire self on the line for it.

Declare the Need for Prophecy

Prophecy has been for some time the key missing ingredient in most churches and their ministries, and the absence of prophecy contributes significantly to declining memberships in mainstream white denominations. Heschel said over thirty years ago that, "one of the saddest things about contemporary life in America is that the prophets are unknown."[14] They are among the forgotten of history. Who reads and studies the prophets today? "They have not touched the mind of America,"[15] said Heschel. Most pastors avoid the prophets like they would the bubonic plague, preferring to preach from those passages of scripture that stress only the love and grace of God. They fail to understand that this, apart from the prophetic message of God, gives one an incomplete understanding of the God of the prophets and of Jesus Christ. It is necessary that pastors grapple with the truth that one cannot adequately understand divine love and grace apart from divine justice and wrath. Although this book emphasizes ethical prophecy, it does not do so to the exclusion of acknowledging the importance of the priestly office of the church. The latter is already stressed in a million different ways in seminaries and in churches. To further support this claim, one need merely examine the private libraries of pastors during and after their seminary training. One will find few, if any, commentaries and critical studies on the Hebrew prophets. This is not difficult to understand when it is remembered that few seminary professors

---

[13] Abraham J. Heschel, *The Prophets* (New York: Harper, 1962) 5.

[14] See Carl Stern's interview with Heschel in *Moral Grandeur and Spiritual Audacity*, ed. Susannah Heschel (New York: Farrar, Straus, Giroux, 1996) 399.

[15] Ibid., 400.

challenge their students to do ministries that are grounded on principles of Hebrew prophecy.

The prophetic voice is the necessary complement to the priestly voice. David Walker never rejected the priestly or more pastoral voice of the church. He simply stressed the prophetic side of the Christian faith, since its emphasis is on justice and compassionate living. It is very unlikely that Walker spent as much time as he did at the A.M.E. Church in Charleston listening to and quite possibly participating in the planning of the Vesey conspiracy, without also hearing prophetic sermons on a regular basis. White enslavers did not take prophecy seriously at all. No one knew this better than Walker, who essentially took them to task for their shortcoming in this regard.

It is likely the case that most churchgoers today do not know who the eighth-century prophets were, let alone what they prophesied, and why they did so. Heschel said that the prophets were the most disturbing people who ever lived.[16] And so they were! The prophets need to be rediscovered, preached, taught, and modeled in churches and the world today for just that reason. The prophets' message is that God takes persons seriously, unceasingly searches for them, and at the same time demands that justice be done in a spirit of lovingkindness.

We have seen how seriously David Walker took the message of the Hebrew prophets, even though he did not frequently cite their names in the *Appeal*. But the fact that he spoke so often of the need for justice to be done, and for compassion to be displayed toward the enslaved, suggests he was greatly influenced by the prophets. That David Walker was so concerned about the condition of his people in history; that he was so concerned about politics and social justice, is evidence enough of the importance of the prophets in his ministry.

At this juncture in the twenty-first century, there is a dire need to declare again the reality of and the need for ethical prophecy in the church at large. Those called to ministry should make this declaration, loudly, passionately, and frequently. Should the called fail and keep silent, laypersons, seminary professors, agnostics, and others who know the significance of prophecy can—indeed, ought—to declare its importance and necessity. In the end, it matters little *who* makes this declaration. *That* it be made is the most important thing. This declaration,

---

[16] Ibid.

done often and energetically, will speak to the most vulnerable people in a way that most preaching and teaching in churches today does not. It will be the spice that is lacking, and the honey that attracts and holds the people's attention to the Word of God.

Stress the Dignity and Preciousness of Persons

David Walker declared the dignity and preciousness of persons in general, but most especially that of African Americans. In this regard, he was without peer. There is no question that many who claim to be Christians have lost their sense of the sacredness of persons as such. Most seem unwilling to ascribe inviolable sacredness to those who are outside their own group. Therefore, the sense of the preciousness of persons is not as obvious as it should be among many proponents of Christianity. But this contradicts God's intention, which is that all persons be recognized and treated as sacred beings, inasmuch as all have in them a trace of God. It therefore stands to reason that persons are sacred and precious to God. Sacredness and preciousness are inherent in persons because God creates us in love, and loves each of us more than we could ever imagine—loves us in spite of ourselves! Perhaps the closest thing that comes to such love is that which a truly loving mother has for her child.

That persons are precious and sacred to God explains why God's pursuit of persons has been and continues to be unending. Persons matter to God. All persons are important and infinitely valuable to God, or none are. Yet knowledge of God's unyielding pursuit does not excuse the inhumane practices that some engage. Our infinite value to God does not mean we can do whatever we want, and then try to easily justify it by making the claim that God still values us highly. Because persons are so valuable to God, prophetic ethics reminds us that when the weak and vulnerable are mistreated, we are obligated to intervene on their behalf.

Where do we hear preaching and teaching on the dignity and sacredness of persons today? We hear more about the dignity of animals! On nearly any given Sunday, in almost any church building, we seldom hear anything said in sermons—beyond generalization—regarding the sacredness of persons. And yet our children, our young African American boys, die in the streets everyday as if they were dogs, and are just as quickly forgotten. Still the word about their preciousness and sacredness is not forthcoming from most pulpits, black or white. Any church today that has hopes of being rejuvenated and relevant will have to hear again the prophets' word about the preciousness of persons. Surely God implies the sacredness of persons when God declares through the prophet Hosea to a hard-hearted, disobedient, and unfaithful people: "How can I give you up...?" (Hos 11:8) Only the pastors and churches that declare the preciousness of persons, and do ministry accordingly, will be able to avoid what many have not been able to avoid today—the scandal of getting used to black on black violence and murder among young African American males; the scandal of getting used to the abuse of children and women; the scandal of getting used to gay, lesbian, and bi-sexual bashing, etc.

We need to be both honest and clear about this. There are not many proponents of the Christian faith, black or white, who are noticeably disturbed when the media reports on the murder of one black boy by another, or by a group of black boys. The reaction, more often, is one of indifference. This is the scandal—indifference! Most people have gotten used to the daily murders among young black boys; murders that can happen in any moment, at the very least provocation—an accidental bumping against, a certain look on an unsuspecting person's face, a certain verbal response that is interpreted as being an insult to a young boy's "manhood." His manhood! He's still a boy of 13 or 14. But somehow he believes that his manhood has been insulted.

It just does not upset many Christian adults that boys kill boys, especially if perpetrator and victim are black. Until the voice of ethical prophecy is recovered, this trend of indiscriminate murder among young African American males will continue indefinitely, since the lives of these boys does not matter to most of us, no matter how much we pretend otherwise. God hates, abhors, and condemns most of all, murder. God cannot be pleased with the daily murders of young black boys, even if they are the very ones pulling the triggers of the automatic weapons that take the lives of their peers.

Today we must learn anew what David Walker knew in the 1820s. Every person—African, American Indian, Asian, European, Latino/a—is worth more than any human has ever known, and perhaps can know. We are not really capable of accurately calculating our value or worth, either to ourselves or to God. What we learn from David Walker's emphasis on the dignity of African Americans is that every person is of inestimable value to God, inasmuch as God calls each into being and loves each one.

Perhaps we get our best clues to the worth of the person by working to enhance her well being. A famous preacher once said that by serving persons we get a clearer sense of their preciousness. They become all the more precious the nearer we come to Jesus Christ, "and see them more perfectly as He does."[17]

Somehow we need to find ways of convincing every African American boy, *while he is still a little boy*, that he truly is a prince.[18] We need to convince every African American girl that she is truly a princess to us, and to the God of the prophets. If no one else will deliver this message to black children, black pastors and churches should do it every Sunday, and any other day of the week that the saints are gathered, until they begin to "get" the message. That is, until the children themselves begin to believe that we adults know that they are princes and princesses, and that they matter, to God and to us.

Ethical prophecy is about making a difference in God's world; making a difference in the concrete blood and guts issues that affect the lives of God's people. But in order to do this, prophecy may sometimes have to offend the sensibilities of otherwise good and loving church people. No one harms, maims, or abuses that which he loves, assuming that he has a healthy sense of what it means to truly love self and the other.

There are plenty of "backwards thinking" persons who swear their love for the children and the women that they abuse. Because such persons are in need of therapy, we cannot accept that they love truly, no matter how much they say they do. There is no way to convince a right thinking person that a man truly loves the woman that he beats to a pulp every weekend. The same can be said regarding the maiming and murders of black boys in this society. If we recognize the preciousness of these boys and truly love them, we would never in a million years allow even one of them to be sacrificed. Yet, hundreds are sacrificed to homicide all over the country virtually every week. We have to come to terms with the fact that God is not pleased about these sacrifices, for in

---

[17] Phillips Brooks, *Lectures on Preaching* (Grand Rapids MI: Zondervan Publishing House, 1877) 281.

[18] Here I borrow from Heschel, who wrote "every child is a prince." See his essay, "The Religious Message" in *To Grow in Wisdom: An Anthology of Abraham Joshua Heschel*, ed. Jacob Neusner with Noam M. M. Neusner (New York: Madison Books, 1990). 155.

the final analysis these boys, like all other persons, belong to God. Therefore, they are as precious to God as are all other persons. And, who do you think God holds responsible for these senseless losses of human life?

Know the Community

David Walker knew what was going on with his people, both in the nominally free black community of his day, and in the community of enslaved Africans. He knew, because he was frequently out among the people. He 'hung out' with the folk. Although his nominally free status meant that he did not have to live among the enslaved, he always identified himself with all black people of African descent, whether in this country, in Africa, or other places. Whether in Wilmington, North Carolina, where he was born and raised, or in Charleston, South Carolina, where he spent several years before moving on to Boston, Walker was in close contact with the community of the enslaved, always in touch with the folk. In this sense he knew firsthand, rather than having to be told, how the enslaved were treated by white enslavers. It is difficult, if not impossible to be prophet to people one does not know. The prophet Micah, for example, was one of the peasant farmers of the countryside, and became, in the presence of the rulers, the voice of the poor and oppressed. Micah prophesied as he did and made such scathing criticisms of the rulers and the well to do because he knew firsthand how unjustly the people were being treated. In any case, one does not earn the right either to prophesy to or to be heard by those whom she has not gotten to know on their terms.

There is no way to overstate the importance of getting to know the people and the community among which one hopes to minister as an ethical prophet of God. This is especially true for the local church that wishes to live up to its prophetic calling. Every church should know the community where the church building is located, even if most of the members are long distance commuters. The way to do this is for the pastor, and those committed to the ministry of a given local church, to get out among the people and to basically hang out with them on the street corners or in the bars; socialize with the neighborhood people on their own turf, on their own terms, in the places they hang out. This does not mean one unthinkingly behaves in ways that compromise the faith when learning the ways and customs of the local community. There indeed must be limits. If one of the favorite hangouts is the local bar, this does not mean that a pastor or elder has to drink self into a drunken stupor in order to "identify" with her neighbors. But this is certain: if one does not know the community, she cannot do effective ministry, prophetic or otherwise. David Walker knew his people and the communities they lived in.

Stress Black Self-Determination

Discussed above (chapter 4), black self-determination is so critical to prophetic ministry among African Americans that it must again be lifted up. Blacks must look primarily to themselves to orchestrate their survival, liberation, and empowerment. This means they must find the means of getting in touch with their lost sense of dignity and self-determination.

There are two men of black African descent who immediately come to mind when the subject of black self-determination and black dignity comes up. These are David Walker and Malcolm X. Others have, of course, stressed self-determination and dignity during the black African presence in this country. None have done so quite like Walker and Malcolm. Each of these men preferred to give his life, rather than betray his people. Neither man could be at peace with himself as long as he was aware that his people possessed a low estimate of their own self-worth, or worse, accepted whites' diminished portrayals of who they were as beings created by the one God of the universe.

Walker and Malcolm knew the importance of a positive sense of self and of one's worth as person in the struggle for black liberation. As long as blacks possessed a low self-appraisal of themselves as persons, this would seriously impede progress toward full emancipation. As long as many blacks lacked a healthy sense of their own worth, and that of others in the black community, there was no reason to think that they would be able to muster the needed self-determination required for the struggle against racial prejudice.

By stressing self-help and uplifting the race, black foremothers and forefathers of the nineteenth century were also emphasizing the need for self-determination; the need to decide for oneself, regardless of outward circumstances, which course one would take. Would one bow down to racial injustice and slavery, or would one be determined to overcome it by whatever means appropriate to the case? Even Booker T. Washington, when he urged blacks to lift themselves by their own bootstraps (notwithstanding the fact that many of them did not even have boots!), understood that an important key to black liberation was self-determination to overcome the odds against them.

A survey of contemporary African American communities offers few signs of black self-determination, especially among young males. Only a fool would pretend that there are not legitimate reasons for the deep despair, sense of meaninglessness, mean-spiritedness, and lovelessness that hovers ominously around so many of these boys who have never had a childhood. But even so, as desperate as their situation is, there is no doubt that the message of David Walker's ethical prophecy is that the committed of the black community must insist on the need for self-determination anyway—even among young black males. Considering what they have always known and had to contend with in the urban battle zones of this country, it is likely such insistence will be difficult for many black boys to appreciate They will not know where such self-determination comes from, since it is not often enough modeled for them.

In the likes of David Walker, Maria W. Stewart, Ida B. Wells-Barnett, Jo Ann Robinson, Martin Luther King, Jr., Fannie Lou Hamer, Malcolm X, and many other African American forefathers and foremothers, past and present, we have personalities worthy of emulating. Likewise, there are not a few ordinary persons in local black communities who, as knowledgeable and distraught as anybody regarding the plight of young African American males, still insist on the need for self-determination. For example, a layman in his mid-sixties who is member of a Disciples of Christ congregation in Indianapolis, with vast experience in the construction industry, recently lamented the fact that African American men have been so beaten and crushed by this society. On the other hand, he brooded over the fact that so many have just given up, rather than look to and believe in themselves and in their inheritance from black foreparents. This man knew that the pain and frustration that many black males—young and old—experience is very real and must be acknowledged. Yet he also wondered out loud about what has happened to that spirit of self-determination that black foreparents modeled and passed on. "Can we recapture this," he asked?

David Walker would respond that if the race is to continue, i.e., survive, in order to be around to continue the work of liberation and empowerment, the spirit of self-determination will have to be recaptured. In this, African Americans have no choice. It is do or die—period. There is nothing that has happened to African Americans in the past thirty years that would cause anyone with seeing eyes to believe that blacks can long endure in society without adamant, vigorous, relentless self-determination. Even with such determination in place, blacks know that they cannot afford to pause and rest, for the beasts that are racism and economic exploitation does not rest from their insidious labors, ever.

We should be honest and confess that presently many black children are taught little in their homes about the need for self-determination. In part, this is because their parents—many of who are very young and without adequate parenting skills—were not themselves taught. This means that there has been significant erosion of some of the most important historical values among African Americans. Not least of these is the will to overcome obstacles, and the conviction that if one is self-determined and fearless, she can overcome most things that might otherwise be a nuisance and hindrance. Far too many black children today know nothing of the importance of deciding on a particular constructive course of action and staying the course until the goal is achieved. It is much too easy for most to give up when the going gets rough. Too many prefer to sit back and wait for some magical window of opportunity to appear. Windows of opportunity do appear periodically for African Americans—young and old—but they appear too infrequently and remain open for very brief periods of time; too briefly for significant numbers to take advantage of the opportunity, even if they wanted to. And too often, when these windows do open, we find that too few young blacks have done what they need to do by way of preparation to take advantage of the short-lived access to new opportunities.

David Walker admonished his black contemporaries not to sit around waiting on God or some messiah-like figure to liberate them from slavery. Rather, he taught, they were to take their destiny into their own hands. This also must be the message from black churches to black congregants and members of the black community today. It has to be the message of real hope to black boys, many of who are not optimistic that they will even live to the age of eighteen. The message of ethical prophecy is that we should neither depend solely on God, nor on other persons—especially those outside the black community—to do for us what we can do for ourselves, if we reclaim the potential power of self-determination.

From his experience in the Charleston A.M.E. church, Walker saw firsthand that large numbers of his people were not content to wait for the appearance of a messiah-liberator. Denmark Vesey and his comrades in the liberation struggle were determined to do what they could to obtain their own freedom. Each looked to self as liberator. Walker, who had already decided before leaving his home in Wilmington that he would spend the rest of his life fighting to eradicate slavery by any means at his disposal, was surely influenced and encouraged by the spirit of black self-determination that he witnessed at the Charleston church. He did not forget this when he settled in Boston. He continued the struggle from there.

If present day African American youth learn little or nothing of the importance of self-determination in their homes and schools, then black churches are good places for this process to begin. Even in a local church with 25–50 members, the pastor has an audience to which to preach and teach about the importance of self-determination—and how important it is for adults, in all that they do, to model this for children. The black church has the responsibility of saving the image and the humanity of God that, in this case, is our children.

Surely David Walker loved the A.M.E. Church in Charleston for its bold participation in planning the Denmark Vesey uprising. That church exhibited the principle of black self-determination in action. It is true that some persons, including Vesey, were executed when the plot was discovered by whites. But what better way to go down is there than fighting for the recognition of one's humanity, dignity, and freedom?

Insist on the Need for Well Meaning Whites to Repent

It is naive to expect progress in the matter of racial reconciliation until African Americans come to terms with their own humanity, dignity, and sense of self-determination. Without some sense of these, there is no basis for reconciliation with even the most well-meaning whites. Reconciliation can take place only among equals. This means that all parties must first be certain of their own sense of personhood and dignity. Many African Americans still have a long way to go in this regard, which means that there is much intra-community work to do before worrying about whether or not reconciliation with whites is even possible. But not only do blacks have prerequisite reconciliation work to do. Whites do as well.

Most whites today would likely say that they themselves did not do what their ancestors did during and after American slavery, and therefore have nothing for which to repent regarding the issue of racism. This is frequently the stance of otherwise well meaning whites, who counsel African Americans to forget about the slavery, racial prejudice, and economic exploitation of the past, and begin where they are today. Of course, they are never quite certain about what is to be done about present day racial prejudice and economic exploitation. They are certain that they themselves should not be implicated in the wrongs of the past that were committed by their ancestors against the forebears of present day African Americans.

This matter of white repentance has always been a sore spot in black-white relations. But until such repentance occurs, there is no real basis on which to proceed toward reconciliation. The truth is that in the minds of many African Americans the refusal of whites to repent is tantamount to saying that there is nothing for which they (whites) can be held responsible regarding wrongs committed by their ancestors. It is also tantamount to denying that they continue to benefit from systematic racial discrimination.

What well meaning whites need to understand is that this is not simply about an individual white person, e.g., Joe Doe. It is about wrongs committed against an entire race of persons by another race, which benefited and continues to benefit from the harvest of those wrongs. No one can deny that there have been individual whites throughout American history who were not explicitly involved in the exploitation of persons of African descent. The Grimké sisters of South Carolina are excellent examples of such persons. The issue is not individual white people as such. The issue is that even the most liberal, progressive, well meaning white person benefits financially and otherwise from wrongs committed against African Americans. The real issue is the other side of racism, or white privilege.[19]

Few nineteenth-century whites were as radical as John Brown when it came to fighting the slavocracy. Not many white abolitionists were willing to risk their own lives and those of their families, as Brown did in

---

[19] See the excellent anthology on this subject, *White Privilege: Essential Readings on the Other Side of Racism*, ed. Paula S. Rothenberg (New York: Worth Publishers, 2002).

the Harpers Ferry, Virginia, incident in 1859. But even though he despised the system of slavery, and the harm it did to both the Africans and the whites, John Brown benefited from slavery by virtue of being white and male.

As excellent as is the scholarly work that the likes of Joe Feagin and Andrew Hacker (both white males) are doing regarding the issue of racism in this country today, it must be admitted that Feagin (a sociologist) and Hacker (a political scientist) benefit from the very racism they so courageously address in their work. These white men have acknowledged that they have benefited from both past and present day racism, and that it is because of this benefiting that they must repent; not for what their ancestors did, but because they are the recipients of the bounty that their ancestors built up at the expense of the forced, uncompensated labor of blacks. They understand that although they themselves are not guilty for what their ancestors did, they are responsible for how they respond to what they did. They have not lived and developed in a social vacuum. Many of their educational, social, economic, and political privileges came as a result of the stolen labor of African American ancestors during American slavery and the ongoing employment and other forms of discrimination against blacks today.

So, it does not matter very much that individual whites do not do what their ancestors and less well-meaning whites do. ALL whites continue to benefit from racism. This is what well-meaning whites who desire reconciliation between the races must come to terms with. Until this happens, until they are willing to acknowledge and repent for their complicity in racism and discrimination and alter their lifestyle accordingly, reconciliation between blacks and whites will remain at best an elusive phantasmagoria.

That so many whites, even of the well meaning variety, see no need for repentance goes a long way toward explaining why so few hardly make any effort at all to eradicate institutional and other forms of racism today. Why should they? After all, in their mind they themselves have done nothing wrong. If one is confident (as many whites are!) that he has done nothing wrong, it's pretty hard to convince him that he needs to work on his attitude and behavior. What well meaning whites need to understand is that this is not about an individual well meaning white person here and there. It is about well meaning individual whites acknowledging that they benefit from wrongs done—and still being done—to African Americans. It is about these whites accepting responsibility for responding to this in ways that will be liberating for both themselves, their posterity, and for blacks.

Ethical prophecy always requires repentance for wrongs done. But it is also true that often persons have to be shown how they have been wrong. It was not difficult to do that during American slavery. David Walker was persistent in seeking the repentance of white enslavers. One would think the issue was cut and dry in those days. There were persons who claimed to be Christians, who also enslaved Africans. Many of those enslavers did not believe that slavery was wrong, let alone a sin against humanity and against God. It does seem, however, that the issue has gotten more complex several generations removed from slavery. At least this seems to be the case for many whites, for whom the clearest thing in their minds is that they, as individuals, never enslaved anybody; never mistreated Native Americans; never exploited anybody's wages; etc. But as long as whites think about these matters this way, they will never be able to come to terms with their complicity in this tragedy, inasmuch as they benefit from all of the wrongs—historic and present—even today. Without legitimate recognition of these things, and without the repentance of well meaning whites, there will be no significant movement toward racial reconciliation.

Insist on the Need for Black Pastors to Repent

We have seen that there were a number of preachers, including Morris Brown, who might have been involved in the planning of the Denmark Vesey rebellion in Charleston. David Walker would have known most of these preachers. Because they had already figured out the socio-political responsibility of the church, they were not among the black preachers who needed to repent. There is, however, a type of black minister who needed to repent in that day, as well as today. During the years of slavery, for example, such a one was frequently a proponent of an otherworldly religion and not too disturbed about blacks' plight on earth. One's true reward comes only after she leaves this world, or at least that was the prevailing line for the otherworldly Christian.

Today, we have the case of the mega-church black pastor who is often a theological fundamentalist and lacks a clear vision of the church's social responsibility. This, despite daily news of the murders of young black boys by other young black boys. The basic emphasis of their ministries is providing spiritual comfort for the people, rather than bringing the church's resources to bear on the problems that daily crush and maim them in both spirit and body. For many of these pastors, the church exists as an end in itself. This is why so much of the church budget goes toward beautification of the building (under the pretense that "God needs a nice place to be worshipped"). It explains why pastors of large churches are always in the market for a bigger, more modern, and extravagant building, or are desirous of building a new one. Many Christians have learned to be suspicious of such pastors and of such models of ministry. The provision of equal energy to raise funds for providing community-based, critical ministries as to raise new edifices would perhaps do much in helping people replace suspicion with trust and a partnering commitment in ministry.

As seen in Andrew Billingsley's study, *Mighty Like a River: The Black Church and Social Reform*,[20] many black pastors do good ministry with the resources at hand. Yet, most do not consistently do ministry in ways that take the prophetic tradition of the church seriously. It is for this reason that there is need for black pastors to repent. Until they themselves take prophecy seriously, and consistently do ministry based on the principles of ethical prophecy, there can be little hope that there will be churches relevant to black communities in the face social realities such as the daily murders of black boys throughout the nation.

The standard that David Walker left for ethical prophecy in ministry is not an easy one to follow. In light of the uncertain futures of black children, however, we have to try harder than we have to date. There is no doubt that prophetic ministry is *go for broke ministry*. It holds nothing back, it puts everything on the line. Participants in such a ministry know that neither church nor ministry is an end in itself; that it exists for the purpose of doing God's will in the world. God's will is that the sacredness and preciousness of every person be acknowledged, and that justice be done. God's will is that persons return to covenant relation with each other and with God, that all live together as one people in a community of respect, equality, and sharing, i.e., a beloved community.

---

[20] Andrew Billingsley, *Mighty Like a River: The Black Church and Social Reform* (New York: Oxford University Press, 1999).

The testimony of the Bible, and of generations of Christians, is that God is faithful and will not give up on persons. This notwithstanding, ethical prophecy teaches that persons bear much responsibility for what happens in God's world.

Select Bibliography

Aptheker, Herbert. *One Continual Cry*. New York: Humanities Press, 1965.

————. "Negro Slave Revolts in the United States, 1526–1860." In *Essays in the History of the American Negro*, 1–70. New York: International Publishers, 1945.

————. *The Negro in the Abolitionist Movement*. New York: International Publishers, 1941.

Baldwin, James. *Blues for Mr. Charlie*. New York: Dell, 1964.

Baldwin, Lewis V. *There Is a Balm in Gilead: The Cultural Roots of Martin Luther King, Jr.* Minneapolis: Fortress Press, 1991.

Bennett. Lerone, Jr. *Before the Mayflower: A History of Black America*. Chicago: Johnson Publishing, 1970.

Bergman, Peter M. *The Chronological History of the Negro in America*. New York: Harper & Row, 1969.

Bertocci, Peter A., and Richard Millard. Chapter 26 in *Personality and the Good*. New York: David McKay, 1963.

Billingsley, Andrew. *Mighty Like a River: The Black Church and Social Reform*. New York: Oxford University Press, 1999.

Birch, Bruce C. *Let Justice Roll Down: The Old Testament, Ethics and Christian Life*. Louisville: Westminster/John Knox, 1991.

Birch, Bruce C., et al. *A Theological Introduction to the Old Testament*. Nashville: Abingdon Press, 1999.

Bishop, Jim. *The Days of Martin Luther King, Jr.* New York: G. P. Putnam's Sons, 1971.

Boesak, Allan. *Walking on Thorns*. Grand Rapids: Eerdmans Publishing, 1984.

Bonhoeffer, Dietrich. *The Cost of Discipleship.* New York: 1937. Reprint, Macmillan, 1959.

Bowne, Borden P. *Metaphysics.* 2nd edition. New York: Harper & Brothers, 1898.

———. *The Principles of Ethics.* New York: American Book, 1892.

Branch, Taylor. *Pillar of Fire: America in the King Years 1963–65.* New York: Simon and Schuster, 1998.

———. *Parting the Waters: America in the King Years 1954–63.* New York: Simon and Schuster, 1988.

Breitman, George, editor. *Malcolm X Speaks.* New York: Pathfinder Press, 1965.

Brightman, Edgar S. *Moral Laws.* New York: Abingdon Press, 1933.

Brockman, James R. *Romero: A Life.* Maryknoll NY: Orbis Books, 1989.

Brooks, Phillips. "The Value of the Human Soul." Chapter 8 in *Lectures on Preaching.* Grand Rapids: Zondervan Publishing House, 1877.

Brown, Joanne Carlson, and Rebecca Parker. "For God So Loved the World?" Chapter 1 in *Christianity, Patriarchy, and Abuse: A Feminist Critique*, edited by Joanne Carlson Brown and Carole R. Bohn. Cleveland OH: Pilgrim Press, 1989.

Browne, Joseph W. *Personal Dignity.* New York: Philosophical Library, 1983.

Brunner, Emil. *Faith, Hope, and Love.* Philadelphia: Westminster Press, 1956.

———. Chapter 9 in *The Divine Imperative: A Study in Christian Ethics.* Translated by Olive Wyon. London: First English translation, 1937. Reprint, Lutterworth Press, 1961.

Burrow, Rufus, Jr. *James H. Cone and Black Liberation Theology.* Jefferson NC: McFarland Publishers, 1994.

———. *Personalism: A Critical Introduction.* St. Louis: Chalice Press, 1999.

———. "Personalism, the Objective Moral Order, and Moral Law in the Work of Martin Luther King, Jr." Chapter 5 in *The Legacy of Martin Luther King, Jr.: The Boundaries of Law, Politics, and Religion*, edited by Lewis V. Baldwin. Notre Dame IN: University of Notre Dame Press, 2002.

Buttrick, David. *Preaching Jesus Christ.* Philadelphia: Fortress Press, 1988.

Carson, Clayborne, editor. *The Autobiography of Martin Luther King, Jr.* New York: Warner Books, 1998.

Carson, Clayborne, editor, et al. "Conversation with Martin Luther King." In *Eyes on the Prize Civil Rights Reader*, 393–409. New York: Penguin Books, 1991.

Ceplair, Larry, editor. *The Public Years of Sarah and Angelina Grimké: Selected Writings 1835–1839*. New York: Columbia University Press, 1989.

Chambers, William. "We See, In Effect, Two Nations—One White and Another Black." In *Antebellum American Culture*, edited by David Brion Davis, 278–82. Lexington MA: D.C. Heath, 1979.

de Lubac, Henry. *Teilhard de Chardin: The Man and His Meaning*. New York: Mentor Books, 1965.

de Tocqueville, Alexis. *Democracy in America*. Volume 2. New York: Vintage Books, 1945.

Douglass, Frederick. "The Constitution of the United States: Is it Pro-Slavery or Anti- Slavery." In *The Life and Writings of Frederick Douglass*. Edited by Philip S. Foner, 2:467–80. New York: 1950. Reprint, International Publishers, 1975.

————. *Life and Times of Frederick Douglass*. New York: 1892. Reprint, Bonanza Books, 1962.

Downing, Frederick L. *To See the Promised Land: The Pilgrimage of Martin Luther King, Jr.* Macon GA: Mercer University Press, 1986.

Commager, Henry Steele, editor. *Dred Scott v. Sanford* in *Documents of American History*, 339–45. New York: Appleton-Century-Crofts, 1963.

Dulles, Avery. *The Survival of Dogma*. Garden City NY: Image Books, 1973.

Fosdick, Harry Emerson. *The Meaning of Service*. New York: Association Press, 1921.

Frankl, Viktor E. "Logotherapy Approach to Personality." Chapter 8 in *Psychology of Personality: Readings in Theory*. 2nd edition. Edited by William S. Sahakian. Chicago: 1965. Reprint, Rand McNally College Publishing Company, 1974.

————. *Man's Search for Meaning: An Introduction to Logotherapy*. New York: 1959. Reprint, Pocket Books, 1973.

————. *The Unheard Cry for Meaning*. New York: Touchstone Book, 1978.

Franklin, John Hope, and Alfred A. Moss, Jr. *From Slavery to Freedom*. 40th anniversary edition. New York: Alfred A. Knoph, 1988.

Fretheim, Terence. *The Suffering God: An Old Testament Perspective*. Philadelphia: Fortress Press, 1984.

Fromm, Erich. *The Art of Loving*. New York: Bantam Book, 1967.

Garnet, Henry Highland. "A Brief Sketch of the Life and Character of David Walker." In *Walker's Appeal/Garnet's Address*. Preface by William Loren Katz. New York: Arno Press and the *New York Times*, 1969.

Garnet, Henry Highland, and David Walker. *Walker's Appeal and Garnet's Address*. Nashville: 1848. Reprint, James C. Winston Publishing, 1994.

Garrow, David J. *Protest at Selma: Martin Luther King, Jr., and the Voter Rights Act of 1965*. New Haven CT: Yale University Press, 1978.

Geaney, Dennis J. *The Prophetic Parish*. Minneapolis: Winston Press, 1983.

Genovese, Eugene. *Roll Jordan Roll: The World the Slaves Made*. New York: Vintage Books, 1974.

Giddings, Paula. *When and Where I Enter: The Impact of Black Women on Race and Sex in America*. New York: Bantam Books, 1984.

Gladden, Washington. *Recollections*. Boston: Houghton Mifflin, 1909.

Glock, Charles Y. Chapter 9–12 in *Religion and Society in Tension*. Chicago: Rand McNally, 1965.

———, et al. "Ministerial Guides: The Sounds of Silence." In *Religion in Sociological Perspective*, 163–86. Belmont CA: Wadsworth, 1973.

Glock, Charles Y., and Rodney Stark. "Prejudice and the Churches." In *Religion American Style*, edited by Patrick McNamara, 305–14. New York: Harper & Row, 1974.

Grimké, Angelina. "An Appeal to the Christian Women of the South" and "Colonization." (Letter 6). In *The Public Years of Sarah and Angelina Grimké: Selected Writings 1835–1839*, edited by Larry Ceplair, 36–79; 164–68. New York: Columbia University Press, 1989.

———. "An Appeal to the Women of the Nominally Free States." In *Root of Bitterness: Documents of the Social History of American Women*, edited by Nancy F. Cott, et al. Boston: Northeastern University Press, 1996.

———. *Letters to Catherine E. Beecher*. Boston: Isaac Knapp, 1838.

Grimké, Sarah M. "An Epistle to the Clergy of the Southern States." In *The Public Years of Sarah and Angelina Grimké: Selected Writings 1835–1839*, edited by Larry Ceplair, 90–115. New York: Columbia University Press, 1989.

Gutman, Herbert G. *The Black Family in Slavery & Freedom*, 1750–1925. New York: Pantheon Books, 1976.

Harding, Vincent. *There is a River: The Black Struggle for Freedom in America*. New York: Vintage, 1981.

Harkness, Georgia. *The Sources of Western Morality*. New York: Charles Scribner's Sons, 1954.

Heschel, Abraham J. "Choose Life." In *Moral Grandeur and Spiritual Audacity*, edited by Susannah Heschel, 251–56. New York: Farrar, Straus, Giroux, 1996.

———. *God in Search of Man: A Philosophy of Judaism*. Foreword by Susannah Heschel. Northvale NJ: Jason Aronson, 1987.

———. *Man Is Not Alone*. New York: Farrar, Straus & Young, Inc., 1951.

———. "Prophetic Inspiration: An Analysis of Prophetic Consciousness." In *To Grow in Wisdom: An Anthology of Abraham Joshua Heschel*. Edited by Jacob Neusner with Noam Neusner, 53–69. New York: Madison Books, 1990.

———. *The Prophets*. New York: Harper & Row, 1962.

———. "Religion and Race." In *The Insecurity of Freedom: Essays on Human Existence*. Philadelphia: Jewish Publication Society of America, 1966.

———. "The White Man on Trial." In *The Insecurity of Freedom: Essays on Human Existence*. Philadelphia: Jewish Publication Society of America, 1966.

Heschel, Abraham J., Robert McAfee Brown, and Michael Novak. "The Moral Outrage of Vietnam." In *Vietnam: Crisis of Conscience*. New York: Association Press, 1967.

Hine, Darlene Clark, and Kathleen Thompson. *A Shining Thread of Hope: The History of Black Women in America*. New York: Broadway Books, 1998.

Hinks, Peter P. *To Awaken My Afflicted Brethren: David Walker and the Problem of Antebellum Slave Resistance*. University Park: Pennsylvania State University Press, 1997.

Hyde, Lawrence. "Radhakrishnan's Contribution to Universal Religion." Chapter 8 in *The Philosophy of Sarvepalli Radhakrishnan*. Edited by Paul Arthur Schilpp. New York: Tudor Publishing, 1952.

Jackson, Mattie J. "The Story of Mattie J. Jackson as told to L. S. Thompson." In *Six Women's Slave Narratives*, 5–42. Introduction by William L. Andrews. New York: Oxford University Press, 1988.

Jacobs, Harriet A. *Incidents in the Life of a Slave Girl*. Edited by Jean Fagan Yellin. Cambridge MA: Harvard University Press, 1987.

Jefferson, Thomas. *Notes on the State of Virginia*. Edited by William Peden. Chapel Hill: University of North Carolina Press, 1982.

Jones, William A. *God in the Ghetto*. Elgin IL: Progressive Baptist Publishing House, 1979.

King, Martin Luther, Jr. "The Ethical Demands For Integration" and "A Christian Sermon on Peace." In *A Testament of Hope: The Essential*

Martin Luther King, Jr. Edited by James M. Washington, 117–25; 253–58. New York: Harper & Row, 1986.

————. "Rediscovering Lost Values." In *A Knock at Midnight*, edited by Clayborne Carson and Peter Holloran, 5–19. New York: Warner Books, 1998.

————. *Stride Toward Freedom.* New York: Harper & Row, 1958.

King, Martin Luther, Sr, with Clayton Riley. *Daddy King: An Autobiography.* New York: William Morrow, 1980.

Knudson, Albert C. *The Prophetic Movement in Israel.* New York: Methodist Book Concern, 1921.

————. *The Beacon Lights of Prophecy.* New York: Eaton & Mains, 1914.

Lecky, William E. H. *History of European Morals.* Volume 2. New York: D. Appleton, 1879.

Lerna, Gerda, editor. *Black Women in White America: A Documentary History.* New York: Vintage Books, 1973.

Lerner, Gerda. *The Grimké Sisters from South Carolina: Rebels Against Slavery.* Boston: Houghton Mifflin, 1967.

Lincoln, C. Eric, and Lawrence Mamiya. *The Black Church in the African American Experience.* Durham NC: Duke University Press, 1990.

Machiavelli, Niccolo. *The Prince and the Discourses.* New York: Modern Library, 1950.

MacIver, Robert, editor. "What We All Can Do." Chapter 12 in *Unity and Difference in American Life.* New York: Harper & Brothers, 1947.

Malcolm X. *The Autobiography of Malcolm X*, as told to Alex Haley. New York: 1965. Reprint, Ballantine Books, 1992.

Marable, Manning. "The Military in the Black Experience: Towards a Theory of The Racist/Capitalist State." Chapter 6 in *Blackwater: Historical Studies in Race, Class Consciousness and Revolution.* Dayton OH: Black Praxis Press, 1981.

Mbiti, John S. *Introduction to African Religion.* 2nd edition. Oxford: Heinemann Educational Publishers, 1991.

McConnell, Francis J. *The Prophetic Ministry.* New York: Abingdon Press, 1930.

McLaurin, Melton A. *Celia A Slave.* Athens GA: University of Georgia Press, 1991.

Mott, Stephen C. *Biblical Ethics and Social Change.* New York: Oxford University Press, 1982.

Muelder, Walter G. "Autobiographical Introduction: Forty Years of Communitarian Personalism." In *The Ethical Edge of Christian Theology*, 1–42. New York: Mellen Press, 1983.

————. *Foundations of the Responsible Society: A Comprehensive Survey of Christian Social Ethics*. New York: Abingdon Press, 1959.

————. *Moral Law in Christian Social Ethics*. Richmond VA: John Knox Press, 1966.

Niebuhr, Reinhold. *Leaves from the Notebook of a Tamed Cynic*. New York: Willet Clark & Colby, 1929.

Nygren, Anders. *Agape and Eros*. Translated by Philip S. Watson. Philadelphia: Westminster Press, 1953.

Ofari, Earl. *"Let Your Motto Be Resistance": The Life and Thoughts of Henry Highland Garnet*. Boston: Beacon Press, 1972.

Quarles, Benjamin. "Abolition's New Breed." In *Afro-American History Past and Present*. Edited by Henry N. Drewry and Cecelia H. Drewry, 50–60. Princeton: Princeton University Press, 1971.

Raboteau, Albert J. *Slave Religion*. New York: Oxford University Press, 1978.

Rauschenbusch, Walter. *Christianity and the Social Crisis*. New York: Macmillan, 1907.

Richardson, Marilyn, editor. *Maria W. Stewart, America's First Black Woman Political Writer: Essays and Speeches*. Bloomington: Indiana University Press, 1987.

Rossides, Daniel W. *Social Stratification: The Interplay of Class, Race, & Gender*. 2nd edition. Upper Saddle River NJ: Prentice Hall, 1997.

Rothenberg, Paula S., editor. *White Privilege: Essential Readings on the Other Side of Racism*. New York: Worth Publishers, 2002.

Sartre, Jean-Paul. *The Age of Reason*. Translated by Eric Sutton. New York: Bantam Books, 1967.

————. *Being and Nothingness: An Essay on Phenomenological Ontology*. Translated by Hazel E. Barnes. New York: Philosophical Library, 1956.

————. *Existential Psychoanalysis*. Translated by Hazel E. Barnes. Chicago: Gateway Edition, 1962.

————. "Existentialism is a Humanism." In *The Existentialist Tradition: Selected Writings*. Edited by Nino Langiulli, 391–419. New York: Anchor Books, 1971.

Schneier, Marc. *Shared Dreams: Martin Luther King, Jr. and the Jewish Community*. Woodstock VT: Jewish Lights Publishing, 1999.

Scott, Ernest F. *Man and Society in the New Testament*. New York: Scribner's Sons, 1946.

Snaith, Norman H. *The Distinctive Ideas of the Old Testament*. London: Epworth Press, 1944.

Socrates. "Socrates' Defense (Apology)." In *The Collected Dialogues of Plato: Including the Letters*. Edited by Edith Hamilton and Hunting Cairns, 3–26. Princeton NJ: Princeton University Press, 1971.

Stewart, Maria. "An Address Delivered at the African Masonic Hall." In *Spiritual Narratives*. Edited by Sue E. Houchins, 63–72. New York: Oxford University Press, 1988.

————. "An Address Delivered before the Afric American Female Intelligence Society, of Boston." *Spiritual Narratives*, 56–63.

————. "Religion and the Pure Principles of Morality," *Spiritual Narratives*, 3–22.

Stuckey, Sterling. "David Walker." In *Dictionary of American Negro Biography*. Edited by Rayford W. Logan and Michael Winston, 623. New York: W.W. Norton, 1982.

————. *Going Through the Storm: The Influence of African Americans in History*. New York: Oxford University Press, 1994.

————. *Slave Culture: Nationalist Theory and the Foundations of Black America*. New York: Oxford University Press, 1987.

Thielicke, Helmut. *Theological Ethics: Foundations*. Volume 1. Philadelphia: Fortress Press, 1966.

Thurman, Howard. *Jesus and the Disinherited*. Nashville: Abingdon-Cokesbury Press, 1949.

Tillich, Paul. *Love, Power, and Justice*. New York: Oxford University Press, 1960.

Turner, James. Introduction to *David Walker's Appeal*, 9–19. Baltimore: Black Classic Press, 1993.

Von Rad, Gerhard. *The Message of the Prophets*. New York: Harper & Row, 1965.

————. *Old Testament Theology*. Volume 2. New York: Harper & Row, 1965.

Walker, David. *Appeal to the Colored Citizens of the World, But in Particular, and Very Expressly to those of the United States*. In *Great Documents in Black American History*. Edited by George Ducas and Charles Van Doren. New York: Praeger Publishers, 1970.

Williams, Delores S. *Sisters in the Wilderness: The Challenge of Womanist God-Talk*. Maryknoll NY: Orbis Books, 1993.

Wiltse, Charles M., editor. *David Walker's Appeal*. New York: Hill and Wang, 1965.

Wogaman, J. Philip, and Douglas M. Strong, editors. *Readings in Christian Ethics*. Louisville KY: Westminster John Knox Press, 1996.

Wolf, Naomi. "The Racism of Well-Meaning White People." In *Skin Deep: Black Women and White Women Write About Race*. Edited by Marita Goldman and Susan Richards Shreve, 37–46. New York: Anchor Books, 1995.

Young, Henry J. *Major Black Religious Leaders: 1755–1940*. Nashville: Abingdon Press, 1977.

Index

Abernathy, Ralph 190
Abolitionists 140
abolitionists-feminists
absolute immanentist view 97
action-reflection 143
activity-potentials 112
Adair, R.T. 189, 190
African Repository 155
agapé 150, 162
alcohol 75
Allen, Richard 79, 148
American Colonization Society
    140, 155
Amos 5, 14, 77, 80, 85, 107, 179,
    180
Angelou, Maya 118n68
Anthropotropism 8
Aptheker, Herbert 18n1, 20n10, 21,
    22, 22n20, 23, 24, 144n23
Ashmun, Jehudi 140
Auld, Hugh 95

Babbie, Earl 72n62
"bad boys" Preface
"bad faith" 134
"bad nigger" 171

Baldwin, James 104n47
Baldwin, Lewis V. 64n46189n10
Bathsheba 6
Beatitudes 4
beloved community 56, 204
Bennett, Lerone Jr. 31n49, 118n71
Bergman, Peter M. 118n69
Bertocci, Peter A. 43n3, 112n62
Bibb, Henry 157, 158
Billingsley, Andrew 204
Birch, Bruce C. 5n8, 85n19, 184n5,
    186n7
Black Consciousness Movement
    146
Black Liberation Theology
    Movement 94, 148, 166
black nation 152, 154
Black Nationalist, 15, 152
black radicalism
black self-determination 15, 197-
    200
black self-hatred 119
black self-love 118-119
black unity 151, 152, 154
"blackwater" 153
Boesak, Allan 65, 65n52

Bohn, Carole R. 57n25, 108n56
Bond, L. Susan 88, 88n25
Bonhoeffer, Dietrich 50, 50n13,
    51n14, 57
borderline situation 136
Bosnia 180
Boston 13, 15, 19, 21, 22, 26, 79
Boston University 12
Bowne, Borden P. 43n3, 44n4,
    111n61, 137n14
Branch, Taylor 11n13 and 15,
    190n11 and 12
Braun, Joanne Carlson 57n25,
    108n56
Brightman, Edgar S. 43n3, 137n15
Brooks, Phillips 195n17
Brown, Denny 68n56
Brown, John 153, 201, 202
Brown, Morris 183, 203
Browne, Joseph W. 120, 120n73
Brunner, Emil45, 45n8, 52n16
Burrow, Rufus Jr. 12n17, 64n46,
    165n8
Butler, Eliza 20, 21
Buttrick, David 65-66, 66n53, 71

Cain 168
Caldwell, Elias B. 165
Calvin, John 149, 149n31
Campbell, Alexander 116n65, 173
Carson, Clayborne 11n14
Celia 114-114, 119, 120, 136
Ceplair, Larry 33n53
Chambers, William 151
Charleston AME Church 13, 26,
    79, 80, 183, 192, 200
cheap grace 50
Christian ethic 52
Christian Theological Seminary 9
classical Greek view 7
Clay, Henry111, 162, 163, 166
Colonization 163, 164, 165

colonization plans 152, 165, 173,
    174
communitarian ethics 43
complex unity 112
condemned to freedom 62
Conference on Religion and Race
    10
Constitution 37, 38, 77, 155, 173
Cooper, Anna Julia 35
Cornish, Samuel 20
costly grace 50, 51, 57
cost of prophecy62, 78-84
Corr, Charles 183
counter-cultural 183
counter-status quo 54, 179, 188

David-Zion tradition 5
de Chardin, Teilhard 105n49
decided agency 137
Declaration of Independence 36,
    37, 39, 77, 155
de Lubac, Henri 105n49
democratic principle 110
Deutero-Isaiah 5, 92
Dexter Avenue Baptist Church 189
dignus 107
Disciples of Christ 116n65 116n65,
    173, 198
divine call 78-84
divine holiness 85
divine image 32, 167
divine immanence 97
divine impartiality 99
divine imperative 178
divine justice 84-88
divine pathos 4, 7, 8, 9, 12, 88,
    184-191
divine wrath 87, 88-91, 99
doom 92, 93, 186
Dorsey, Douglas 157
Douglass, Frederick 36, 95, 96n38,
    144, 148, 157, 158

Douglass, Grace 60
Douglass, Sarah 60
Drayton, Henry 183
Dred Scott vs. Sanford 37
Ducas, George 18n5, 75n1
Dulles, Avery 55, 55n21, 72n62
Drewry, Cecelia 20n8
Drewry, Henry N. 20n8

eighth century prophets 3, 4, 12,
    39, 47, 77, 80, 82, 176
emancipation 61
eros 150
ethical prophet 9, 183, 196
ethic of radical transformation 70
Ethiopian Manifesto 142
ethos of slave culture 24-26
evil of indifference 7
existential analysis 130
existentialist thought 176
Exodus-Sinai tradition 5
Ezekiel 5, 80, 99n42, 105

Feagin, Joe 202
federal census 21
Fosdick, Harry Emerson 5, 5n7
Frankl, Viktor 130, 131, 132, 134
Franklin, John Hope 30n43, 31
free blacks 24, 26
Freedom's Journal 15, 19, 24, 155
Fretheim, Terence 58n27
Fromm, Erich 150
fundamental humanity 104, 114

Garner, Margaret 114, 118-120
Garnet, Henry Highland 22, 23, 82,
    154, 154n41
Carrison, William Lloyd 61
Geaney, Dennis J. 69n58
Genovese, Eugene D. 171, 171n11
George's ultimatum 115-118
Giddings, Paula 33n54

Gladden, Washington 44, 44n4
Glock, Charles Y. 54n18, 72n62
God needs persons 7, 101
God's faithfulness 86
God's justice 86-88
God's point of view 46
God's righteousness 86
go for broke ministry 204
gradual emancipation 174
gradualist 174
Greek 94, 95, 103, 104n47160, 185
Greeks 159
Grimké, Angelina 59, 60, 61, 65,
    140, 172, 173,
Grimké, Sarah 59, 60, 61, 65, 140
Gruening, Martha 20, 20n10
Gutman, Herbert G. 119n72

Hacker, Andrew 202
hall of fame
Hall, Prince 2, 88
Hamer, Fannie Lou 198
Hamilton, William 143
Hannah, William W. Preface
Harding, Vincent 29, 29n40
Harkness, Georgia 93, 93n36
Heschel, Abraham Joshua 6, 7, 68,
    82, 139, 185n6, 191, 191n13,
    195n18
Heschel, Susannah 10, 187n9,
    191n14
Heterosexism 13
higher morality theory 4, 12
Hine, Darlene Clark 34n57
Hinks, Peter P. 2n2, 17, 18, 21, 23,
    24-25,76-77, 79, 112-113,
    155n44, 183n4
homicide disease 177
hope for repentance 91-94
Horton, George 20
Hosea 5, 14, 77, 85, 180
human dignity 163

Hyde, Lawrence 106, 106n53
"hypocritical religion" 157
hypothetical imperatives 92

image of God 123, 124, 181
immanent God 97
improper Christianity 76
individuality 97
individualistic ethics 43
individuals-in-community 125
Institutes of the Christian Religion,
    149n31
interdisciplinary integration, 9
intra-community violence 176, 179
Iraq 180
Isaiah 5, 14, 54, 77, 78, 80, 85, 105,
    179, 180

Jackson, Mattie J.158, 158n2
Jacobs, Harriet A. 51, 51n15, 116,
    116n66, 157, 161, 161n6, 174
Jameson, John 116n65
Jefferson, Thomas 39, 100, 109,
    110, 110n57, 112, 121, 122,
    143, 146, 159, 160, 161
Jeremiah 5, 14, 58, 58n28, 62,
    72n62, 77, 78, 80, 85, 90, 92,
    180
Jewish Theological Seminary 11
Johns, Vernon 189, 190, 191
Jones, Jim 14
Jones, William A. Jr. 183, 183n3
judge of the universe 44

Kant, Immanuel 150
Katz, William Lorenz 20n10
King David 6
King, Martin Luther Jr. 10, 45, 56,
    62, 63-64, 66, 72-73, 137n15,
    156, 190, 198
King, Martin Luther Sr. 48, 48n10
Koresh, David 14

Knudson, Albert C. 12n17, 81n9,
    91n32, 92n33
Küng, Hans 72n62

Lane, Lunsford 157
Lecky, William 105, 105n48, 106,
    106n54
Lerner, Gerda 60n31, 118n70
Liberator 22, 33
Liberia 140
Lincoln, C. Eric 72n62, 79n6
"living dead" 131
logotherapy 130
love of self, 149
Luther, Martin 49

Machiavelli, Niccolo 70
MacIver, Robert 66, 66n54
Malcolm X 28, 29, 94, 100,
    100n43, 108, 144, 151-55,
    166, 197, 198
Mamiya, Lawrence 72n62, 79n6
Marable, Manning 145n24, 153
Massachusetts General Coloured
    Association 32
Mason Temple, 63
Mbiti, John 96n41
McConnell, Francis J. 12n17, 107,
    107n55
McLaurin, Melton A. 115n64, 116-
    117, 173n14
meaning therapy 130
Micah 5, 14, 46, 77, 78, 80, 84, 85,
    89, 91,179, 180, 196
Middle East 180
Middle passage 158, 165, 179
Millard, Richard, 43n3
Ministry 47, 48
"monster Prejudice" 174
moral experience 171
moral Govenor 44
moral law 44

moral nature 171
moral pretentiousness156, 163,
    165-66, 173
moral responsibility
moral superiority of blacks 167-72
moral unit-in-community 43
Moss, Alfred A. 30n43
Mott, Stephen 87, 87n24
Muelder, Walter G. 9, 41n1, 43n3
Muhammad, Elijah 152n38, 154,
    155
Mulligan, Robert A. Preface
murder-suicides 119

Nathan 6
Nation of Islam 154, 155
"natural enemies"
Neusner, Jacob 8n10, 195n18
Neusner, Noam M.M. 8n10,
    195n18
new order of things 56, 69-73
Newsom, Robert 114-116
Niebuhr, Reinhold 52n17
Nietzsche, Friedrich 131
Nonperson 159
Nygren, Anders 149-50

Ofari, Earl 30, 30n44
Omnibenevolence 100, 103
Omnipotence 100, 103
Omnipresent 100
Omniscient 100
"Othello" 2

Pan-Africanists, 125, 155
Parker, Rebecca 57n25, 108n56
Paul, Nathaniel 2
Peculiar institution 19
Pprsonal-communal 42
personal-communal ethic 126
personalism 12
personalistic ethics 43

Phillips, Ulrich B. 161, 161n5
poll tax 18
"pretended" Christians 156
"pretended preacher" 161
priestly 52
proper Christianity, 76, 164
"proper" religion 157
prophet and priest 54-59
Prophetic and Ethical Witness of
    the Church 9
prophetic daring 78
prophetic ethics 1, 41, 45, 49, 181,
    184, 187, 193
prophetic ministry 10, 83, 182, 186
prophetic religion, 8, 182
Prosser, Gabriel 31, 76, 144
protest tradition, 178

Quarles, Benjamin 20n8
Query XIV 100, 161
Query XVIII 122

Raboteau, Albert J. 76n3, 158n1
racial uplift, 147
racial reconciliation 42, 200, 203
racism 13, 19, 42, 65
rape 114, 115
Rauschenbusch, Walter 3, 4, 5,
    182, 182n2
Realm of God 4, 71
repentance 93, 200-205
Richardson, Marilyn 33n52
Righteous works 52
Ringer, Benjamin 72n62
Roberts, Keith A. 72n62
Robinson, Jo Ann, 198
Roman 94, 95, 103, 104n47, 160,
    185
Romans 159, 160
Romero, Oscar 59, 72n62
Rossides, Daniel W. 68n56
Rothenberg, Paula S. 201n19

Royce, Josiah 56
Russwurm, John 20
Rwanda 180

sacred and secular
sacredness of persons 104-126,
    193-96
Samuel 54
Sartre, Jean-Paul 62, 130, 132, 133,
    134
Schneier, Rabbi Marc 11n16
Scott, Dred 37, 39, 64n47
Scott, Ernest F. 105, 105n50
seed of Cain 168
self-defensive violence 153
self-determination 5, 100, 101, 108,
    135-39, 145, 146, 148, 149,
    150, 156, 199, 200
self-direction 108
self-hatred 119, 150, 155
selfish individualism 43
self-love 111, 119, 149, 150
Selma 10, 62, 64
Separatist 155
Sermon on the Mount 4
"servile deceit" 127, 137, 144-45,
    149, 154
sexism 13
sexual exploitation 115
Sierra Leone 140
similarities between Walker and
    Malcolm X 153-155
shared suffering 57
Sharp, Granville 140
Snaith, Norman H. 87, 87n23
Snowden, Samuel 79
social critic 53, 56
social gospel 182
social physician 56
Socrates 58, 58n26, 67
Solomon 166
Stark, Rodney 54n18

Stern, Carl 187n9
Stewart, James 32
Stewart, Maria W 32, 33, 34, 147,
    157, 174, 198
Strong, Douglas M. 1n1, 3
Stuckey, Sterling 22, 22n22, 25n29,
    89, 96, 152n37, 156, 156n47,
    167, 167n10

Taney, Chief Justice Roger B. 37,
    38
theist-creationist 185
theocentric 95, 169
theological anthropology 104
theological social ethics 181
theological social ethicist 9, 181
The Rights of All Men 24
Thielicke, Helmut 136
Thompson, Kathleen 34n57
Thurman, Howard 178, 179n1
Tiennamin Square 180
Tillich, Paul 91n31
Tocqueville, Alexis de 110-111,
    111n60
"true Christianity" 157
Truth, Sojourner 35
Tubman, Harriet 35
Turner, James 83-84, 84n16
Turner, Nat 76, 77, 153

Uriah 6

van Doren, Charles 18n5, 75n1
Vesey conspiracy 26, 31, 79, 142,
    144, 172, 183, 192, 200, 203
Vesey, Denmark 76, 31, 200
vocation 181
von Rad, Gerhard 5, 6, 8, 83,
    83n15, 90n29

Walker, Anthony 18
Walker, Edwin 21, 22

Walker, Lydia Ann 21
Washington, Booker T. 197
"well meaning white people" 43
Weld, Theodore 60
Wells-Barnett, Ida B. 198
Wheatley, Phyllis 20
*White Privilege: Essential
    Readings on the Other Side of
    Racism* 201n19
white repentance 200-03
Williams, A.D. 48
Williams, Delores 57n25, 108n56
Wiltsie, Charles M. 81n11
Wogaman, J. Philip 1n1, 3
Wolf, Naomi 43, 43n2
womanist movement 35
works righteousness 49, 52

Young, Henry J. 31n48, 103,
    103n46
Young, Robert Alexander 142